Steve Braunias has won over 30 national writing awards as a journalist, satirist, author and television writer, including fellowships to Oxford University and Cambridge University. He works for the *New Zealand Herald*, and is the proprietor of Luncheon Sausage Books. He lives in Te Atatu with his partner and their young daughter.

Also by Steve Braunias

Fool's Paradise (2001)
How to Watch a Bird (2007)
Fish of the Week (2008)
Roosters I Have Known (2009)
Smoking in Antarctica (2010)
Civilisation: 20 places on the the edge of the world (2012)
Madmen: Inside the weirdest election campaign ever (2014)

THE SCENE OF THE
CRIME

STEVE BRAUNIAS

HarperCollinsPublishers

To May Mackey

HarperCollins*Publishers*

First published in 2015
by HarperCollins*Publishers* (New Zealand) Limited
Unit D1, 63 Apollo Drive, Rosedale, Auckland 0632, New Zealand
harpercollins.co.nz

Copyright © Steve Braunias 2015

Steve Braunias asserts the moral right to be identified as the author of this work. This work is copyright. All rights reserved. No part of this publication may be reproduced, copied, scanned, stored in a retrieval system, recorded, or transmitted, in any form or by any means, without the prior written permission of the publisher.

HarperCollins*Publishers*
Unit D1, 63 Apollo Drive, Rosedale, Auckland 0632, New Zealand
Level 13, 201 Elizabeth Street, Sydney, NSW 2000, Australia
A 53, Sector 57, Noida, UP, India
1 London Bridge Street, London, SE1 9GF, United Kingdom
2 Bloor Street East, 20th floor, Toronto, Ontario M4W 1A8, Canada
195 Broadway, New York, NY 10007, USA

National Library of New Zealand cataloguing-in-publication data:

Braunias, Steve.
The scene of the crime / by Steve Braunias.
ISBN 978-1-77554-083-0 (pbk.)
ISBN 978-1-77549-120-0 (ebook)
1. Murderers—New Zealand. 2. Violent offenders—New Zealand.
3. Criminal psychology. 4. Criminal investigation—New Zealand.
I. Title.
793.31993—dc 23

Cover design by Christa Moffitt, Christabella Designs
Cover image by shutterstock.com
Typeset in Bembo Std by Kirby Jones
Printed and bound in Australia by Griffin Press
The papers used by HarperCollins in the manufacture of this book are a natural, recyclable product made from wood grown in sustainable plantation forests. The fibre source and manufacturing processes meet recognised international environmental standards, and carry certification.

A law court has its own peculiar power of attraction, don't you think?

— Fräulein Bürstner, in Franz Kafka's *The Trial*

Contents

Introduction	1
1 Mark Lundy: Operation summer	13
2 That summer: Victor Wasmuth	38
3 The bogan ninja: Antonie Dixon	54
4 That spring: 'Mr X'	75
5 Falling down: Guy Hallwright	91
6 The lair of the white worm: Derek King	114
7 A naked male riding his bike: Timaru	132
8 Mark Lundy: Killing Christine and Amber	138
9 Mark Lundy: Sleeping	143
10 Made in Australia: Rolf Harris	149
11 Terra nullius: Brad Murdoch	164
12 Sex and Chocolate: 'Bones'	176
13 The Rotorua Three: Clint Rickards	188
14 The killings at Stilwell Road: Chris Wang	210
15 Mark Lundy: The trial	236
Acknowledgements	312

INTRODUCTION

Basically what happened is that a Maori guy stuck a knife between the second and third ribs of an Asian guy, and killed him. A forensic pathologist described the fatal wound when he appeared as a witness at the murder trial in the High Court of Auckland. I looked over at the defence lawyer's desk and saw the photos taken of the victim at postmortem — the tremendous amount of blood on his chest, the mouth wide open in death.

He got stabbed in his workshop. He died in his driveway. In court, it was getting on to four o'clock on a Thursday afternoon in spring, and I was thinking about dinner. It was a boring murder trial, because all murder trials are boring; the court demands it, with its patient reconstructions and re-imaginings of a frantic, awful event. The windowless room, the serviettes neatly folded over the top of glass jugs of water on the lawyers' desks ... But there is something more intense than boredom at all murder trials: misery.

You can always feel the misery of the families of the victim and the accused. It's like a weight. It's crushing. While the pathologist listed his findings at postmortem — the entry point of the knife was 1.9 centimetres; it had passed through skin, fatty tissue, muscle,

and entered the aorta, causing 1.2 litres of blood to haemorrhage —
I looked at the victim's wife. It was as though she was hearing the
bad news for the first time. It was as though she was dying. It was
worse than that: she was re-imagining the frantic, awful event of
her husband's death.

'A grumpy drug deal gone wrong,' said a police detective with
a shaved head and a pleasant face. I had taken him aside and asked
what the trial was all about. The accused was claiming self-defence.
The murder weapon was displayed on an exhibits table: a sharp
kitchen knife, barely long enough to halve an orange.

I closed my eyes. I was happy. Like five of the cases examined
in this book, I chose the stabbing at random. They weren't
assignments; they weren't news. I'd walked in off the street that
Thursday afternoon in spring just to see if anything was happening
at the High Court, just to re-experience the familiar misery.
I needed to immerse myself in the slow, dingy reality of a trial
because I had spent that morning reading about crime writing in
Te Ara, the New Zealand online encyclopedia for children.

The encyclopedia's musings on crime and media had recently
been published. The author was some nobody. 'Crime news,'
Nobody wrote, 'offers the media potent content as it is often
negative, personal, visual, violent, emotional and lacks complexity.'
The rest of his commentary was just as pithy and just as pious, and
it briefly made me want to wring Nobody's neck, but you can go
to prison for that. Worse, you first have to appear in court.

*

The possibility exists — a rough calculation here, a journalist's
tendency to exaggerate just about everything there — that I have
spent an entire year of my life sitting in courtrooms. Strange to
think of it as a block of 365 days. The passing of the seasons, summer
to summer, while sealed inside a zone of other people's horror —

I remember excitedly approaching the wife of a policeman accused of rape, and telling her that my daughter had just been born. *Dad will be home after court.* I've been attracted to the peculiar power of trials for every year of her life.

I've loved it and hated it, and I could seldom tear myself away. All reporting is the accumulation of minor details, and nothing is too minor in a courtroom devoted to a case of murder. There is such an obsessive quality to trials. There is no such thing as courtroom drama, and the idea that a trial is a kind of theatre is facile. It's far more powerful than that. It's a production of sorrow and paperwork, a clean realism usually conducted in a collegial manner, in dark-panelled rooms with set hours of business. The orderliness is almost a parody of the savage moments it seeks to understand. Inside, the black silk robes and the swearing on Bibles; outside, the dirty realism of New Zealand as it goes about its business, the everyday chaos of love, sex and money, for the most part settling into patterns of happiness or droll compromise, sometimes going too fast to stop and ending in violent death.

A court is a chamber of questions. Who, when, why, what happened and exactly how — these are issues of psychology and the soul; they're general to the human condition, with its infinite capacity to cause pain. The question that very often most interests me in court is: where. It's impossible and pointless to try to put yourself in the mind of a killer, but the setting takes you to the scene of the crime, shows you something about New Zealand. It's not the dark underbelly; it's the dark surface, in plain sight, the road most travelled. There goes Mark Lundy, possibly, driving along the Petone foreshore in the middle of the night. There goes Louise Nicholas, possibly, being taken to a house in Rotorua's gruesomely named Rutland Street. Other chapters in this book allow a guided tour of a beautiful Victorian mansion in Auckland, and walk the yellow brick road of that distant suburb of New Zealand, the Gold Coast.

Sometimes I think it's the setting and not the mystery that explains why our most famous murder, the Crewe killings, has such a hold on the public imagination. The rural New Zealandness of the 1970 double-killing offers a parable of the way we lived — the isolation, the hard work, the pioneer spirit. Jeanette and Harvey Crewe were killed in their farmhouse in obscure Pukekawa. It was Waikato hill country, submerged in dense fog. 'The talk was of calvings and eczema spores, stock prices and rainfall,' wrote Terry Bell in *Bitter Hill*, his 1972 book calling for Arthur Thomas's release. No one heard the two gunshots. The bodies were mummified in bed linen, bound with pieces of galvanised wire from the farm, and removed in wheelbarrows. It was a murder case in which a cow served as an alibi. Thomas said that he couldn't have been at the Crewe household because he was with a sick cow, Number 4, which he helped calve that night. The only shot he fired from his rifle that month was to destroy the animal. It took two months for the bodies to surface in the Waikato River; until then, police searched in limestone caves, and also considered the possibility that the Crewes were wandering 'dazed' somewhere in that lonely countryside.

The only vivid detail in the very first case of murder tried in New Zealand — Joseph Burns was found guilty of murdering a couple and their daughter in Devonport, on 22 October 1841 — takes you to the scene of the crime. It was also the same exact spot where Burns was hanged. The courthouse on Queen Street was packed during his trial; a fortnight after his death sentence was passed down, Burns was unshackled in his cell, and escorted by armed guard to the Auckland wharf, and across to Devonport by boat. The scaffold was erected at the Devonport naval base, on the same spot where Burns had hacked the family to death, and burned down their house. Dudley Dyne writes in *Famous New Zealand Murders*, 'Near the tall scaffold ... lay the coffin ready to receive the body of the prisoner. Burns sat down for a rest upon the coffin, a sight that moved the chaplain to tears.'

Dead man resting, on his own coffin, on a Saturday morning on the gently lapping shores of pretty Devonport. Then he stood on the gallows trapdoor and had the rope placed around his neck. He asked the hangman to place the knot a little higher. The trapdoor fell. 'Thus,' penned a watching reporter from *The New Zealander*, 'terminated the first European execution.' I wonder whether the reporter came back for more. I would have.

*

The first time I stepped into a courtroom was in Greymouth. I was 23. I had joined the staff of the *Greymouth Evening Star*, and made court reporter. It was fascinating and baffling and terrifying, and I never really got used to it; I felt on edge, and didn't know what to think. I was afraid of murderers and frightened of men who gave the bash — the most common cases were drink-driving, supply of marijuana, and giving the bash. Pat, a very fat man from *The Christchurch Press*, sat next to me in the press bench. He had seen it all; he sucked on barley sugars, slept, and was extremely helpful.

Most of the time I worried about spelling people's names right. But I also wondered what those days in court were telling me about life in Greymouth. There was a long trial involving two businessmen, one a former policeman, who drove a young guy off the road one dark night and beat him up. The young guy had been following the ex-cop for weeks and gathering information on him on behalf of a friend, whose wife was sleeping with the former detective. The other businessman pushed me against the wall one day during recess. 'I don't like you,' he said. I didn't say anything. He had his hand on my throat.

Punks — 'punk rockers', as I solemnly described them in the paper — were always in brawls. They had come to the Coast from Christchurch for peace and quiet, or for the easy access to dope, cactus and datura. One day they started a brawl in court. The judge picked up the hem of his robes, and legged it from the courtroom. Police reinforcements grabbed at the marauding punks. A girl with spiky hair and laddered stockings, who was awaiting her charge of offensive language, crossed the crowded courtroom and gave me a note. She'd written her name and phone number. She lived in a cold house next to the cemetery.

A man was fined $250 for assaulting a woman at the Golden Eagle, where I drank. Ken was an okay guy. I saw him the night before he hit her. The river had flooded, and poured into the bar. A guy rowed in through the front door on a canoe, and ordered a beer. The next night, Ken brought his dog in to the bar, and a drunk woman masturbated it. Ken knocked her out cold. His lawyer said: 'My client was highly upset, and so was his dog.'

Older, fatter, sucking on mints, I thought back to Greymouth when I recently sat in on a day in court at the Auckland District Court on downtown Albert Street. It was the familiar register of petty crime and bashing. A 24-year-old woman from China had shoplifted $43.84 of cosmetics from Farmers. There was something depressing about her address in Queen Street: apartment number 1002. Hairdresser, 21, caught entering a karaoke bar after it had closed. Sales rep, 38, fined $375 for smashing up a mountain bike after drunkenly pointing at a helicopter. Man, 30, hits partner in Takanini. Man, 50, hits ex-partner in Rosebank. Man, 47, hits partner in Grey Lynn — and also pleads guilty to hitting another woman that same evening …

The dismal little stories, one after another, endless and shabby and mindless. It meant nothing and it revealed everything. It was New Zealand fucked up and out of it, dealt with promptly and efficiently by a court staff of six, a female judge of uncertain years with a private education accent, and lawyers in grey suits with missing threads at the cuffs. The bailiff pushed through the doors, calling for names. He would return and say, 'No appearance, ma'am.' There was only one spectator, a character whose daily rounds also include the Inter City bus depot, where he keeps a close scrutiny on any drivers who pull into Auckland later than scheduled.

Woman, 41, pleads guilty to defrauding a taxi driver. She had been drinking all day in New Lynn; at 6.30pm, she caught a cab to Avondale. The fare was $13. She didn't have any money. She swore at the driver, and then urinated on the front seat. The cleaning charge was $70. Convicted, and ordered to pay the driver $83. Stunned, she said from the dock: 'What, the whole $83?' She was on an invalid's benefit. It was agreed she could pay back the sum at $10 a week.

The town drunk arrived late in the afternoon. Dressed in walkshorts, socks, sandals and a polo shirt, he muttered aloud to himself at the back of the court, and rustled inside a plastic bag to fish out his wallet, which was empty. Finally, his case was called up. His barrister, chewing at a grimy strip of sticking plaster on the little finger of his right hand, apologised for his client failing to turn up earlier. 'He has gastroenteritis, asthma and eczema problems. He was advised to remain in bed, which explains him not coming to court, ma'am.' And then he added: 'He has a nervous disposition. He can be a difficult character.'

In boisterous spirits and with terrific cheer, the accused approached the dock, and hooted: 'Hello, everybody!' But the only people remaining in court were the staff. The one spectator had left, possibly to run his steely eye over the incoming coach from Coromandel. Never mind; the accused had another public announcement. 'I'm an old boy from the old school!'

His charge of assault was read out. He put on a very convincing display of shadow boxing in the dock. He said to the security guard: 'You'll make an All Black one day!' The judge remanded him to another date. He told her: 'You're fantastic!'

The bailiff walked around the courtroom and collected documents, straightened chairs. But the town drunk had one last message to broadcast. He turned as he left the court, and said: 'I've been on TV. You didn't know that, did you?' His eyes truly sparkled, and his happy laugh was like a reminder that lawlessness can provide the one thing that formal, civilised life in New Zealand so often withholds: pleasure.

*

Much is made of the psychology and pathology that may or may not be laid bare of the accused in major trials. We feel we get to know something revealing and crucial about people defending serious charges, and reach our own judgment on their character. Who did it — the weird paperboy David Bain, or his weird father Robin Bain? Who do you think was more likely to snap? What did you make of Scott Watson, still claiming his innocence for the murders of Ben Smart and Olivia Hope? We watch, we inspect, we somehow divine their true nature.

I think a great deal of this is dangerous nonsense. I think it did for Mark Lundy, and that the jury reached a verdict based partly on a stupid and vindictive reading of his body language.

But the business of a trial is far less concerned with psychology than with an exercise in complicated physics. It's a study of time and mass, meaning that it tries to put people back into a space they may have once occupied where something definitely bad happened. Witnesses and expert testimony are called on to confirm or dispute the equation. The effort and specificity are incredible, and essentially futile — no one can go back in time, no one can ever know the truth of an event.

When in doubt, tell stories. Volumes of court transcripts are filled with fiction. Some of it's intentional — the lying witness, the dishonest cop. Most of it's confused, mistaken, guesswork, half-truths, or just lousy science and long bows. The sum of it is a demented, swirling kind of fiction; with their competing narratives of guilt and innocence, a trial is always going to take on the literary form of an unreliable memoir. I think that's one of the main reasons why I like attending court. I like the way it tells stories. I like the ambiguities, the uncertainties.

But trials end with a verdict, which becomes law, and regarded as fact. A strange phenomenon then immediately occurs in the media. Until the verdict, court reporting is typically cautious; it's stenographic, recording what was said by who. After the verdict, all bets are off. Verdict equals law equals fact, and guilt becomes absolute guilt. Suddenly, you can say what the hell you like, because you know he did it. This bilge, after Lundy's first trial in 2002: 'He is a hefty, rubbery figure with a huge bulge in the middle, like the Michelin Man. When he walks, his palms face backwards instead of in towards his sides … His eyes swam behind thick lenses, like lazy fish in two small tanks … He was a keen watcher of crime documentaries on Sky and the Discovery Channel. He planned the crime carefully and contrived an alibi. The planning was cold-blooded.'

Well — possibly. I doubt it. I don't know. But I hate the certainty of it, and it was the only thing I promised Lundy when I met him before his second trial — that if he was found guilty a second time, I wouldn't declare some sudden knowledge of his movements and motives when I came to write about it. It wasn't because I particularly liked him. And I wouldn't have felt all that bad about betraying him in print if I had come to think he was guilty and that the verdict was correct. The horror of the killings and the pity for Christine and Amber Lundy were more important than respecting a murderer's feelings. But accepting his guilt is different from claiming an absolute knowledge of how he went about killing his wife and daughter. In any case, he didn't pay much attention to my pledge. He thought he'd be acquitted.

In law, Lundy is a murderer. In law, Clint Rickards, the former senior policeman accused of taking part in the gang-rape of Louise Nicholas, is innocent. He was acquitted in that trial, and another verdict of not guilty was delivered at a similar, subsequent trial. But it cost him his career, his reputation, his name; whereas Nicholas was referred to in a 2015 news story as a 'rape victim'. In law, that's false. But the certainties have moved on, and remain firmly on Nicholas's side of the story.

I drank beers with Lundy on a porch. I had a cup of tea with Rickards in a café frequented by the mentally ill. I smoked cigarettes with Nicholas in an adobe house. And then there was the time I met Chris Wang, accused of killing two men with a steak knife bought from the Made In Japan $2 shop on Queen Street. I went there and bought the same knife. The packaging reads: 'Always hygienic since blade is stainless-steel. Achieves a professionally cut surface!'

I never really knew what I was doing with any of these people. Freedom was at stake for Lundy and Wang. Something else was at stake for Rickards and Nicholas, something vital and important: belief. I was just passing through.

I've worked the past 15 or 20 years in journalism as a kind of writer at large, rarely assigned to anything, mostly just choosing stories that seem interesting. When at a loss, I'll walk into a courtroom. I always feel at home the second I take my seat. I wait for the misery, the ambiguities, the accumulation of minor details.

'Crime does pay, for the media at least,' announces the nobody from *Te Ara*, in its section on crime writing. 'Editors, journalists, television and radio producers know that there is an appetite for morbid, horrific and macabre news stories … The media's crime coverage is highly selective … The most heinous or bizarre murders get the most media coverage. For example, a stabbing will receive little media attention compared to a man who kills his family.'

Fair call. No one else from the media bothered to attend the stabbing trial that spring afternoon. It was a slow day. I recognised one of the clerks in another courtroom. She said, 'I've had a woman accused of killing her husband.'

I could have gone there, but I felt an important point was about to be reached in the case of the Maori guy who stuck a knife between the second and third ribs of an Asian guy, and killed him. The pathologist took the jury through his postmortem. The victim's chin, he said, had an 'irregular tearing'. He said it was consistent with falling face-first on the driveway. In the public gallery, the dead man's widow fainted.

Court was adjourned. An ambulance was called. 'Crime news … lacks complexity' according to *Te Ara*. In fact, it deals with the most complex subject in life. The subject was addressed quite directly by the pathologist when court was resumed, and he described the deceased. '51 years of age. 74 kilos in weight, and 169 centimetres in length.' A life reduced to statistics, the image of flesh on a slab: slowly, profoundly, we were being told what it's like to be dead.

Chapter 1

Mark Lundy: Operation Summer

> ... the high authorities we serve would not order such an arrest without gathering exact information about the reasons for the arrest and about the person to be arrested. There's no room for mistake.
>
> — *The Trial*, Franz Kafka

1

It was a curious summer. Once a week I'd visit Geoff Levick at his beautiful rural property west of Auckland in Kumeu, with its dark pond and its plum trees, and sometimes we'd sit on the back porch with his house guest, Mark Lundy. There was an apple orchard next door, and a line of pines straight ahead, above a narrow creek. I went for a wander one day and surprised a pheasant. A harrier circled the orchard on the afternoon I first met Lundy.

'Hawk,' I said.

'Yes,' he said.

We sat in silence. There was another attempt at New Zealand small talk — cricket, the weather, Winston. He was under instructions from his legal team not to discuss his impending trial for the murder of his wife and child, but after five minutes that was pretty much all we ever talked about. Everyone else was doing it; for the better part of 15 years, the subject had formed part of the national conversation. The killings were so awful, so brutal. Christine Lundy was hacked to death in her bed. Amber Lundy, seven years old, had her head cracked open with the same weapon, which has never been found. The murders were conducted in their Palmerston North home at an unknown time of night, by person or persons unknown or by someone they knew and loved. You could walk a long day's march before you found anyone who thought it wasn't Lundy — the fat man who fucked whores, who murdered his own family for an insurance cheque, who staged it to look like a burglary gone wrong, who was found guilty and should never have been let out on appeal to stand retrial. Levick and Lundy were quite likely the only two people in a very wide radius who maintained his innocence. They occupied a kind of parallel universe in that sunny, idyllic corner of farmland and vineyard.

Lundy was a big man, slow, pale, very angry, very bitter. He almost looked gaunt. He was 43 at the time of the murders, fat and soft-skinned, with a lousy fringe. Fifteen years later, he'd lost a lot of weight and most of his hair. There was a peculiar goatee. He was assertive, verbose, nervous. We had a beer or two. Levick preferred a balanced diet of instant coffee and cigarettes. I liked Lundy, not overly; I liked Levick, a lot. The two of them were in such intense cahoots — they were fighting to clear Lundy's name, to beat the murder charges in court — but they made an odd pair. Levick was small, with startling blue eyes set in a red face, and his conversation revealed a brilliant, nimble intellect. Lundy lumbered in gait and mind. It was difficult to imagine them meeting in any circumstances other than their shared obsession with proving Lundy's innocence.

I said, 'Do you two actually have anything in common?'

Lundy spoke first. He said, 'Nothing.'

He helped out around the place. The next time I visited, he was up on a ladder, peering into a water tank. It didn't have much water in it. The ground was hard, and turned brown by the end of January. The creek nearly went dry. The surrounding countryside was parched and the roads were empty. I loved heading out that way, past the prime minister's Helensville electoral office with the big picture of Key's gormless face, past the strawberry fields and the roadside stalls — watermelons $4.99, six cobs of corn $5. It was horsey and fruity. A new dementia unit was due to open. There was the famous sign with its berserk apostrophes advertising YUCCA'S BROMELIAD'S ORCHID'S SUCCULENT'S. There were the famous wine estates of Nobilo and Soljans. They were very pretty on the eye. Also, though, they mocked Lundy's own hapless schemes to create a vineyard on prime land in the Hawke's Bay. His dream came to nothing. Police regarded the venture as evidence in his prosecution; it went to motive — he needed money, fast. 'There's another way of looking at that,' Geoff said, that first afternoon on the porch. He had two packets of Winfield Green beside the ashtray. He whittled them down while he explained that the wine venture contained the answer to the riddle: if not Lundy, then who killed Christine and Amber? It involved root stock, a frightened woman who called the police, an outstanding debt … Geoff liked to re-enact conversations, and he started to shout when he took on the role of his prime suspect. 'Keep your voice down,' Lundy said. A man was driving a tractor in the orchard. Levick padded into the house to put on the jug for more coffee.

I said to Lundy, 'Who do you think did it?'

He said, 'I don't know. I don't think too much about that. I just want to know why. Why would you kill them? They were my life. In a way, they still are. It's all I think about. They're with God, waiting for me. I know I'll see them in Heaven.'

He wept. Levick had come back with his mug of coffee. He said, 'You all right, Mark?'

Lundy said to me, half in wonder, 'I've talked to two other journalists, Mike White and Jared Savage. They didn't make me cry. *You* do.' The other half felt like rage.

2

These were his halcyon days. He was a free man, at large and on bail, not exactly happy, often tense, but hopeful that his retrial would get him the right result — not guilty, at last, of the murders of Christine and Amber on 30 August 2000. He was found guilty at his first trial in 2002. He successfully appealed to the Privy Council — thanks in large part to the incredible efforts of Levick, who didn't know him and simply took an interest — and his conviction was thrown out in 2013. He bail conditions allowed him to travel to Kumeu, and he'd also driven to the cemetery in Palmerston North to visit the graves of his wife and daughter.

I said, 'Were you nervous someone would see you there?'

He said, 'Oh, shit yes. Terrified.'

He'd sat and talked to them, he said. 'My girls.'

I imagined him sitting there, asserting his right to grieve. The text on the headstone was in his words. It was like a touching tribute to himself. It read: FOREVER LOVED BY HUSBAND AND FATHER MARK. And underneath, from the terrible song: UNFORGETTABLE. THAT'S WHAT YOU ARE. Palmerston North writer Peter Hawes, who attended the first trial and filed an extraordinary report to the *Manawatu Standard*, mentioned the headstone when we spoke on the phone. He hated the thing. 'Not only do they get hacked to death,' he said, 'they get lumbered with banality.'

We spoke on a day when I happened to be visiting Levick and Lundy. I took the call in the trees by the creek, and talked in a low voice. It felt like an abuse of hospitality to talk with Hawes. He was in possession of one of the most original minds in New Zealand literature, but he echoed what everyone else thought when he said, 'I know full well he is absolutely guilty.' He had studied Lundy in court, tried to examine his pathology. He failed. He said, 'I couldn't get at him. I couldn't find the gap in his brain. I couldn't find why he did it.'

And then he said, 'Amber's death was an act of love.'

I said, 'What?'

Hawes said, 'A kid can't live after seeing that. He killed her to save her.'

From his story in the *Standard*: 'I sank my brain into the doings of this crime — it affected me greatly. My wife was afeard of me, she hid axes and tomahawks and feared for my sanity as I tried to descend to Lundy's. Because he did these murders, of that, dear reader, have no doubt. He waddled into that bedroom dressed in freezing work overalls with mask and perhaps a snorkel. Then he set about her. He took away her face in 17 blows, in order to expunge her from the memory of his and the human race. His daughter, alarmed by the affray, then rushed into the room and in a gush of sheer parental love, Mark Lundy chased her down the hall and, in three jagged blows, sent all memories of what she had seen to heaven.'

Hawes and I spoke for about half an hour. I hiked to a low ridge, and sat down on the pine needles. I said in a low whisper, afraid that Levick or Lundy might overhear, 'Have you considered the possibility that he's innocent?'

Hawes said, 'That would be an interesting intellectual exercise.'

Levick tried to get me interested in that intellectual exercise back in 2005. It was a kind of fishing trip: I was working at the *Sunday Star-Times* back then, and Levick was wanting a journalist to look into the material he'd gathered that raised questions about Lundy's conviction. I demurred. I said it wasn't really my cup of tea, but I forwarded the email to the incomparable Donna Chisholm, my esteemed colleague at the newspaper. She wrote a couple of stories. I gather it must have been her whom Lundy was referring to when he wrote to Levick from prison, 'A pet reporter is a good idea. You seem to have found one.' He hadn't. Donna moved on to other subjects.

I eventually came on the scene long after I was needed: that summer, awaiting the retrial. I packed a lunch for my weekly outings to Kumeu, and spent most of those long, hot days inside a small room off the garage. Levick had filled the shelves with massive amounts of paperwork from his diligent and genuinely awesome investigation into the Lundy case. I opened up manila folders marked PAINT and PETROL and TIME OF DEATH, took notes ('M and C buy $29.95 chickwheat-shade lampshade at Lighting Direct, last time sees her alive … $83.40 room fee Foreshore Motor Lodge, hooker $140'), and slowly began to make some sense of the formless narrative told by Levick's documents. I suppose I was getting embedded. I daresay I was forming sympathies. The journalist and the murder accused, hanging out on Levick's porch in the afternoon shade, another time driving down the road to an ice-cream shop. A child dropped her ice cream, and cried. There was a prickly pear in flower. The three of us spooned creamy goodness into our faces as we relaxed outside the store in gorgeous sunshine.

'How's yours?' Lundy said.

'Delicious,' I said.

We sat in silence. It didn't seem like a good idea to discuss the case in public. Blood splatter, autopsies, whores — so much of the whole saga was garish, explicit. So much of it was banal, domestic. The setting was a kind of quintessence of boring New Zealand life; the family were overweight and cheerful, very popular, very social, into Scouts and Girl Guides and Pippins, messy, guzzlers of junk, normal, living in a weatherboard house with green trim. A 43-year-old kitchen sink and tap salesman in Palmerston North kisses his wife goodbye one morning and drives to Petone, near Wellington, to see clients. He stays overnight in a motel, eats a roast-chicken dinner from Pak'nSave, polishes off most of a bottle of rum, and calls an escort from The Quarry Inn to his room just before midnight. They have sex. She leaves. These were the undisputed facts, and Lundy's version of events — it was just a routine business trip; even the assignation with a hooker was part of his routine — sounded entirely plausible. But the police inquiry, Operation Winter, formed a mosaic of evidence pulled from all sorts of places — McDonald's, Texas — and some of it sounded kind of plausible. Lundy drove from Petone and killed them with a tool from his garage (police argued that paint flakes in Christine's hair matched the paint he used to mark his tools), then drove back to the motel. A man from Texas who practised a novel form of forensic science claimed that a stain on the sleeve of Lundy's shirt was brain tissue. Goes to motive: the wine venture was about to collapse, and he needed the life insurance pay-out. Goes to character: his behaviour was thought of as really fishy.

3

Why do some cases fascinate, why do others fail to engage? What stories do they tell us about ourselves? Very often they offer a commentary on the range of our hatred. It's rare that we remember the names of victims. It's as though our sympathies can't match the depth of the loathing we reserve for a criminal élite whose names we never forget. Rewa, Dixon, Weatherston … The crux of the Lundy saga — its special appeal, the thing that gave it an enduring power and resonance — was his perceived role as a shocking phoney. He was scorned as a fake, and much of it came down to his display of grief at Christine and Amber's funeral. He wailed, he heaved great sobs, he had to be held upright. A slow-motion clip of Lundy howling at the funeral featured in the opening credits of long-running TV satire *Eating Media Lunch*. In the catalogue of grave sins, Lundy's exhibition that day was held in only slightly less odium than the murders.

He had lost his wife and child. They had been brutally murdered. 'How is a man,' he asked at his trial, 'supposed to grieve?' It was a good question. Had he committed some other affront? Was there a resentment that he had transgressed the New Zealand code of remaining taciturn or at least laconic at all times? Open displays of grief are permissible at a tangi. Not at a funeral in sensible and provincial Palmerston North, not collapsing, losing it. 'The funeral, for me, was something of a disaster,' Lundy wrote in a letter to Levick from Manawatu Prison in 2005. 'I had co-ordinated & organised everything, the extra seating, the extra sound system for outside, the order of proceedings, pallbearers, eulogies, songs, hymns, the whole works. At 12.45 I arrived at the back of the church, [his sister] Caryl driving me, and I couldn't get out of the car. I totally lost it. I have vague recollections of seeing people but that's all. My next memory of consequence was … around the corner at the Rose & Crown. In the bar were at least 200 family and friends from all over the country. I was told later that I was grabbing everybody and hugging them, not shaking hands. I was babbling out something like, "I'm missing out of Christine and Amber hugs, so I need to get them from somewhere." I am told that I was hugging strangers, who were there just as sticky beaks, and refusing all handshakes. I have no recollection of all this. When I saw the 6pm news I was both shocked & embarrassed at what I saw.'

There were other reports of Lundy's behaviour — said in court, and in the media — that received a lot less attention. After the murders, he told police he was having thoughts of suicide, and wanting to drive his car at speed into a wall. That's an acceptable exhibition of grief, isn't it? This hardly counts as forensic credibility, but a psychiatric assessment of Lundy was made by James S. Howard III, an American forensic psychiatrist based in Southland, 'as determined from New Zealand newspapers'. Howard wrote, 'He stated he would curl up in a ball for hours. He became sullen and withdrawn. He kept away from the house, neighbourhood, and papers. That does not fit a profile of a killer of this type ... There is nothing which leads me to believe anything other than that Mark Lundy did not kill them.' Howard's 'assessment' was made during the six-month police search for the killer. He concluded: 'Let us hope Mark Lundy will not be the scapegoat in this unresolved police matter.' Police arrested Lundy in February 2001. Howard's report was never referred to again.

Howard had the psychiatric expertise, but had never laid eyes on Lundy. In contrast, there was memorable evidence given by someone who knew Lundy, and who offered his version of that hopeless but popular science known as body language. Detective Allan Wells appeared as a witness for the prosecution. He had known Lundy for 20 years, and described himself as a 'friend'.

Crown prosecutor Ben Vanderkolk: 'You have come along to this Court about what Mark Lundy was like at the funeral, as if that has got something to do with his guilt or innocence?'

Wells: 'Yes.'

He was asked to describe Lundy's behaviour at the funeral. He said, 'He had both his arms over the support people as if they were carrying his weight for him, and he farewelled Christine and Amber in the hearses. They drive off, and he walked around the corner of the church. I noticed he seemed to come to grips with himself pretty quickly ... It was a totally different mannerism.'

Meaning, Lundy dropped the act when he thought no one was looking. The evidence was considered revealing, and played to the widespread feeling that Lundy was acting a role. Wells further described that Lundy lifted his shoulders and stood upright. Geoff Levick asked Lundy about the episode in a letter. He replied, 'I have no idea what he [Wells] was on about. If I did in fact change my posture though, I would not be too surprised. I am an extremely emotional person and my family and friends were soothing me somewhat. I was constantly putting on a brave face and disappearing so as to totally lose it when I had to. It is quite possible that I did in fact lift my shoulders so as to bluff the many in the house so they would leave me alone to grieve in my own way. (Shit, I'm actually losing it even now recalling those times. Told you I am an emotional idiot.)'

His worst character reference came from another 'friend', who went with Lundy and a few others on a fishing trip about six weeks after the murders. They had beers at the Ohingaiti Tavern. They had beers at the Oasis in Waiouru. They stayed at the Sportsmans Lodge in Turangi, and Lundy switched to spirits. 'He said we had beer, and good company, and the only thing missing were whores.'

Prosecutor: 'Did he make any other remark about the whores?'

'Just the fact that he rated himself and what his abilities were.'

Lundy and the whores. It wasn't a good look. His brother was horrified when he was told; he later came to believe that Lundy was guilty, and even changed his name to avoid association with the surname his brother had made so hated. Police questioned Lundy at length and with disgust about his use of escorts in Petone and on other trips; the interviews were played in court. He chose to give evidence at the first trial. It could not be said that he presented himself as a faithful husband, or a widower incapacitated by mourning.

Prosecutor: 'Do you have any guilt over hiring the escort on the night Christine and Amber died?'

Lundy: 'It sickens me to a certain degree.'

'And yet on a subsequent business trip you could go back to the same motel with another prostitute?'

'I did.'

'The same circumstances, the same sort of celebrations, alcohol, as you did on the night your wife and child died?'

'I just said I did.'

'You can do that, can you?'

'I did do it.'

All of which proves ... what, exactly? None of these matters — that he'd grieved too much, grieved too little, grieved inappropriately — tied him to the crime. But all of these matters played to the suspicions that he was dreadfully, profoundly insincere. The lie was that he loved his wife; the truth was that he wanted shot of her, he had big dreams, he fancied himself as the prosperous owner of a vineyard, and Christine was holding him back. Hence, according to this folklore, the over-acting. It was as though he never knew how to be normal. It was as though he was intensely self-conscious. There was something about him which consistently played a false note. I was struck by these doubts, too, when I met him that summer. I wanted to warm to him — God almighty, what if he was an innocent man, who had experienced the trauma of losing his wife and daughter in violent, shocking circumstances and then was blamed for it, and banged up in jail? — but his manner didn't make it easy. One afternoon we were standing around Levick's bare and rather depressing kitchen, and the subject of wine came up. Lundy had been a wine buff, and belonged to a wine club in Palmerston North. I said I was more like his brother-in-law, Glenn Weggery, who used to tag along with Lundy to the wine club but brought his own beer. Lundy then launched into a long story about meeting a stranger at a scouting convention. There was a great variety of wine, and the bottles had been opened. The man said he fancied himself as an expert taster, and challenged Lundy to a blind-tasting duel. Lundy mimed going around the table, taking sips, and not only naming the label, but also its year and the exact vineyard. The challenger was left open-mouthed. He had met his match. He was in the presence of a master. It was a long and fairly boring speech, the monologue of a braggart; and when it finally ended, we stood in awkward silence until Levick changed the subject. All of which proved ... what, exactly? So he was good at wine tasting. So he chose to tell a self-serving story. So why was it that it made me feel uncomfortable, that it had something to do with his guilt or innocence?

4

In between monologues and gelato ice creams, Lundy would disappear into his small room with the single bed at the end of the hallway to study another million words about his case and prepare notes and questions for his defence team. There was a lot of fresh scientific evidence and police disclosure coming through that summer, and the prosecution had prepared its list of 144 witnesses — which was fascinating as much for its absences as its inclusions. A number of crucial witnesses from the first trial would play no part in the retrial. I felt disappointed. In particular, I really wanted to see the amazing Margaret Dance on the stand. Reading the transcript of her evidence in the first trial was like reading the report of a séance. In that hot little room off Levick's garage, with my salami sandwiches peeling in the sunlight and ants marching towards my chocolate biscuits, I marvelled at her lyrical imaginings; here, at last, in this den of blood-spatter findings and autopsy reports ('The jaws were removed, cleaned and inspected'), there was something playful, something childish.

Dance told the court that she saw someone matching Lundy's description wearing a woman's wig and running from the scene of the crime on the night of the murders. 'My first impression was, "I wonder what she is running away from?" Then I saw it was a he, and [he] had a let-me-get-out-of-here-quickly sort of expression ... I have a very photographic memory. I recall an impression of intensity on the person's face, like he was wanting to get somewhere.'

Later, after she heard news of the murders, and wanting to help police find the killer, she gave the matter a lot of thought, or, as she put it, 'musing'. She was asked in cross-examination: 'Can you explain this musing process?'

'It's just allowing things to run through my mind.'

'Do you have any particular ability in this area?'

'Occasionally, yes.'

'Can you explain what that is?'

'It's usually called ESP … Whether it is accurate or not I have no idea.'

'Are you saying this psychic ability may not be accurate?'

'It's been very accurate on occasion,' she said.

By 'musing', and 'allowing things to run through my mind', she wrote down the words HANDS DARK. This was helpful, because it narrowed down the police hunt for the killer to a man wearing a woman's wig and with dark hands. She also wrote the words SKIP BIN TAWA. She explained, 'I wondered where the bloodstained clothes had been put, and those were the words that I got.'

Ludicrous. Dance belonged to a wider farce — the police theory that Christine and Amber were killed not long after 7pm. It required so many blatant fictions. Margaret Dance's vision of Lundy fleeing from the murder scene at around that time was merely the most playful. The foundation myth for the time of death was courtesy of Dr James Pang, who conducted the autopsies. He claimed the absence of the smell of gastric juices in the stomach was proof that the digestion process hadn't begun — meaning they were killed about an hour after they ordered their last supper, a McDonald's meal, at 5.43pm. Pang's time-of-death estimate created immense challenges. Police had to put Lundy at his home in Palmerston North at about 7pm.

They rose to the challenge with flair and wit. Calls made to Lundy's Motorola cellphone put him in Petone at 5.30pm, and again at 8.29pm; he didn't have an alibi for the two hours and 59 minutes between the calls; ergo, or *reductio ad absurdum*, it gave him the time to make the return trip to Palmerston North, where he slaughtered his family at roughly 7.15pm. Although Christine and Amber never missed an episode of *Shortland Street*, which began at 7pm, and although Amber didn't go to bed until about 8pm, police advanced the notion, in all seriousness, that the reason they were in bed was because Lundy had persuaded Christine to undress and wait for Big Daddy in bed at 7pm so they could have sex. The two had spoken on the phone at 5.30pm. The Crown prosecutor said at trial: 'Why was she naked? The eight-minute call is the key.' And so Lundy headed home, although it meant he had to drive all the way from Petone, and then return to the motel where he had booked a room for the night — oh, and although, also, the Lundys' Hewlett Packard home computer was manually turned off at 10.52pm. Police got around that last one when its computer 'expert' Maarten Kleintjes said it was possible that Lundy had cleverly manipulated the clock. Most remarkably of all, according to police, Lundy managed to make the 300-kilometre round-trip in a ground-speed record of two hours and 59 minutes (the 'Lundy Five Hundy', as it was later immortalised), as well as find the time to chop his wife and daughter to death; fiddle with the computer; stage a break-in; run down the street in a wig and women's clothes; dispose of said wig and women's clothes, the weapon, Christine's jewellery box, and his blood-splattered clothes — he drove like a maniac, killed them like a maniac. In Lundy's final police interview, when he was arrested for the murders, Detective Inspector Steve Kelly crowed: 'No doubt about it, Christine and Amber were murdered during the period you have no alibi … Caught you, buddy, absolutely caught you!'

The drive released him. Without it, Geoff Levick would never have taken an interest in the case; and without Levick, it's doubtful Lundy would ever have had his conviction quashed by the Privy Council, and been set free to wander that beautiful property in Kumeu, where he once noted 24 different bird species in one day, including kookaburras. Lundy owed Levick his freedom. It was an incredible achievement. When Levick first sent me that email back in 2005, I dismissed him as a madman. Of all the cases to take on, he chose Lundy! The modern history of New Zealand policing was rotten with false arrests for murder; they framed Arthur Thomas, the cases against David Bain, David Tamihere, John Barlow, Scott Watson and Teina Pora were variously dubious or downright rubbish; but surely they got it right with Lundy? I assumed his guilt. He was gross, despicable; there was the matter of his wife's brain on his shirt. He appealed the conviction. He came before the Court of Appeal in 2003. It didn't go well. The judge said, 'Amber must have died with the awful injuries to her mother as her last living memory. The trial judge did not give this aspect enough weight. He really only mentioned the involvement of Amber in passing. The murder requires denunciation and demonstration of society's abhorrence at a very high level.' The sentence was increased from 17 years to 20 years. When Lundy returned to prison that day in a state of shock, he walked past the cell of serial rapist Malcolm Rewa. At that time, Rewa laid claim to the second-longest sentence in New Zealand. He was given 22 years; another serial rapist, Joseph Thompson, had been sentenced to 25 years. Rewa called out to Lundy, as if it were a boast: 'You're still only the bronze medallist, Lundy …'

He was left to rot. Just about everyone loathed Lundy. Levick, too, thought much the same — until a story by Paula Oliver, in *The New Zealand Herald* on 10 January 2003, caught his eye.

The article was about an effort by some friends of Lundy, 'a stoic few', to reinvestigate the murders. I later met the closest friend, the most stoic. He had remained loyal to Lundy all those years, and it had cost him dearly. He suffered a nervous collapse and depression, he fled Palmerston North, he desperately wanted to 'fly under the radar', as he put it, and not have his name used in print. That seemed fair. He outlined the history of his campaign to free Lundy. He approached David Yallop, the author of *Beyond Reasonable Doubt*. Nothing came of it. Then he approached Bain's belligerent advocate, Joe Karam, who advised him 'to seek out media interest'. The subsequent *Herald* story in 2003 pointed to discrepancies and assorted weirdnesses in Lundy's prosecution, including the matter of that manic drive. Levick had driven that same exact route many times. He did the maths. He didn't think it was possible. In fact, he was *convinced* it wasn't possible. It made him wonder about the entirety of the case against Lundy, and soon he began to adopt the mantra of all campaigners: 'There's something not quite right here.'

5

The weeks leading up to the 2015 retrial were increasingly tense. Lundy suffered terrible headaches every day. Levick seethed and stewed, although that was his usual manner. He had spent 10,000 hours of his life and around $100,000 of his money on the case, and it had turned him into an obsessive. I'd ask him a question and he'd give an answer that was epic in length and discursive in narrative and scornful in feeling — he'd come to hate the police. Levick always apologised for talking too long. He was exceptionally generous, and I never left the property without a great big bag of plums. When he talked about cricket, he would relax. He wouldn't touch alcohol, but his red face told another story of past boozings. He muttered that it had something to do with a recent separation, and talked about his wife with longing. He had moved into a new house, and it felt empty and sad. The bathroom was stocked with two bars of Knights Castile soap and little else; the walls were bare except for a photo of a racehorse he used to own. Levick and Lundy moved like old bachelors through the house; separated and widowed, they were joyless, certainly determined, intensely serious, lonely.

I wasn't much fun. I shut myself away inside the small room reading up on the case, and sometimes I wondered whether Levick's magnificent effort was futile and wrong-headed. His Post-it notes read FFS, LIES, CRAP. In his mind, there was no room for doubt, or nuance; Lundy had been framed, the charges were bullshit, the police had lied and twisted the evidence. The clearest distillation of his investigation was in the folder marked GEOFF'S BOOK. He had written it for publication. No one could ever publish it. It was libellous and furious. The constant use of bold type, capital letters and exclamation marks were immediate signs of an obsessive at work, expressing himself in the typography and language of vitriol. 'Chapter three: Bladder full. Chapter four: Exposed banana. Chapter six: What car? What woman? What wig?' And yet much of it was completely accurate. Piece by piece, he took apart the 7pm question — Dance's crazy evidence, the impossibility of the drive, the vacuity of Pang's time-of-death theory, the absurdity of manipulating the clock on the computer. The book reads like a prophecy. On 26 January, two weeks before the retrial, the police told Lundy's defence team that they had thrown out the time-of-death theory of 7pm — and with it, Margaret Dance and all the rest of their fanciful notions that cast Lundy as a cold-blooded killer and master criminal racing through the Manawatu flatlands in the early evening.

Levick had called his book 'Meticulous, or Ridiculous?'. The police conceded that the latter option was the correct one when they finally admitted that they were wrong with their wretched 7pm theory. The scenario had changed in the new police inquiry, Operation Spring. They now put the time of death as sometime well after midnight, perhaps 3am. In essence, though, nothing had changed. It had simply been a case of wrong time, right man. Everything else remained in place. Lundy was the murderer. He did it for the insurance. He staged a break-in. And, most damningly — the one piece of evidence that put him at the scene of the crime, what it all came down to — the stain on his shirt was tissue from Christine's brain.

'Fucking Miller,' Levick said. He meant Dr Rodney Miller, whom he loathed even more than anyone from the police. Miller was a specialist in diagnostic pathology, based in Dallas, Texas, who had tested Lundy's shirt and identified the presence of brain tissue. It was a novel approach — Miller worked in the field of immunohistochemistry, or IHC, primarily in cancer research, and his tests had never previously been used in a forensic crime investigation. By chance, he had attended a pathology conference in Palmerston North in August 2000, just three days before the murders. He was a keynote speaker. His speech was titled, 'Achieving reliability of immunostains', and it addressed techniques of tissue transfer. This was exactly what the police needed during their investigation into Lundy. A scientist from Medlab in Palmerston North, who remembered Miller's talk, wrote to him in January 2001: 'I've got a curly one for you!!! We are involved in a homicide investigation in which a mother and daughter were slain using a tomahawk … The husband/father is the prime suspect. His shirt has 2 smears of nearly invisible material on it … One smear was dampened with water, and imprinted on a slide. It shows tissue fragments including intact blood vessels. We feel it is probably brain.'

Miller replied, 'Wow! That is really a nasty case, and it would be great to nail the bad guy.' And then: 'Maybe we could use tissue transfer media to remove the cellular material from the shirt, and do immunostains on that.'

Head of the police inquiry, Detective Sergeant Ross Grantham, personally took the samples to Miller's laboratory in Texas. He later claimed in an affidavit: 'I was not shopping for an expert who could tell me that it was brain tissue.' He wrote to Miller: 'It is vitally important for our case to be able to positively identify the material as originating from Christine Lundy.'

Miller wrote an entertaining narrative, published on his laboratory website, about the testing. 'The week before Detective Grantham came, I was rinsing off a fresh chicken to be used for dinner, and noticed spinal cord tissue protruding from its severed neck. I thought this presented an excellent opportunity to see whether we could use IHC to detect tissues smeared on shirts, so I smeared chicken spinal cord, kidney, and liver on portions of an old shirt ... Little did the chicken know that she would be contributing greatly to putting a guilty man behind bars.'

Yes, if only chicken little could talk. Miller's immunostains proved positive for chook tissue; likewise, his testing on Lundy's shirt 'showed unequivocal tissue on the areas of the stain'. He wrote: 'This provided unequivocal evidence that Mark Lundy had brain tissue on his shirt, from an area that also contained Christine Lundy's DNA. This was the critical piece of evidence that allowed an arrest to be made.'

Miller remarked near the end of his breezy crime yarn that Lundy was sentenced to 20 years without parole. 'I think we all know that if he committed this crime in Texas, his punishment would be a bit different.' Miller's evidence would have sent Lundy to his death. There is a note of regret, a kind of sigh, in his 'I think we all know ...'

The police had found their smoking gun. The supposition was that Lundy wore overalls or something similar at the murders, but small traces (described at trial as 'bigger than a speck of sand, smaller than a grain of rice') of Christine's brain somehow found their way onto the shirt he was wearing underneath. Strange, perhaps, that other tell-tale traces weren't found on his shoes, jewellery, glasses, or anywhere in the car. Crown prosecutor Ben Vanderkolk told the jury at the 2002 trial: 'It clothed the body of the killer. It is the silent witness to the killing. Do not let this shirt leave your side.' Lundy's defence team blandly agreed that it was evidence of Christine's brain, thus consigning their own client to Hell. They put up a little bit of a fight, but they picked it badly when defence lawyer Mike Behrens accused Grantham of planting brain tissue on the shirt. It was a disastrous tactic. Behrens yapped in court about 'a most corrupt plan of the most rotten kind'. To Grantham, he asked, 'Did you put the brain tissue on the shirt?'

Grantham replied with force: 'That's the most disgusting thing I have heard in 23 years.'

Judge Anthony Ellis told the jury in his summing up: 'The presence of Christine's brain matter is not in dispute.' Well, where do you go after that? What need to say much else? His summing up took exactly 38 minutes. The jury returned its verdict in just under six hours.

Levick put more time into investigating the validity of Miller's testing than any other issue relating to the case against Lundy. He declared it was unreliable science, that the stains were so degraded they couldn't possibly reveal evidence of tissue. There's a thrilling moment in his notes when he first had an inkling that IHC staining might be deeply flawed. Not long after he came onboard the campaign to free Lundy, he wrote an email to another supporter, on 25 August 2003: 'I reckon I'm on to something. We have a man in prison for a murder we fervently believe he did not commit. He was wrongly convicted on a stain.'

Levick was vindicated in 2013 when the Privy Council accepted that the jury at the first trial should have heard evidence that seriously challenged Miller's testing. It was one of the major reasons why his conviction was quashed. At a pre-trial hearing in September 2014, though, an expert called by the defence agreed with Miller's tests — that the shirt did reveal traces of central nervous system tissue. Miller was right. Just as damagingly, police introduced a new scientific testing of molecular material known as mRNA. 'It's a brand-new test they've come up with just for this case, exactly like they did with Miller's immunostains,' said Levick. 'Same old, same old. More smoke and mirrors ... So what they've got is this: one, the ESR [Institute of Environmental Science and Research] says it's Christine's DNA on the shirt stain. Two, Miller's IHC tests says it's central nervous system or brain tissue. Three, the mRNA tests says it's human. One, two, three: gotcha.'

Lundy's defence said the stain might be from meat — a hamburger pattie, a chop, something like that. They objected to the mRNA testing, and argued at a pre-trial hearing that it shouldn't be put in front of a jury: 'It cannot be said to be accepted by the scientific community.' Justice Stephen Kos dismissed their argument: 'The novelty of a scientific technique is not a per se basis for exclusion.' They took their fight to the Court of Appeal in November 2014. Three judges made their ruling. Justice Ellen France wrote, 'The proposed evidence that the brain tissue on Mr Lundy's shirt sleeve is probably human is pivotal evidence.' She noted 'the absence of international standards', and ruled it was inadmissible. She was outvoted 2–1 by the other judges. It would stay. *Gotcha*. There were further crises to come for Lundy's defence.

6

The last time I saw Lundy before the trial began, he said, 'I'm like a haymaker inside.' The trial in Wellington was due to open in a fortnight. We had a beer on the back porch. The weather had been wonderful all January, and grassy Kumeu shone like an emerald. Levick bit down on his Winfield and said he wasn't going to go to Wellington for the trial. 'Don't think I could bear it,' he said. He said he'd have to be held back when Dr Miller took the stand. Lundy said to him, 'But you *will* be there at the end, and we *will* go out and celebrate. There are no ifs and buts about it.'

Then he said to me, 'And there might be room for two journalists.'

He also meant Mike White, from *North & South*, who wrote a remarkable 18-page story about the Lundy case in 2009. Catchy headline, too: 'Meticulous, or ridiculous?' White had gone through all the paperwork that Levick had accumulated, researched the science, conducted difficult interviews, and produced a masterpiece of careful thinking and thorough inquiry. It was also crucial in gaining Lundy's release. The story had come to the attention of David Hislop QC, a New Zealand criminal lawyer based in England. I spoke to Hislop during the trial and asked him what he thought when he read the story. 'Wow,' he said. It got him hooked. He agreed to take on the case, following in the footsteps of previous barristers Mike Behrens, who mounted a thin defence at the first trial, and the famed Barry Hart, who was engaged for a few years on Lundy's behalf, and unearthed some important pieces of discovery from the police, but with whom things eventually soured. Letter from Lundy, 2007: 'I do not want Barry Hart to represent me any more. If it were not for Geoff and the team, absolutely nothing would have been done for my appeal … We just need the right lawyer to seal the verdict and take the glory and appreciation of those who believe in me. I am an innocent man. I need help!'

Hislop took it to the Privy Council, which expressed serious concern over the 7pm theory and also Miller's tests, and declared, 'The verdict is unsafe.' It ordered a retrial. Lundy was released on bail. Hislop headed a team including former Crown prosecutors Ross Burns and Julie-Anne Kincade, and private investigator Tim McKinnel, who successfully fought for Teina Pora's release. The team did not include Levick. There was a twist in the tale of Lundy's defence: the man who had done more than anyone to secure a retrial had been given his marching orders after Levick clashed with Hislop once too often about the direction they should take at the trial.

Letter from Levick: 'I had in mind a full-out, all-guns-blazing attack on Miller … I have seen nothing to indicate that such a tactic would not have worked.'

Letter from Hislop: 'You continue to impugn the manner in which we have sought to conduct the case on this issue … I think the time has come when Mark must make a decision. Either he trusts the legal team or he does not — if he does not, then we go, simple as that. I do not intend conducting this trial with you condemning our every decision.'

Reply from Levick: 'I will not take any further part in this case except to debate matters with ML [Lundy], if he asks … This is a no-reply email. I will not take bullshit like that.'

It was a sad and even tragic ending to Levick's involvement, but also kind of inevitable. I could easily imagine him losing his rag, voicing his opinion in a stroppy, scornful manner, driving Hislop up the wall. He didn't think like lawyers; he went his own way, he was a maverick. But the defence had lost the man who knew more than anyone about the many and various intricacies of Lundy's case. Hislop was taking a very big risk in getting rid of him.

I went out to Kumeu one last time in February. It was a week before the trial. Lundy was at his sister's house in Taupo. I phoned him the next day and wished him luck; I wouldn't see him again until he appeared in the Wellington High Court. I sat in the small room and read through some documents, but it felt desultory. All of Levick's homework wasn't going to help Lundy or play a part in the trial. I took a few notes and left to talk with Levick on the porch. The silvereyes had scoffed the last of the plums. The ground was as hard as a rock. His passionfruit vine had been diagnosed with black leg, a killer fungus, and was due for the chop. There were the hawks, and a kingfisher perched above the dark pond.

I said, 'Well — what d'you think's going to happen next week?'

Levick said, 'Whatever is going to be said and done next week is set in concrete. The strategies are done. That's it. Now the battle starts, and I can't do anything about it. I basically got fired at the end of October, which I find very strange. I could do a hundred times more than what I'm doing. But my commitment to Mark Lundy and his family was to get it to the Privy Council, and I did. I've done all I can do. I have no responsibility now. If anything, I'm relieved. I'm not worried about it. Other people can worry about it. He's stressed to the eyeballs, but there's nothing, *nothing* I can do.'

But he wasn't relieved, and he was extremely worried. He said, 'I think it will swing on the same thing as it did in the first trial: the shirt. If I was on the first jury, I'd have argued the drive, and said it was impossible, but I'd have caved in on the shirt, and found him guilty. Well, the drive's gone, but we've still got the shirt. And we're not going to attack that, which I think we should. But how much of the science will the jury understand, anyway? And will they even think about it that much? It's unbelievable how fast people make up their mind. They'll be told he killed his wife and daughter. I have no doubt some members of the jury will make up their mind within three minutes of the trial that they won't like him. And I don't know what the hell I can do about that. Nothing. There's nothing I can do …'

He had a file of police suspects on the table beside him. It was compiled before Lundy was arrested. I asked him about it, and it lifted his spirits. He was back on familiar ground — the puzzle, the mystery of the killings, the interesting possibilities. We went through the list of persons of interest. There was a P addict who rented near the Lundy house: 'He's from a family regarded as the worst in Palmerston North.' There was a man who knew Christine, described as 'unstable', and who had stabbed his mother. There was a schizophrenic who saw his father kill his mother with an axe. There was a Maori guy whose stepfather was in jail for rape, and whom police visited and found asleep on a mattress in the lounge at 11am. An officer recorded their brief dialogue.

Police: 'How about you sit up and talk to us?'
Man: 'Nah. Get fucked.'

He stormed out of the room, holding his blanket around his waist.

Were any of these characters the killer? Or just blameless low-lifes? Levick talked about suspicious sightings of a white van seen on the night of the murders. Then he talked about the kind of weapon used to kill Christine and Amber. He said, 'As an aside, a couple of years ago I saw an interesting jemmy bar for sale at The Warehouse, and bought one. It was quite short, able to be hidden in a pair of trousers. I used it to attack a watermelon, a pumpkin and some old dog bones. Sorry for the imagery. A full-on blow cleaved the pumpkin in half. The watermelon was disintegrated. Quite a deadly weapon. Flailed, it will break bones, I have no doubt. A jemmy bar was used to gain entry into the Lundy home that night …'

He wasn't treating it as any kind of forensic detail. There was probably nothing in it. Like he said, it was just 'an aside'. But perhaps everything was. Maybe the truth was in black and white.

One day inside that little shop of horrors in Levick's garage, I reached for a folder marked SUTHERLAND. This was the name of the ESR scientist, Bjorn Sutherland, who had examined the crime scene. Sutherland was an important figure in the case. He'd discovered the two microscopic stains on Lundy's shirt. I opened the folder. It contained photocopies of various ESR forms that Sutherland had completed. Further on, it contained photocopies of photographs taken of Christine and Amber, dead.

They showed what happened to Christine that night when her murderer struck her head and face many, many times. The photocopies were black and white; most of the images were black, with blood. Christine was killed in bed. Her face was black. Amber lay on the carpet in the doorway. The back of her head was black. She had got out of bed to see what was going on, and was killed as she turned to escape. She wore a nightie and little white socks. She was seven years old, for pity's sake, and her left hand was curled beside her head.

I remember I was standing up when I looked at the pages. I remember a terrible silence in the room, and feeling very tired, and thinking: did *he* do that?

Chapter 2

That summer: Victor Wasmuth

Summer in New Zealand is the story we tell to ourselves to make us feel good, the annual regatta, the wide blue yonder of sea and sky and sunlight — it's got Christmas in it. It's the holidays. It's the whanau on a porch. There's sand on the pavements and the worship of food. There's maize waist-high in the fields and a van broadcasting the strangely melancholic chimes of 'Greensleeves'. It's got outdoor flow. It's island time. It's all on for young and old. It's the national ideal, a wonderful time to be alive, a favoured time to kill.

Intolerable summer, with its high sun sizzling, the light too bright, the nights too hot to sleep, too dry, too sticky — something's got to give. Better to stay inside and fester. But summer brings it all out in the open. The empty country roads going nowhere, the fizz of waves on coarse black sand. The moths. The cicadas. The dogs barking in boarding kennels. The dogs barking in boarding kennels. The dogs barking in boarding kennels.

'For some years I have been certain that I have been persecuted,' wrote Victor Wasmuth. 'Details of this business are best known to myself, but unfortunately I cannot prove any particular incident. In any case, I decided there would have to be a showdown to have the whole matter thrashed out.'

Summer surrounded him like a narrow ledge. He stepped over it on 7 January 1963. The dogs barking in boarding kennels at the back of a neighbour's property, howling through the long, slow days and moonless nights in a dusty corner of Auckland. West, at Bethells Beach, a long and winding metal road cut through the hills towards the coast. The painter Don Binney lived out that way. There was a hermit in the valley, an old forestry worker who lived in a tip. Bethells was peaceful, obscure. It sagged in the heat. The summer of 1963 burned like a fire across New Zealand: passengers fainted on Wellington commuter trains when delays were caused by tracks buckling in the sun, temperatures were the highest in Christchurch for 101 years, concerns of a drought led to hose bans in Gisborne.

Wasmuth lived in the shade of a macrocarpa in a small fibrolite bach at the top of a rise. 'We were two doors down,' said John Porteous, 'and I was 13.' He boarded at St Paul's in Ponsonby, and was home for the holidays. There were 10 children in his family. His parents had separated. 'Father Cronin helped us deal with the situation,' he said. 'He was a great guy, the most amazing man I've ever met. He gave everything away. He always said life wasn't about money, or fame, or any of those things. It was all about your immortal soul. He was all priest.'

Father Cronin was inside the house, playing cards with John's sisters. Their mother had gone to visit their father. It was a Sunday. 'I used to make bows and arrows out of branches and dry ferns,' John said. 'I was in the block of land between our place and the kennels, drying out these bits of fern in the sun. And all of a sudden there were police cars everywhere. Father Cronin said, "Get inside. There's a bit of a problem up the road."'

John's brother Paul Church said, 'I was seven. It was quite exciting. I was outside by the garage. It was just a lazy Sunday. Nothing ever happened at Bethells.' Trucks from the Duck Brothers' quarry bounced up and down the road every day. You could hear the train coming into nearby Waitakere station. Sometimes you could hear the surf. And then there was the matter of the dogs at the unromantically named Gorseland Kennels, owned by Jim Berry, between Wasmuth's bach and the house where John, Paul and the other eight children lived with their mum.

The kennels accommodated 12 dogs. One belonged to the governor-general. Paul and his sister Frances would walk over to the Berrys' to buy fresh eggs, and visit the kennels. He said, 'She was terrified of dogs. "Oh, just pat them, they're all right," I'd say to her. I remember Mr Berry showed me the pups one day. A couple of weeks before it happened, he asked Mum if they bothered her and she said no. He said, "The guy up the road is always complaining. But we were here first."'

We were here first. So much of the New Zealand way of life bristles in that remark. Wasmuth had emigrated from England. He had worked as a builder. His name was listed in census records in Christchurch in 1928, Onehunga in 1946, Waitakere in 1949, and Rodney in 1956. He was married and had two daughters, but the couple divorced. He remarried, to a woman with two children of her own. They separated, and Wasmuth was living alone by the summer of 1963. Newspaper photos taken of him in police handcuffs show a tall man with a superb physique, like a sprinter — his singlet and shorts reveal shapely legs and ankles, a narrow waist, lightly muscled arms. He looks tanned. He had lost the hair on top of his head, and his eyes are wild and staring.

Stories continue to be told about him by people at Bethells Beach. They said he was a recluse. They said he was a crack shot. They said he walked the road at night with a rifle under his oilskin coat. A man who bought the property two doors down said: 'I heard he had a kid who was a mongol.'

*

Wasmuth was mad. 'Grossly insane', a psychiatrist told the court, in the unrestrained language of the time. His craziness rose with the temperatures that intolerable summer. There was an incident with tomatoes at Christmas. He complained that someone was stealing the fruit right off his plants, and accused Jim Berry's wife, Kathleen, of knowing who was behind it. Seething, paranoid, alone, he sat at his kitchen table in his singlet and shorts and worked on a book — he was a murderer with a fancy prose style. When he appeared in court, he listed his occupation as 'Novelist'. He was a published author, with several short stories appearing in magazines in Australia. His latest project was an epic poem.

I searched for people who might have known him, and called a woman in Northland. 'Well,' she said, 'I'm his daughter.' We didn't talk for long. 'He had literary aspirations,' she said, 'but his poem was pretty much nonsense. It was like blank-verse poetry. There was an awful lot of it — pages and pages. It was impossible to make sense of it. He was an intelligent person; it had what you'd call classical references in it. He'd ask people for their opinion. But nobody could understand it. I've still got some somewhere. Haven't looked at in years, and no desire to.'

A misunderstood genius? The only available document in Wasmuth's oeuvre is his statement to the police. I was shown it in the lobby of an Auckland hotel where I met the late Bill Brien, a former detective who led the inquiry. He gave me a photocopy. The heavy typewriter keys had left ink over the pages; a round stamp from a police inkpad described a circle, like a stain from the bottom of a teacup. It was three pages long and it gave off a kind of crackle of lunacy and violence. You couldn't make this stuff up because it was so artless. There was nothing contrived about it. It was dreamy, almost whimsical. It told a narrative of elisions. Important facts were missing. It skated over the events of the day, was more concerned with the suspicious behaviour of others. It began: 'For some years I have been certain that I have been persecuted …' It ended: 'I have no regrets because I think that the whole thing may have been staged. Except for a pain in my arm, I feel in good health and mentally balanced.'

I visited May Mackey in her apartment in Parnell. She was 92, and claimed: 'I'm fading out.' In fact, she was agile and alert. She made a pot of tea, and put out a plate of custard squares. In 1963 she was married to Detective Inspector Wally Chalmers of the Auckland CIB. 'He was a real Scotsman,' said May. He was pipe major of the police pipe band, a big, barrel-chested man with a soft heart. During the war, when there was a shortage of staff, he worked shifts as a police cook in the Auckland barracks; after making arrests, it was his habit to climb the stairs to the fourth-floor kitchens and make a meal for himself and the arrested man. Days before he was called out to Bethells, he led a party to disarm a 22-year-old plasterer, who was holding a couple hostage in their home in Ellerslie.

May grew up in Dunedin. She was christened Hughina. May and Wally married late in life — she was 40, he was 44 — and adopted. 'We put our names down, and they gave us Huia, our daughter. Then they rang again, and said. "We've got another one." A baby boy, only 11 months old.' They called him Wallace.

They lived in a police house on Forfar Road, Glendowie. I asked her about that summer's day in 1963, and she said, 'The children looked so beautiful that day. I had a pram to carry the two of them, and I thought I'd go for a walk to meet Wally. I phoned the station to find out which route he was coming home. They said, "Sorry, he's not here." He only went out when there was trouble. The next thing, I get a visit.' Wally was 46.

They put her on tranquilisers. The funeral at St David's Church in downtown Auckland was a vast public ceremony with thousands of people lining Khyber Pass Road, and a cortège that went for 5 kilometres. The police band piped the hearses the length of Khyber Pass. May didn't remember much about it. 'I was confused at the time. Grieving. Totally stunned over what had happened. So it's not terribly clear.'

I phoned Valerie Bright in Paihia. In 1963 she was married to Detective Sergeant Neville Power. She said, 'Nev was very studious. He always had his nose in a police manual. Loved cryptic crosswords — he'd puzzle them out over the phone with his dad.' His father was assistant commissioner of police, and his three brothers were also in the force. He was regarded as a rising star, and was a well-liked, attractive man, tall with fair hair.

They lived in Alma Street, Te Atatu South. I asked her about that summer's day in 1963, and she said, 'I was feeding my six-month-old daughter and 18-month-old son their breakfast. Nev pecked me on the cheek and said, "See you later." I was at a friend's house that afternoon when Nev's parents came around. They said, "You need to sit down." It was a weird feeling. I thought it might be a vicious joke on someone's part.' Neville was 25.

Valerie didn't remember much of the funeral, either. She was in a haze of sedatives and grief. Her husband's brothers — listed in the paper the next day as Constable OW Power of Ohakune, Constable BW Power of Te Kuiti, and police cadet KW Power of Trentham — carried the coffin. Valerie said, 'When the casket was lowered into the ground, I felt I was going to go down with it.'

Life back at Alma Street was an agony. 'My son, Ross, stood at the window and waited for his dad to come home. "Daddy come home. Daddy come home." He did it for ages. It tore me apart.'

She sold the house the following year. 'I couldn't get away quickly enough.' I asked her about her husband's killer, and she said, 'I hated Wasmuth. Hated him. His picture is imprinted in my mind. I can see him now.'

I was to visit May Mackey twice, in 2012 and again in 2015. I liked her so much; there was such a kindness to her, and she always spoke from the heart. She had arthritis, and one arm was bad. I poured the heavy teapot, and followed her orders to cover it with a 'coat', as she put it, to keep the pot warm. We sat next to each other on a narrow couch. She laughed easily, and wasn't sentimental; she was more practical and honest than that.

She said about Wally's murder, 'Well, it's history now. But it's always heavily there. That was my life. Wally and I were soulmates. That's how it always was with us. I was left alone with two young children, and a totally broken heart.'

May spoke in a very clear voice. She said: 'My Christian faith helped me through.' It gave her strength, and purpose, and led her towards Wasmuth.

*

I went out west to Bethells on a beautiful day in late summer. The main road leads up and over hills to black sand and a dramatic surf. It was swampy and scruffy, with pukeko rampaging in the scrub, and the rusted shells of cars dumped in land no good for farming, no good for anything much.

There was Wasmuth's bach at the top of the rise. There were fruit trees down the back; Wasmuth's daughter remembers visiting and seeing plums for sale at the front gate. But now the front gate was decorated with barbed wire and held by two padlocks; there had once been a letterbox in the middle of it, and it looked like a wild animal had clawed it out.

I talked to neighbours. People said the man who now lived at the bach Wasmuth built was a recluse. They said he'd cut off his phone. They said he was strange. One neighbour claimed two people lived there: 'We call them the Weird Brothers.'

The kennels next door were overgrown with gorse — it really was Gorselands. Terangimarie Blake and her two children lived in the homestead once riddled with bullets. She grew lettuces in a wheelbarrow, and gave an articulate speech about why she preferred to be called queer and not lesbian. She was very beautiful.

Nehe Reuben lived on the other side of the bach. He opened the door fast and hard; all of a sudden, there was a Maori man standing there with a full moko. He was very pleasant. When he moved in five years ago, he said, the house was haunted. It was the year Wasmuth died. 'The birds weren't singing. My son was getting visitors at night. The ex, too. They were fucken levitating, mate. I got the Maori ghostbusters in and all that shit. The birds sing now.'

You could see the bach through bushes on the side of the road. It was small and dark, with the roof at a 15-degree angle. Two tea towels dried on a line tied across the verandah. It was from there that Wasmuth started shooting. Out of the blue, he fired his .303 Enfield rifle on a complete stranger, Harry Petit, who had come to collect his dog from Gorselands. Petit was shot in the arm at the doorway of Jim Berry's house. Wasmuth continued shooting. Kathleen Berry and Neil Falconer, a 16-year-old who worked at the kennels, crawled on their stomachs into the house as bullets hit the fridge. They phoned the police. Wasmuth went inside his bach, and came back out to empty his teapot.

Petit was dragged to safety. Wasmuth shouted, 'Get some Elastoplast, that'll fix it.'

The dogs barking in boarding kennels. Jim Berry stepped onto the road to see where the shooting was coming from, and was shot in the heart. He was 37.

His wife told the police, 'My husband collapsed in the middle of the road. I ran back to him but he never spoke to me.'

Wasmuth said in his statement, 'Berry made a perfect target of himself. I aimed, fired and he fell to the ground.'

Wasmuth made a pot of tea. Then: 'Shortly afterwards a man came up to my bach. I do not know who he was, and [he] asked me where there was a phone as a man was dead on the road. I told him there was a phone at the Reynolds' place. I had no desire to shoot him, so I let him go.'

The dogs barking in boarding kennels. He waited in his small, dark, hot fibrolite box. 'I stayed inside and more or less expected the arrival of the police.'

Constable Norm Sowter was dispatched to pick up Detective Sergeant Bill Brien from his home in St Heliers. I phoned Sowter in Ahipara. He said, 'It was a magnificently sunny day. Not a cloud. I shot out to get Bill, but it was such a lovely day, and you know what it's like on a Sunday in Mission Bay. Crowded, packed. I was permanently on the horn, driving on the footpath, doing anything to get there as quickly as I could.' Police had temporarily banned the use of sirens.

Another car was sent to get Detective Ross Dallow. I visited Ross at his home in Te Atatu; he is the father of newsreader Simon Dallow, and there were family photographs of his famous son throughout the house. Ross said, 'I was doing some gardening around the back of the house, and suddenly heard a commotion at the front. I saw a police car taking off. Plain-coloured car. Unmarked car. I was part of a rapid-response team, so I got on the phone to central. I had a very quick shower, and the next car came in about five minutes. I was told there had been an incident, that it was very serious.'

The first policeman Wasmuth shot was Neville Power. He approached Wasmuth's bach with Constable John Langham, and fired a tear-gas canister through a window. Wasmuth stepped out onto his porch, and shot Power through the corner of the bach. Wall particles and bullet fragments were found in his heart at the autopsy.

Wasmuth, in his statement: 'He exposed most of his body from behind the corner of the bach, and he too made a perfect target. At this stage I didn't care who I shot, and whether they were policemen or not.'

Power lay dying. He called out to Langham, 'Help me, John.'

Langham called back, 'Stay where you are, Neville. Don't move.'

Wasmuth went outside and stood over Power's body. Langham heard him say, 'Is it cold down there, sonny?'

And then the killer went for Langham, who was hiding in long grass. He would have executed him. But Wally Chalmers arrived, and shouted at Wasmuth to get his attention. He saved Langham's life and sacrificed his own. He retreated, tripped in a ditch, and fell backwards. Wasmuth advanced with his Enfield rifle. Chalmers died within minutes.

Wasmuth, in his statement: 'I saw a big man with red or fairish hair. He was about middle-aged and dressed in a light-coloured shirt. He stumbled and fell. I shot him as he lay on the ground.'

Langham managed to get to Neville Power. He told the coroners court, 'I lifted his head and turned him around. He shuddered a couple of times and died in my arms.'

Paul Church — the seven-year-old mucking around by the garage — saw the police arrive. In all, 16 officers were at the crime scene. He said, 'They came straight through the front gates, they were in the bush — they were just everywhere. More and more. Something was escalating quite quickly. They wanted a word with Father Cronin. They asked him to minister the dead. He said, "Yes, of course." He got his purple stole and said, "Stay here." I remember him walking up the road.'

The priest in his purple stole — 'all priest', 'the most amazing man' — walking up the valley of death that Sunday in the Waitakere Ranges to give the last rites to Berry, Chalmers and Power. He was in full view of Wasmuth. 'But he didn't shoot,' Paul said. 'Maybe there was still some decency left in him. He could easily have killed the Father.'

The dogs barking in boarding kennels. Dallow was still racing to the scene. He heard that his fellow officers had been killed over the car radio. They travelled the rest of the way in complete silence. He remembered that very clearly. He said, 'Even now, I …' He put his head in his hands.

Detective Constable Graham Johanson arrived. I called him at his home. He said, 'After Wasmuth shot Wally, he walked up the road to where I was. Our NCO said, "Take cover!" Officers ran for the ferns on the side of the road.'

Johanson, a former air-force marksman, was armed with a .32 Browning semi-automatic. He was 40 feet away. He fired at Wasmuth's legs, then his torso, and the third bullet hit Wasmuth's elbow. He said, 'I was shooting to kill.'

I said, 'Did you regret you didn't kill him?'

He said, 'Very much so. He killed my mates. Neville was a good friend. We visited him and Val at their home. He was a gentleman.'

Later reports claimed Wasmuth came at Johanson swinging his rifle like a club, and fought like a tiger when he was arrested. 'Rubbish,' said Johanson. 'Total rubbish. But he was quite wild. His looks were scary. He said, "Look out. I'm a dangerous man. I'll spit in your eye."

'That day was the worst thing in my 25 years in the police. It hit me hard for months and months. I did it cold turkey — they didn't have counselling then. I couldn't attend the funeral. Just couldn't. Even today, I …' Like Dallow, he gasped for breath. Two weeping ex-cops, 50 years after that slaughter in the bush.

Norm Sowter went with Wasmuth to hospital. He said, 'I remember him well. Tall guy, strapping build; well put together. He was very serious in everything he said. A very, very dour sort of guy. He just didn't give a stuff. He was complaining about his arm and all that sort of shit. The nurse grabbed his arm, gave it a bit of a twist, and said, "Is that where it hurts?" I'd have liked to have given her a medal. That was quite pleasing.'

Ross Dallow remembered arriving at the killing fields in Bethells. The whole scene struck him as feral. 'No one went to Bethells then. It was like going to Great Barrier Island! So you get there that day, and you had the heat, you had the flies, you had the sound of the dogs wailing and crying down there — I thought, "I wouldn't want to live here." You wouldn't have slept all that well at night.

'There'd been a heavy summer shower that afternoon. It was sticky and steamy. You know what Auckland's like up in the hills.'

*

Poor Jim Berry's death has been recorded almost as an aside to the shootings of the two policemen. He was a casualty of madness and isolation and summer; his death was a private affair. The deaths of Chalmers and Power were public. It shocked the nation, and led directly to the formation of the Armed Offenders Squad (AOS) in 1964. Wasmuth's massacre was a pivotal moment in New Zealand policing history.

'It changed the whole of the history of the police insofar as firearms are concerned,' as Bill Brien put it, in a letter he sent to me before we met at an Auckland hotel to talk about the killings, and where he gave me Wasmuth's crazed statement. Brien was in charge of the police inquiry, and subsequently wrote a report calling for the AOS to be established.

One of the New Zealand ways of death in public life is to fashion a plaque on a great big rock. Two great big rocks are dedicated to the two policemen at Te Atatu's Neville Power Park, named in 1965. There was no reference to Wally Chalmers until volunteer park ranger Christine Julian took action. She said, 'I thought it was fitting that the two men who died together should be memorialised together.'

She chose Wally's rock from the quarry at Bethells. 'I thought that the rock should come from the place where he died. I went to the quarry, and the manager was about to drive me in and look at thousands of rocks, when I saw a particular rock leaning against his hut. I said, "That's the one." It has a certain presence to it.'

The inscriptions on the rocks for Neville Power and Wally Chalmers read: KILLED ON DUTY. The massive slabs face the blue, smoky hills of the Waitakere Ranges, towards Bethells.

*

What do you do when lives are broken and shattered? What kind of shape do you make when you reassemble the pieces?

Wasmuth stayed broken. He was all sharp edges, scattered. He was declared mentally unfit to stand trial. 'I was 17 at the time of the killings,' his daughter said. 'I went to see him in prison. He was joking about it, saying it was a lot of bother over nothing. "It'll all go away soon," he said.'

They locked him up in Auckland's Oakley Hospital and more or less threw away the key. A psych nurse who knew him said, 'He was in the right place. He was a nutter. He was quite well-spoken, but he talked shit the whole time.'

His daughter visited. 'You could talk to him like a normal person, but then he'd start raving and saying things that were totally unrealistic.' He told her they let him out at night. Like the nurse, she said he refused to take medication.

He was in the M3 ward, or Male Three, which housed patients with severe psychiatric disorders. When Oakley closed in 1992, Wasmuth and the others were cuffed and taken by bus to the Lake Alice asylum in Whanganui; when that closed in 1999, he returned to Auckland, by aircraft, to the Mason Clinic ('Improving Lives through Responsive Forensic Services').

Another psych nurse, who knew him at Mason, said Wasmuth could do one-armed push-ups well into his eighties — that splendid physique, the sprinter's body. He was eventually released to a rest home with a secure unit in New Lynn, and then to a similar facility in Red Beach, on the Whangaparaoa coast, to be near his younger brother.

'He never gave up on my father,' said Wasmuth's daughter. 'He was allowed to take him home and for outings. He was very loyal.'

The daughter of a lunatic and a killer; the daughter of a man who sold plums at the gate, tried to write, caused immense suffering, and died at the age of 95. 'He was a difficult person,' she said. 'He wasn't very warm. I couldn't say I loved him at all.'

John Porteous, who watched the drama from his home at Bethells when he was 13, said that Father Cronin visited Wasmuth at Oakley Hospital. 'He was concerned for the man. He was the perpetrator of the act, but Father looked past that and looked at the man himself, and his relationship with his Creator.'

Someone else tried to visit Wasmuth: May Mackey, Wally Chalmers' widow.

In her small apartment in Parnell, over the tea and custard squares, she said, 'Right from the beginning I wanted to see Wasmuth, to talk to him. I had always that yen to see him, because I never had anything against him, none at all. I felt he might have needed something. It was my attitude to people. That's why for 30 years I've visited people in prisons.

'Lake Alice closed down and they moved them to Mason Clinic. I was in there visiting, and heard about Wasmuth. I asked permission to see him. But they wouldn't let me. They said it would not be in his best interests. And that was that.' She said this during my visit in 2012.

I went to see May again in 2015, a few days after she turned 95. She wore slacks and a cardigan. 'My right arm is feeling sorry for my left arm,' she said. It could only hold things with difficulty, and she couldn't play the piano in her sitting room. But she was in great cheer, and walked out to the street to greet me. May was always out and about at the Parnell shops; earlier that week, she said, she was walking up Parnell Road when Teina Pora jumped out of a café to embrace her. Pora had only recently been released from prison for a wrongful conviction of murder. She remembered him on his first day in prison. 'A little person holding his grey blanket, being led to his cell.' They became friends in the last 10 years of his imprisonment.

She again brought out the custard squares and the teapot with its coat. May was a good listener, with a very keen memory for detail. The complete lack of dementia and her good physical health meant that the only thing that made her eligible for a rest home were her 95 years. She preferred her freedom. She was a little old lady but there was such a strength and calmness about her, and something else, something just as striking — it was as though she'd changed race, and had become Maori. She looked Maori. She spoke Maori place names with flair. Once a week, she said, she made herself a boil-up — pork bones, with spinach. She was a kuia, wise and ancient.

As Hughina Garnett, she was raised in Dunedin, and took a job in a clothing factory. She told the story of her conversion to Christ in a beautifully sensitive profile by Anglican Church media officer Lloyd Ashton in the church magazine *Anglican Taonga*. She was riding to work one day in 1937 with a friend. They spotted a booklet on the footpath. It was called 'The Reason Why'. May's friend read the Christian tract aloud as they cycled along. Then and there, May told Ashton, she had a kind of an epiphany; the word she used was 'convicted'.

She studied as a missionary with the Bible Training Institute, and prepared for mission work in somewhere like Africa or Asia. But she holidayed with the Northland whanau of a fellow student, Emma Kake. It was a profound experience. May told Ashton, 'I thought, "I'm not looking overseas. I'm not moving out of Maori-land."'

She met Wally Chalmers when she worked as the matron of the Shelley Beach Maori Girls Hostel in Ponsonby. Wasmuth's killing left her a widow for five years. She remarried, to Dave Mackey, of Tainui. In 1982, she started visiting inmates at Mt Eden Prison. She said in the magazine, 'You sit with them and you just ask, "So where do you come from?" And when they tell you, you say, "Oh. I know your relations." And you just mention some names. This is the Maori world. It's all whanau stuff.'

I asked her more about her visits. They had ended with the death of her friend Ben Dickson, who drove her to prison. But she stayed in touch with the prisoners by phone, and had passed on a list of 10 particular prisoners to a new visitor. She said, 'I showed him the list. "These are special people," I told him. They were Willie Bell. Malcolm Rewa. And others, including a man called Jeremy. He sent me a card on my birthday this week. He said to me one day, "If you'd met me 20 years ago, you wouldn't have come near me."

'And that's all I know about why he's in prison. I never ask about their crimes. Or if they did it. Willie said to me, "No one's done what I've done." People hate his insides. He hates himself. But I just sit with them, and we talk. Not about God, or religion; just talk. The only message I have is the message of redemption.'

From Wasmuth, through to contemporary monsters such as serial rapist Rewa, and Bell, who bashed three people to death in an RSA in 2001 — May's life these past 50 years was a kind of brief history of violence in New Zealand, in Maori-land. She was so serene.

Chapter 3

The bogan ninja: Antonie Dixon

> There was no hair on his head — none to speak of at least — nothing but a small scalp-knot twisted up on his forehead. His bald purplish head looked like a mildewed skull.
> — Ishmael's first encounter with Queequeg in *Moby Dick*, by Herman Melville

1

Dixon was mad. He was every kind of crazy, a bogan ninja, bringing down the blade of a Samurai sword in a flash of silver once, twice, then three, four, five, six, seven, eight times in a partially successful attempt to sever the hands of two screaming women on an early summer's evening near Thames, killing a stranger with a gun later that night in Auckland and inviting suicide by cop, all the while smoking awesome amounts of P and opening his mind to exciting possibilities of chaos. He was disturbed, disordered, mentally diseased. In diagnostic terms, he was fucked in the head. There was only one question of interest at his lurid and depressing seven-week trial at the High Court of Auckland in 2005: was he mad, or bad? But the answer was obvious. He was both. He was so nasty, resolutely vicious and absolutely remorseless, but he should never have been found guilty of murder, attempted murder, kidnapping, and eight other relatively benign charges. The jury rejected his insanity defence. He got a life sentence. It was a death sentence. He needed a straitjacket, or whatever psychiatric restraints — ECT, a lobotomy — that were available in mental health units. He was sent to prison, and his doom. He killed himself in his cell. Antonie Ronnie Dixon was 40.

The state — the police, and Crown prosecution — jeered at Dixon, and said that he was a sane person pretending to be mad. The paradox is that he was a mad person pretending to be mad. When he made his first sensational appearance on the opening day of his trial, he was like a master satirist. He was a parody of a lunatic.

Queequeg's queer 'scalp-knot' and blotchy pate remained the most incredible haircut in New Zealand history — if we accept the widely held theory that Melville's tattooed Polynesian was Maori — until Dixon was shown into Courtroom 6 that Monday morning in February at the High Court. All eyes were on his eyes, which he rolled in his head, bulged, widened, zigged this way in their sockets, and then zagged that way. But the haircut was even more amazing. It looked as though he had borrowed it from a small boy. Bowl-cut a few inches above his ears and all the way around, it rested on the very top of his shaved head like a light nest. So light that at times it almost seemed to hover above his head — it was a haircut which wanted out, but was doomed to follow him around.

It came with him as Dixon, 36, wide-hipped, 5' 8", pale and flabby, clutching at the waistband of his baggy green shorts, was led into the dock; it disappeared with him as he ducked his head, and hid from view of the jury, when the court was played an excruciating 111 emergency call made on the night of 22 January 2003.

The date marked Dixon's long day's journey into night. It began when he took to his lover Renee Gunbie and ex-lover Simonne Butler with the Samurai sword as they sat, terrified, at the kitchen table in a house in Pipiroa on the Hauraki Plains. It was another intolerable New Zealand summer. Mosquitoes roamed the banks of the nearby Piako River. Heat rose in waves above the long, flat, melting roads. Crime scene photos showed two bottles of Lion Red and a packet of Round Wine biscuits on the dining table; on the floor, there was blood in the cat bowl, and shoeprints in blood. There was also a clump of black hair. He had tried to scalp Gunbie. The two women were left to bleed to death. They were lucky to live. That attack — perhaps the most original in modern New Zealand criminal history; so much about Dixon has to be measured in superlatives — was distilled in court as two counts of attempted murder, and two counts of intent to cause grievous bodily harm.

Almost incidentally, he was also charged with murder. James Te Aute, 25, was shot and killed in a carpark behind a Caltex service station in Highland Park, near Pakuranga in Auckland. He had driven there in his wife's Ford Telstar. The couple had been together for 11 years, and had three children. Her brother, Jackson Lemalu, said in court that Te Aute was his best friend: 'The only person I could talk to about things.'

He was with Te Aute on the night of the murder. They had met that morning, 'mucking about in his garage, fixing his car', then they had driven to Manurewa, to Mt Wellington, to Pakuranga. Two friends joined them; one was looking after 'a mate's little boy', who he thought was aged nine or 10. The boy was still with them when they parked behind the Caltex in Highland Park. It was sometime after midnight. A stolen Caltex card had been used to fill up with gas; the licence plates on the Ford Telstar had been switched; and Te Aute had bought and smoked methamphetamine, or P.

Stoned at midnight at the Caltex with a little boy in the back seat — it was a cameo of urban Maori youth, a portrait of Auckland life. The only thing to do in the circumstances was get wasted.

Dixon just happened to come along. He hated Maori, Asians, Pacific Islanders. He was white trash, a car thief by trade; the car he parked was stolen that evening from Hamilton. He sat in darkness, grinding his teeth in the methamphetamine reflex. Te Aute was about to die. Dixon had decided it on a whim. The two P freaks — both married men, both fathers — were ships in the night.

Dixon's defence lawyer, Barry Hart, to Lemalu: 'It's fair to say that James was addicted to P and loved it, isn't it?'

Lemalu: 'Yes.'

'He'd go looking to score, and pick you up, is that correct?'

'Yes.'

'How much was he going through? What sort of quantities?'

'Small amounts.'

'Enough to get fried on. Correct?'

'Yes.'

Te Aute went to a house that night to buy P. Lemalu waited in the car.

Hart: 'When he got back in the car, you could tell he was flying, is that correct?'

Lemalu: 'Yes.'

'Wide awake and pumped up. Is that fair to say?'

'Yes.'

'Is it fair to say you were hanging out to have some P?'

'Yes.'

Lemalu told the court that a car had pulled up beside them in the carpark behind the Caltex. The driver gave them the finger.

'We thought we might have known him. We wanted to know what his problem was, so we got out of the car. Before we even approached him, I noticed him raise his arm, and just the way he raised his arm made me react, so I hit the ground.'

He heard shots. The car drove off. Lemalu saw his brother-in-law lying on the ground. 'I went to see if he was all right. I lifted him up, and noticed he had all these holes in him.'

He dialled 111. The tape was played in court. It went on and on, loud and panicked and screaming: 'My mate's been shot! He's been shot, man! Come on!'

Operator: 'How many times has he been shot?'

Lemalu: 'One ... two ... three ... four ...'

'Four times in total?'

'Nah. More than that.'

He sat in the witness box with his head in his hands, gulping, as the call went on and on; Te Aute's wife fled the courtroom in tears; and Dixon's incredible haircut descended, and sunk from view.

2

Dixon's sword was inside a glass case on the floor at the front of Courtroom 6. I wanted a closer look. At a lunch break one day, the court crier obliged by balancing the exhibit on top of the witness stand. The weapon was very slender, with a straight blade snapped in two at the tip. Its black handle was long enough to be gripped by both hands. The blade was smeared with swirls and drips of dry brownish flakes.

I said: 'Is that rust?'

'No,' said the crier, a young fellow with delicate sideburns, 'that would be blood.'

And then he brought out a gun. This other exhibit was the murder weapon. In court, senior constable and dog-handler David Templeton had remarked, 'It's a strange-looking gun.' Short-barrelled, with a 10-round magazine and a Beamshot scope and laser, assembled with parts from about four different guns, it looked as light as a handbag. Dixon's sleek little accessory weighed in at just 2.04 kilograms.

After he shot Te Aute, Dixon led police cars on a chase through Manukau. It was cat and mouse; the distinct possibility is that he was really enjoying himself. He would accelerate, then put on the brakes at speed. He would drive on the wrong side of the road. He would turn off his lights and hide in darkness, then suddenly come up behind the cops, then beside them, and then open fire. One round hit the side of a police car. Another just missed an officer who couldn't move — he was wearing body armour so heavy and bulky that it trapped him in the passenger seat.

The chase ended when Dixon pulled into a cul de sac in East Tamaki, and broke into a house. He held the homeowner hostage. The siege lasted overnight. Dixon came outside and surrendered just after dawn.

Detective Constable Craig White was called as a witness. He said he sat next to Dixon in a police car after reading him his rights.

Crown co-prosecutor Richard Marchant asked, 'Did he say anything to you?'

'A variety of things,' replied White. He consulted his notes, and read out this variety.

> What the fuck are you cunts looking at? I'll cut you up as well.
>
> What's it like being in a car with a murderer?
>
> If I had a better fucking gun, you cunts would be dead.
>
> I cut those sluts up real good.

Detective Constable Michael Hayward was also called to the witness stand. He had spoken with Dixon for about an hour on the day of his arrest. Again, Dixon addressed a variety of subjects.

> Do you want me to bite your fucking nose off?
>
> Fucking sword broke. I want a refund.
>
> You fucking cocksuckers. You and your fucking meth programmes.
>
> I'm going to the big house. I'll fuck those cunts up as well.

Another voice was heard in Courtroom 6 while Hayward read from the thoughts of Dixon. It was Dixon himself. He set up a low muttering from the dock. It was strange to hear him actually speak; here was the man whose script was being read out by police officers to the court, but now Dixon himself was talking. In a high, quiet voice, he said: 'Conspiracy. It's a fucking conspiracy.'

And then he was quiet again.

Detective Sergeant Peter Jones was the seventieth and final witness in the prosecution's case. Jones said he had sat with Dixon and Hayward at the police station. 'I asked the accused, "Where is the sword now?" He said he didn't know, but then he asked if it was still in her head.'

3

One day a row of tanned young people with strange accents waited outside Courtroom 6. They turned out to be advanced students of English from a language school. Andre, their tutor, said he immigrated to New Zealand from Cape Town. 'A courtroom is a good place to hear English being spoken,' he said.

He had chosen a good day to expose these new New Zealanders to the formal and informal use of English. Simonne Butler was called to give evidence. She spoke very fast. She was exact, fluent. She used interesting words, such as 'infiltrate', 'appease', 'calibre', and 'flailing'; and slang, too, like 'sleazed' and 'chopped up'.

She was an attractive woman, almost vivacious, despite the setting and the circumstances. She sat in court with the cuffs of her jacket rolled up. They exposed her scarred and mutilated hands. She was the star witness — for the defence. It seemed bizarre that Dixon's victim had been called by defence lawyer Barry Hart, and not Crown prosecutor Simon Moore. Well, she was hardly going to say it was all a misunderstanding. Hart's intent was that she would strengthen his argument that Dixon was insane.

She said she met Dixon in late 1997. She was a telesales rep. He told her he was a mechanic. Hart asked her, 'Was there anything about him that was a little bit different?'

She said, 'Yeah, there was. He would just talk and talk and talk, and you couldn't shut him up. He'd go on about all manner of things. Probably the most hyperactive person I've ever met. Yeah. What was the question?'

'Did you notice anything a little different about him?'

'Very full-on. Very excitable, and a show-off.'

'And then the two of you became emotionally connected?'

'Yeah. He was just charming, and funny, and kind, and … yeah. I sort of fell in love.'

One day in early 1998, she noticed there was an extra razor and toothbrush in her bathroom. He'd moved in. He remained charming, and funny, and kind, but also insane.

'He had quite large mood swings, from being so happy and ridiculous to being agitated, and pacing, and wailing. He constantly thought he was being followed by police. He'd go on and on about Jehovah's Witnesses, and how he was one of the 144,000 Chosen Ones. Oh, first of all he told me he was the Devil, but that was back when I thought he was an idiot.'

She said he misquoted the Bible, and his version of Jehovah's Witness teachings were confused. 'The things he used to say were really wrong. I know a little about it. My nana is a Jehovah's Witness, and I did Bible Studies to appease her from 10 to about 12.'

Yes, she told Hart, she had problems in childhood. 'But not in the same calibre as him.' Dixon 'was always unbalanced, I guess you'd call it'. Hart asked her about his religious 'rantings', and she said, 'Before the end, when I got chopped up and stuff, he was really full-on.'

Hart said, 'We'll get to that day later.'

In March 2002, she bought a home on the Hauraki Plains. She had plans to turn it into a bed-and-breakfast, and run a naturopathy clinic. Meanwhile, Dixon was phoning her 20 times a day, saying that people were trying to kill him. He heard voices in his head. He continued his habit of pacing, 'up and down, back and forth, his arms flailing'. Their relationship — 'tumultuous, a horrible dysfunctional cycle' — came to an end, but in June that year, Dixon 'sleazed his way back into my bed'. She got pregnant, and had an abortion in September.

Her evidence got to that day, on Tuesday, 21 January 2003.

She described the attack. Hart asked her to slow down so that the court stenographer could catch up. She told how Dixon asked her into the dining room. He locked the door behind her and ordered her to sit down at the table. Renee Gunbie was already there. She was bleeding from a cut in her neck. Dixon started screaming, accusing them both of being 'in with' the police, 'working against him', that they had to die, that they were 'sacrifices'.

She said, 'His god had told him we were going to die. The New World Order was taking over. He went on about Allah for a little bit. He was screaming, and bouncing about, just crazy and psycho and horrible. I'd always been able to calm him down in the past, but he just wasn't responding to me.'

Hart: 'And then?'

Butler: 'And then we were all screaming.'

Paramedics estimated that Gunbie was five to ten minutes from death when they arrived. She was handless, scalped, and her throat was slit. Butler's left hand was reattached in a marathon 27-hour surgery. Both women were taken to Middlemore Hospital; a few days after the attack, flowers were sent to their rooms. Gunbie received tiger lilies and gerberas. There was a note. It read: *With love. Sorry. Tony.*

In cross-examination, Butler talked more about the attack. She said: 'I don't know who he went for first. I think he went back and forth between us.' And then she came up with the most evocative line of the entire trial: 'There was just so much screaming and blood and silver.'

The language students were given a powerful lesson in how plain English can seem so cryptic, so loaded with meaning.

Hart asked her about the week leading up to the attack. She remembered she had gone to the Big Day Out concert in Auckland. Jane's Addiction was the headline act. On the following Saturday, she visited Dixon's ex-wife.

'I don't remember Sunday and Monday. And then Tuesday …' She sighed, and said in a flat voice: 'Tuesday was Tuesday.'

4

You don't have to be the world's leading authority on the hallucinogenic stimulant ketamine to be called as an expert psychiatric witness in a trial about a killer under the influence of another mind-blowing chemical, but it probably helps. Dr Karl Jansen was a tall shrink. He loomed at a height of about 6' 6". He wore boots, jeans, a tan leather jacket. He had worked at the Glastonbury rock festival in England as an on-site psychiatrist. At Otago University, he studied the use and consequences of magic mushrooms. His work on Ecstasy was admired. His interest in ketamine partly derived from personal experience: it was given to him as an anaesthetic after a motorbike accident, and it brought on a NDE — a near-death experience. He told an interviewer, 'I had the full effect. Tunnels of high speed, the light, God, life review, out-of-body, the lot.' He published numerous papers on how the ketamine experience mimics the NDE in terms of brain functioning and blockage of neurotransmitters.

Jansen, a New Zealander practising psychiatry in London, was a defence witness at Dixon's trial. His essential position was that Dixon was mentally ill at the time of the killings, and also that his illness predated his use of P. The drug, Jansen said, aggravated Dixon's symptoms, which he listed as 'impulsive … explosive … paranoid … narcissistic … psychotic'.

He spoke at great length about everything. He said everything in the same calm, measured voice. His accent was a kind of masterpiece of fastidious Englishness. He stroked the sound of each syllable; he was careful never to pronounce the first 'h' in the word 'methamphetamine'. The jury surely hated him.

Jansen went too far. It was one thing for his fussy enunciation and polysyllabic replies to make everyone listening feel as they, too, were experiencing a NDE. That made him merely unlikeable. But he walked gaily into the zone of looking completely ridiculous on the day that he speculated that Dixon's bulging, staring eyes at the opening of the trial might have been a symptom of a thyroid condition — that's 'thyroid' with a silent h.

Over and over, prosecutor Simon Moore put it to him that Dixon was faking a mental illness. The word he used was 'malingering'.

Moore: 'Do you accept evidence of malingering, doctor?'

Jansen: 'I accept that. Malingering is present. But it is entirely possible to malinger, and act the madman, and also to have a core of paranoid illness behind that. And once you say he's not ill, he's pretending, you're also saying he doesn't need any treatment. If you're wrong, that's a huge responsibility. There is so much evidence that he is not of sound mind.'

Moore: 'He said before the trial that he thought of turning up in a nightgown, or would claim he was the son of God. Another psychiatrist has told us that Mr Dixon was too crazy to be genuine. Do you accept that?'

Jansen: 'I accept that. He has clearly manufactured some of his symptoms. But Mr Dixon is what was once known as a psychopath, and is now called a dissocial or anti-social personality disorder.'

Moore: 'Mr Dixon has said that God is a triangle. In prison, he claimed he saw a ghost called Sid. The problem, doctor, is that there are some areas which quite clearly are a nonsense and a fabrication. Do you accept that?'

Jansen: 'I accept that. But this is a complex man in a complex case. Mr Dixon has said things to me like, "I've been fucked by 50 men." I thought this was unlikely. But there is evidence he has been abused. It may have been the case. Terrible things have happened to Mr Dixon.'

Dixon grew up among outpatients from Carrington Psychiatric Hospital in a boarding house on Vermont Street in Ponsonby. His mother, a devout but unstable Jehovah's Witness, tied him to the clothesline. He was ordered to bark like a dog. The lunatics sexually abused him. As an adult, he made a good living as a car thief, but was constantly in and out of prison. By 2002, further out of his mind on P, he raved that cop cars were following him everywhere he went, that 747 aircraft trained cameras on him on their flight path over the deserted Hauraki Plains, that secret cameras were likewise trained on him by courier vans and taxis — the kayakers on the brown Piako River were also maintaining covert surveillance. One day, he cut open his leg with a penknife because he wanted to dig out a tracking device.

Barry Hart asked the jury, 'What more do we have to prove that the accused had a disease of the mind?' Jansen and another psychiatrist called by the defence gave their expert opinion that Dixon had a disease of the mind, and was mentally ill. Two psychiatrists called by the prosecution gave their expert opinion that Dixon maybe had a few problems, but was as sound as a bell. Farce was never going to be far away in a dichotomy as clear as that, and it duly arrived when co-prosecutor Richard Marchant meant to ask psychiatrist Dr David Chaplow, 'Is it your opinion that Dixon is suffering from a disease of the mind?' But what he actually asked was, 'Is it your opinion that Dixon is suffering from an opinion of the mind?'

Farce is brief. Tragedy lasts. Backstage, outside the court, Jansen was funny and charming company; it's always exciting to chat with a genius. Inside the court, I loathed him. Dr Jansen, his credentials bringing in another superlative to the trial — world's greatest living authority on a horse tranquiliser — was the hipster quack and exasperating, long-winded bore who looked as though Dixon had pulled the wool over his eyes. I thought: he couldn't tell Dixon was playing him for a fool.

But Jansen was right. He told the court, 'Mr Dixon may yet end his life. I think the risk is high.'

5

One of the remarkable aspects of the Dixon trial was the quality of the lead counsel. Crown prosecutor Simon Moore and defence lead Barry Hart were then in their pomp. Yet more superlatives: they were the best in their field, or the most in-demand — Moore took on all of the big cases, Hart likewise. Courtroom 6 was oftentimes a match of wits between the two bastions. In fact, they were friends. They both belonged to the same hunt club. There was a warmth to their little off-the-record exchanges in court. A kind of nostalgic glow rests over their work on the trial. The well-fed, beautifully spoken Moore, a King's College old boy and one-time Northern Club president, ended up a High Court judge; Hart, small and thin-lipped with a shock of white hair, his gauche manner and Kiwi vowels plainly not to the manor born, was later struck off after he was found guilty of professional misconduct and 'gross overcharging'. He was also made bankrupt, with debts of over $30 million.

Hart was a cold man. He had a black belt in karate, was brisk, unsmiling, vain. But I interviewed him a few years before the Dixon trial, and remember sitting with him in the dark one evening in his chambers while he wept, talking about his mother. 'In the last two years of her life, she actually had both legs cut off. And … It … She … It was really hard for her, being wheeled around and not being active. Yet she became the champion of her rest home.'

At the Dixon trial in 2005, supping from the trough of legal aid ('I'm not exactly crying poverty,' he said to me), his name in enormous letters on the side of his chambers in expensive Herne Bay, a familiar, scary sight in the High Court, Hart was at his undazzling best. No one ever accused him of eloquence or intellectual flair. He did rave and he did rant. He shouted, a lot. 'There stands an innocent man!', etc. His closing address at the Dixon trial was the longest of his career. It was a shocking mess. Much of it seemed extempore, improvised, off the cuff; Hart lost the thread, found another one, went around in circles, and once lost his footing and nearly fell face-first into the lectern.

His best form of defence was always attack. He had a superb eye for advantages. Hart lodged an appeal after the 2003 trial — and was successful in having the conviction quashed. He argued that Justice Judith Potter failed to correctly address issues of insanity, and that she should have directed the jury to consider an alternative charge of manslaughter. He won a second trial, in 2008. It was a replica of the first, right down to the verdict: guilty.

Dixon committed suicide the night before sentencing. The inquest into his death heard that he strangled himself with a piece of cloth torn from something called an 'anti-suicide blanket'. He had been returned to the cell just hours before from a 'tie-down' room, where his hands and legs were restrained to prevent self-harm. He covered the CCTV camera with wet toilet paper. There was blood splattered on the door at head-height and lower, suggesting he'd hurled himself at the side of his cell.

Coroner Garry Evans ruled that Dixon took his own life, and said: 'Had Mr Dixon been moved to accommodation in the Mason Clinic or other mental-health unit, it's unlikely he would have died.'

Before the suicide, Hart had talked of another appeal, of forcing a third trial. He probably would have lost that one as well. Moore was too good for him. Moore, the golden boy of his generation;

Moore, who had survived the humiliation of the media discovering a photo of him wearing a red tinsel wig and a fake pair of women's breasts on a boat coming back from the Pitcairn Islands, where he prosecuted the famous sex abuse case; Moore, with his superior grooming and his thrilling voice, told a more powerful story than Hart. He spoke slowly, carefully, and kept his eyes narrowed.

He told the jury, 'Dixon is not normal. But he was a man in control and in charge. It was just an attack by angry man. This was the extreme end of domestic violence.'

And then he demonstrated the Samurai attack. He raised the imaginary sword above his head with both hands. He held it there. His waistcoat rode up, and revealed a plump tum straining against his white shirt. Farce, briefly; and then tragedy, enduringly, as Moore brought down the pretend lethal weapon fast, again and again, chopping, slicing, miming all that 'screaming and blood and silver', and said: 'He hit them as hard as he could with the intention to kill. This isn't a madman out of control. It's all planned. It's all precise. This is an execution. Nothing this man does is an accident ... This case is all about understanding the human spirit.'

6

I was mooching around inside Courtroom 6 the day after the jury were sent out to deliberate when I heard two soft, really quite polite knocks on a door. It was the jury. They had reached their verdict. It was 11.03am. A junior lawyer was brushing her hair, a detective was reading the sports pages of *The New Zealand Herald*; otherwise, the court was quiet and deserted, as it had been since the jury was sent out at 12.17pm the previous day. And then came those taps on the door. Within 20 minutes, the courtroom was packed, at attention, silent, tense, wondering, waiting for the final word on the seven-week trial.

Seven weeks of beautiful weather, blue day after blue day, cicadas scratching up a racket in the courtyard magnolia. So many other cases came and went. Heavyweight boxer David Tua was there that first week to fight his ex-manager for money. He strummed his guitar in the shade on Parliament Street, and chowed down on $30 steaks at the nearby Hyatt for lunch. There were appearances by the Refugee Status Authority, and Pop 'n' Good Popcorn. *The First Samoan Pentecostal Church v The Door of Hope City Church* was heard in chambers.

Mad, or bad? The pointless question was about to be answered. Two rows of journalists were there. Joyce was there. Thin and giddy, she was a veteran spectator of High Court trials, had seen a lot in her time, but the Dixon trial was something special. I talked to her that first week. She was genuinely excited. 'It's got everything!' she said. 'There's drugs, there's murder, there's maiming, there's kidnapping!'

Joyce's companion, Helga, was there. Joyce was nimble, cheerful; Helga walked stiffly beneath a big black umbrella in the sun, and never smiled. 'I know the boy,' she said. She knew Dixon when he was a child. She was friends with his mother. They were both Jehovah's Witnesses. She said in passing one day to me that evolutionists and psychiatrists were encouraged to practise sodomy.

Kathie Hills was there. She came every single day. She took swigs from a homeopathic remedy to steady her nerves. I don't know whether it did her any good. She is Renee Gunbie's mother.

Hart was there, Moore was there, Justice Judith Potter was there, a gracious lady who was in the ungracious habit of yawning with her mouth open. Dixon was there. His haircut had grown back, and resembled someone normal. But he plainly wasn't well. He had vomited in the police van on the way to court earlier that week; he was given something light to eat to settle his stomach, but then he was rushed from the court, and threw up, loudly and heavily, on his way to the cells. He also had diarrhoea.

He was such a wretch, hopeless and demented, and horrible right to the bitter end. After he was found guilty, Justice Potter remanded him for sentencing, and he was bundled out of the courtroom. Kathie Hills sarcastically said to him on his way out: 'See you later, Tony.' Just before he disappeared, he got in his reply: 'It won't get you her hand back.'

A few minutes later, Courtroom 6 was once again quiet and deserted. A trolley was brought in to wheel out the great stack of court files; police discussed the removal of exhibits, including bullet fragments taken from James Te Aute, the gun, the Samurai sword.

I took away something else. A kind of souvenir, filched from the rubbish tin in Courtroom 6 — Dixon's Styrofoam drinking cup, with his handwriting on the side. He'd given it to Barry Hart while they were waiting for the jury to come in. It was a thoughtful gesture, a kind of condolence. It read: *If anyone's fucked this case it's me.*

7

The last time I saw Dixon was a month later, at sentencing, on a Friday morning. That afternoon, I went to the offices of forensic psychiatrist Dr Ian Goodwin. He said, 'I know Tony pretty well.'

He'd interviewed 'Tony' more times than anyone — 17 sessions, when Dixon was held at the Mason Clinic — and had declared him sane. His opinion was crucial to the verdict, to Dixon's fate. He was affable and gentle, a little bewildered by the media's demonising of Dixon. He said he saw people as damaged as him all the time. It was as though he overlooked the severing of hands.

I asked, 'When did you first meet Tony?'

'When he was admitted to us about 48 hours after his arrest,' he said. 'He asked me to kill him. He was initially quite agitated, and wound up, and paranoid. He was talking about using large amounts of P. He gradually came down.

'And then it all took a really interesting twist. About a year later, Barry Hart had obtained two independent psychiatric reports, one from Karl Jansen and another from Paul Mullin, and they basically said, albeit in rather guarded terms, that the guy didn't seem very well and wasn't fit to stand trial — or, in the words of the law, would have been "under a disability". That's interesting. The court only needed two such opinions; if you're found "under a disability", that's the end game. There's no trial. The Crown was alarmed, so he was transferred to us again, for another assessment, and that's when I cared for him full-time. I ended up with him for 30 days in total.

'That was the time I really got to drill down and see what was going on. There was an observation written about him every hour, regardless of day or night, and I interviewed him incessantly every working day. And things had altered. Things had changed. He still had this core paranoia of being followed, but he kept presenting these really odd symptoms which didn't make any sense. In fact, I was sure after about two weeks that he had been coached. That he'd done some reading, or had been meeting somebody trying to work out how to present certain things.'

'Is he mad?'

'He's not mad in the psychiatric sense. He's a person with a damaged personality and a paranoid view of the world, and has great difficulty maintaining normal relationships.'

I asked, 'Is he interesting?'

'Moderately so,' he said. 'He's not somebody you have scintillating conversations with. But he genuinely does try to make contact with you as a person. He's good at reading people. He's very good at getting information from people. In fact, he's excellent at that.'

'Is he charming?'

'Occasionally, when he was after something, or was just having a good day. He could be quite pleasant. But you do see that a lot in these psychopathic individuals. That they do have the superficial charm, and the ability to engage with people. It's only as the relationship develops over time that the more unacceptable stuff comes out. He was consistently violent in all of his relationships with women.'

'What forms a "psychopathic individual"?'

Dr Goodwin replied, 'His early life was pretty damned miserable. His childhood was awful. He was extraordinarily ambivalent about his mother; she'd beat him, but at one level he probably cared about her. He was certainly upset when she died. He did have some attachment.

'He was exposed to violence from a very young age. Not only from his mother, but from his father when he was around, and the boarders, and people from the Jehovah's Witness — they'd regularly dole out beatings at the instructions of his mother. Violence was something he grew up with. And sexual abuse, too. It gives you a background that everything else is built on.'

I said, 'You diagnosed him as having a severe personality disorder. What does that mean?'

'He sees the world as a place he has to try to control. But the rest of him is functioning. He was a very successful car thief. He was a self-taught mechanic. He had a good work ethic.'

'Was that undone by P?'

'Yes,' he said. 'He had been functioning before that. For instance, he was quite well versed in martial arts.'

I asked, 'Is that why he had a Samurai sword?'

'Well, at the age of 15, he was found with two Samurai swords under his bed. He had a real interest and training in martial arts. But mostly he was interested in cars.'

'What did you find about him that was likeable?'

He said, 'Not a lot I would say was likeable. He was personable, and reasonable most of the time.'

'Do you think he's at risk to himself?'

'When you go to prison, you get control taken away from you. It'll be really difficult for him. If he can't exert some control, I think he does represent a risk to himself.'

'Were you astonished when he appeared in court wearing that haircut?'

He laughed, and said, 'I was! But I thought he'd do something. One time we found he'd secreted a razor blade in his rectum, and he later told me it was his intention to go to court and slash himself up in front of the judge.'

I said, 'The night of the crimes in 2003 — what the hell was all that about?'

He said, 'I've looked for an explanation. In my position, you've got to make sense of it. Here's somebody who has a fairly damaged personality, constitutionally paranoid, all the time, and then he gets heavily into P, and becomes increasingly wired. And rather than it being free-floating, he starts to latch onto specific things that confirm his paranoia. And the thing that really triggered the violence in the end was his conviction that he couldn't trust Renee and Simonne.

'I think once he started it, once it had happened, he realised just how serious it was. And what he started to do was to work out, "Well, I might as well get a bit of notoriety out of this." I think that appealed to him, to keep the night going. I have no doubt his intention was to take out more than one person that night. He was trying to generate a fairly spectacular event.'

'Did he ever show remorse to you?'

'I didn't see any,' he said. 'He never said sorry about Te Aute. I think he did regret what had happened to the girls at one level. But he didn't feel as though he had lost anything in those relationships. Even though he attacked them, it didn't make a great deal of difference from his perspective.

'When he was about 17, he was seen by a psychiatrist. He wrote in his report, "Dixon seems devoid of moral or social conscience." I think that's probably right.'

'Will he have therapy in prison?'

'No.'

'Ought he?'

'If he develops more symptoms, or remains psychotic, he'll be treated. But in terms of actual therapy to change his view of the world, of trying to undo years of abuse and neglect, then, no, that's not going to occur in prison.'

I said, 'That's an appropriately dismal way to end our interview.'

Dr Goodwin said, 'It's a dismal story. It's sordid. It's a sordid little affair.'

That morning, when Justice Potter sentenced him to life imprisonment, Dixon clapped his hands, and shouted: 'Bring back the electric chair!' He wore a smile on his smooth, gormless face. The grinning idiot left the courtroom, and was led down a narrow corridor. They really may as well have strapped him in then and there and released the volts.

Chapter 4

That spring: 'Mr X'

1

For four weeks one spring, a sad-eyed, moustachioed Iranian apple-picker and a cheerful Maori woman who managed an escort agency were forced to sit together in the High Court of Auckland, jointly charged with conspiring to supply methamphetamine, a.k.a. P. It was pitiful and depressing and I couldn't tear myself away.

The public gallery was empty, except for two detectives involved in the arrest and an occasional family member of the two accused. I sat in on the trial by chance. I turned up at the High Court one day to see if a case caught my fancy. I came across a friend who had previously worked in journalism. His appearance — he was a dapper, elegant figure, with silver hair and an ironic smile — beat all the odds by managing to equal his splendidly Victorian name: Hedley Mortlock. He had found work as a court registrar. Black gowns suited him. I asked him whether there was anything juicy marked down for the day. No, he said, it was business as usual. He was right. I did the rounds, walking in and out of trials, until I stopped in at Courtroom 7 for the trial of Gholemreza Nobakht and Gina Rye.

The two 'conspirators', according to the prosecution, intended to supply 768 grams of crystal meth. Police valued the haul at $750,000, at roughly $1000 a gram. 'It was a good intercept,' said the detective in charge. But I only became aware of that later.

I arrived mid-way through the trial. As soon as I took my seat in the public gallery, a prosecutor told the jury that he was going to play a film. You could describe it as secret footage. You could also describe it as very dull, but that would be a wild exaggeration — it was so entirely boring that I was glued to my seat, waiting for something, anything, to happen. Nothing happened.

The film was a 70-minute surveillance tape of Nobakht and another man at Auckland International Airport's arrivals lounge. They, too, were waiting; they, too, experienced the agony of the viewer, because nothing happened. Nobakht ate a burger at McDonald's. He was a fastidious diner. A strong man, slow in his movements, there was almost something dainty about the way he unpeeled the wrapper. His friend sat with him, rolled a couple of Park Royal cigarettes, left, came back. They both looked around, a lot. The friend used his mobile phone, a lot. They hardly talked to one another. On and on the 70-minute film continued, its grainy images projected onto a screen opposite the jury, its apparently meaningless narrative brightened by cameo appearances of other people at the arrivals lounge — a black man poring over a street map, a fat woman wolfing down a burger and fries without pause or napkins.

Hooked by the riddle of that private screening, I stayed on until the trial finished three weeks later, writing down the unimportant details of an unimportant trial, my feet up, sharpening pencils and allowing the shavings to fall on the carpet, sloping outside now and then to smoke a cigarette beneath the magnolia tree in the front courtyard, then sloping back inside into the warmth of the courtroom — yes, I was quite comfortable, thanks. When the trial ended, my troubles began.

I worked for the *Sunday Star-Times*. What sort of story could I write? I wasn't providing the newspaper with any kind of scoop; it had no particular drama, no moral lesson; it fell far short of the standards required of sensationalism.

The opening sentence of my story read, 'An Iranian living in Japan walks into a bar in Bangkok with another country on his mind: New Zealand.' I was very taken with the racy tabloid flavour of that introduction — but it doomed the rest of the story to follow in its footsteps, as I set out to attempt a dramatic narrative of international connections and high intrigue. It was the worst story I wrote in five years employed at the newspaper, a jangling mess — like all racy tabloid prose, it read like bad fiction, an inexpert, constipated thriller (sample: 'The mule was turned into a pigeon'), its eager revelations tugging at the reader's sleeve to get their attention.

But what drew me to the trial, kept me pinned to my seat, was its sheer ordinariness. I was seduced by the flat, seedy New Zealandness of the crime, by the familiar misery of courtroom justice. It was so entirely average, because it was exactly the kind of trial that had moved in like a plague across the high courts of New Zealand. The war on P was hell on court staff.

In 2003, the government introduced legislation that promoted the drug from Class B to Class A; almost immediately, P trials began to overload the court system. They became the meat and drink of the High Court trials, and the press viewed them as much of a shabby muchness. The P trial in the spring of 2006 had nothing. Nothing to set it apart, nothing of news value, nothing to declare except the banality and despair of all P trials — and the riddle of the secret footage.

2

Nobakht was 41; Rye, 36. When I first saw them in court, I assumed they were a couple. Their heads were close together as they sat in the little crate of the defendants' box. Actually, they loathed each other.

To return to that boring surveillance film: police contended that it showed Nobakht lingering at the arrivals lounge to follow a drug courier bringing in the crystal meth to New Zealand. The courier was a Godot who never arrived. He'd already been arrested, at Customs. By the time he was released, to play out his new, undercover role given to him by police, Nobakht had left the airport.

Nobakht was later arrested, and when he appeared at the High Court, enough evidence had been accumulated for the prosecution to label him as 'the overseer', the man in charge of the P once it arrived in New Zealand. He was charged with importing and supplying a Class A drug. The buyer, according to prosecution, was Gina Rye. She was charged with supply of a Class A drug. Like Nobakht, she denied the charges, and pleaded not guilty. Nobakht presented himself as a Hawke's Bay apple-picker. Rye said she ran an escort agency. She could have called herself a madam, but her mischief ran higher than that; the title she preferred was 'mama-san.'

Rye — long-haired and wide-faced, described as 'solidly built' by one police officer who had kept her under surveillance, and, less flatteringly, by another cop on the surveillance team, as 'plump' — was loose, liked a good time; Nobakht was upright, no fun. From his cross-examination:

How do Iranian men view prostitution as a business, run by a woman?

I cannot tell you how bad it is, but it is very very very bad.

His pieties did him no favours. Of course the jury could only consider the evidence presented in court, and the evidence against Nobakht was damning. But it was obvious they found him difficult to like or understand. Closed off, a mysterious Other, he was too … Iranian. He had come to New Zealand in 1998 for political asylum.

He had been a lieutenant in the Iranian Air Force. In the New Zealand social pecking order, an Iranian refugee is near the bottom of the heap; Rye, too, was identified in court as a low-life, a Maori woman with tattoos on her back, a 'mama-san' who ran hookers, and who described herself as a 'transient', but she was one of us, as recognisable by her skin as her speech. Police had intercepted her texts to family: *Luv ya heaps*, she wrote.

Nobakht had no redeeming informalities. From the evidence of a police officer sent to arrest Nobakht at his house in Napier:

Are you able to tell the court anything of Mr Nobakht's demeanour?

He was concerned that we had not taken off our shoes inside his house.

A woman who had visited Nobakht also gave evidence.

You would know that in the toilet you had to put on a pair of slippers to go into the toilet?

Yes.

And step out of them when you left the toilet?

Yes.

Your New Zealand style and Mr Nobakht's eastern style had its differences, do you agree with that?

No, I think that when two cultures come together, people have to learn about each other's cultures and he wouldn't give me time to learn about his culture and he would never try to learn about mine. He expected every New Zealander to become eastern and he would never try to westernise himself. You'd think if he came to this country he should try and do that a little bit.

Her whining reply was the authentic voice of middle New Zealand. It judged Nobakht guilty of another kind of crime: resistance to mend his foreign ways, failure to observe and share in the New Zealand way of life.

When Nobakht elected to give evidence, he asked for a translator. This was repeatedly mocked by the prosecution, who implied it was a put-on, a tactic to give him time to prepare his answers while the translator muttered to him in Farsi — Nobakht had lived in New Zealand for eight years, surely he knew enough English? In any case, it clearly vexed the jury, because it dragged out the trial even more. Even the translator seemed as though he found Nobakht repulsive. Forced to act out his role in court as Nobakht's confidant and amanuensis, he scowled his way through the onerous translation, and couldn't move from Nobakht's side fast enough whenever recess was called.

Nobakht wouldn't speak English, wouldn't assimilate; he wasn't a New Zealander; he wasn't even human — he was likened to a grasping, scuttling, creeping creature of the underworld. From the cross-examination of an arresting officer:

Is it customary for the police when dealing with a large operation to give such an operation a name?
    Yes.
    And the police have named this operation, that this trial is about, Operation Precious, is that right?
    Yes.
    Was this name taken from—
    Prosecution: Objection, Your Honour. Relevance.
    Her Honour: I don't see any relevance.
    Defence: *As Your Honour pleases. I will move on ...*

What this concealed is that Operation Precious was taken from *The Lord of the Rings*. Gholem, an abbreviation of Nobakht's first name, sounds like Gollum: 'My precioussssss ...'

And yet this Gollum who appeared in the High Court of Auckland had a wife and daughter. They sat in the public gallery. Now and then so did someone who knew Rye, a young Maori guy who wore his address tattooed on his forehead: EAST COAST. His presence may not have won the hearts of the jury. But Nobakht's wife was a lovely woman, Maori, asthmatic, bewildered, grieving, and their young daughter was quite frankly an adorable little girl, perhaps three years old, with big, dark eyes, long eyelashes, and beautiful colouring. Together, they made a heartbreaking sight. Nobakht's wife was convinced that her husband was innocent. He picked apples from 6am to 6pm, she said. He was a good provider, a good father. But the prosecution twisted everything, made him look so guilty … We would talk outside the courtroom, her daughter at her feet, playing with a teddy bear. And this was one of the familiar miseries of a trial. I have seen it so many times: the helplessness of the family of the accused.

As a trial grinds on, as the days and weeks pass, the family can only sit and watch, and wait for judgment. They can't do anything, they can't intervene — they can't make it stop. They are surplus to the court's requirements. They are reduced to bystanders. They have nothing to hold on to, and they float away, like kites, always in sight, but always hovering just out of reach. Anxious and exhausted, worn down, their skin takes on a courtroom pallor — pale, bloodless.

Meanwhile, the accused sits on display in the defendants' crate. In front are the rows for lawyers, and then the judge's bench; the jury sits on the left. There is nothing to look at except each other. The room contracts, tightens its grip as the days and weeks pass. All trials are a purgatory, the outcome suspended between verdicts of guilty or not guilty, jail or freedom. Life is put on hold. Something resembling life takes its place. The lawyers swish their gowns, chant their obedience to the judge: 'As Your Honour pleases', 'Yes, sir', 'Yes, ma'am'. Clerks deliver fresh pages of transcript. Slowly, quietly, agonisingly, the court goes about its business, does the paperwork, measures out the exposures as the days and weeks pass ...

Outside the High Court of Auckland, the paved entrance is dominated by an enormous magnolia tree, its flowers as luscious and ripe as a succulent fruit. There is wisteria, too, prettily spreading itself about. The lawns are neatly manicured. It's a very nice part of town, ordered and posh, probably the most Wellington that Auckland gets, with its rare concentration of a lot of men wearing suits and expensive overcoats — the High Court attracts numerous nearby law firms. It's also probably the most English that boisterous, yahooing Auckland gets — Parliament Street, Princes Street, Waterloo Quad. Opposite the court is ye olde Old Government House, and the luxuriousness of the university gardens. The High Court building itself has been superbly restored to its original nineteenth-century design, when architect Edward Ramsey modelled it on the English image of Warwick Castle.

A grand façade. Inside, the 15 courtrooms with their bare walls and their venetian blinds are the usual modern nightmare of office work. Hermetically sealed against the outside world, they are kept in very clean nick, unlike the grubby, graffitied district courts. Decorum is maintained, in keeping with the serious consequences that await within. Signs which instruct NO TALKING add to the repressive atmosphere.

Late on a Tuesday night, after the jury had returned their verdicts on Nobakht and Rye, I heard quiet sobs outside Courtroom 7. It was Nobakht's wife.

I went home to write something exciting about misery.

3

And so, 'An Iranian living in Japan walks into a bar in Bangkok with another country on his mind: New Zealand.' That was how the drug deal began. The unnamed Iranian drug boss living in

Japan travelled to Thailand to find a courier willing to smuggle crystal meth to New Zealand. He found a man whose name remains suppressed. This 'Mr X' agreed on a fee of US$10,000. X was flown to Japan, then put up in a hotel, all expenses paid, for three weeks. He enjoyed himself tremendously — nightclubs, restaurants, a Russian prostitute. A date was set to travel to New Zealand: 6 February, Waitangi Day.

Nobakht also happened to be in Japan that week. He said he was there on business — buying cars at an auction, and importing them to New Zealand. He booked the same flight home as X. But the courier was such a hapless individual that he took the slow train instead of the fast train to the airport, and missed the flight. He also bungled the way he fastened the drugs to his body: a bag burst open, and the precious P began to seep out. X refastened the stash, and booked another flight. Nobakht, meanwhile, cancelled his flight, and rescheduled. Once again, he booked the same flight back to New Zealand as X.

Already, Nobakht was under suspicion. Police figured it was his job to shadow the courier into New Zealand, keep watch, and set up meetings. X and Nobakht arrived in Auckland on Air New Zealand Flight 90 on 8 February. Customs officials were waiting. X was pulled aside — traces of cocaine were found on his luggage. A body search revealed the P. Facing a maximum penalty of life imprisonment for importing a Class A drug, he agreed to act undercover for the police. Those negotiations took nearly two hours, while Nobakht sat in McDonald's, watching the exit signs, unwittingly starring as a lead performer in one of New Zealand's most boring films. Operation Precious was in motion.

So, too, was X. For three days he led a double life, and both of those lives must have felt like hell. Welcome to New Zealand: it was a lovely week in summer, warm and relaxing, but before X left the airport he had been busted, turned, forced to wear a body wire, and sent out to get hold of drug contacts he'd never met in a country he'd never visited. Instead of carrying powerful narcotics, he was now a condiments salesman: police replaced the meth with rock salt. They allowed him to keep 5 grams of the real stuff. They followed him out of the airport — Nobakht had just left; he'd missed X by 10 minutes — and took him to the Auckland central police station for further debriefing. Acting on instructions from the Iranian in Japan, he booked into the Skycity Hotel.

X changed his clothes. Stepping out into the casino, he looked like just another rube wearing the uniform of British tourists — an England football shirt. He soon made contact with the man who had waited at the airport arrivals lounge with Nobakht. They met at the casino bar. Surveillance revealed that Nobakht was also at the casino that night, and even went up to X and asked if they knew each other. No, said X.

His goose cooked by police, his skin itching with wires, X's first night in New Zealand just kept getting worse. He was told two prostitutes would be sent to his hotel room. The women failed to keep the appointment — they had either knocked on the wrong door, or X was asleep. The latter was unlikely. Earlier, he'd walked to a downtown café with Nobakht's friend. From his evidence as chief witness for the prosecution:

Having used the downstairs toilet, did you go back to the table?
At the point I went downstairs, he [his contact] felt my back and felt the battery pack of my wire.
What did he do?
Basically put his hand over it and felt the wire. And back at Sky casino, he embraced me in a hug and also felt the wire there, in the first meet.
At the café, you say he put his hand on your back?
Yes. I knew he felt the wire, so I take the wire off in the toilet, come back, and he's disappeared.

At which point you might expect that the drug deal was off. But greed is a powerful narcotic: despite X's contact feeling the wire, the deal continued. X met another contact the next day. They drove to Rotorua in the man's car. Police followed, noting the Audi made brief stops at a Papakura gas station and the Te Poi pub. The two men arrived in Rotorua just after 9pm, and booked into Room 24 of the Ascot Motel. X's second night in New Zealand just kept getting worse, too. In the motel room, the driver of the Audi asked to test the P. By mistake, the hapless X gave him some of the rock salt. The man smoked it in a glass pipe, and pronounced that in his opinion the drugs weren't especially strong. He decided it might be better if he smoked it out of tinfoil, so he went to a Countdown supermarket and bought a roll of foil for $1.50. When he returned, X was able to give him some of the five precious grams of real meth. Crisis averted. From X's evidence:

> *What happened when he tried it?*
> It burnt properly.
> *Did he say anything to you?*
> 'This is good.'

It turned into a long night of the alphabet: X also smoked some P, and the two men experienced Rotorua nightlife — a meal at Frodos, drinks at The Grumpy Mole, flesh at Alexandra's Strip Club until 4am. They returned to the Ascot with a six-pack of Steinlager and stayed up drinking. Two women knocked on the door at 7am. It was Rye, and a prostitute called Nicky, who wore a nose piercing and a tattoo on her ankle. Nicky brought a bag containing lingerie and sex toys. She spent the rest of the day with X in his bedroom. From his cross-examination by Rye's lawyer:

> *You had a lot on your mind at the time?*
> Sure.

You were pretty tense?

Yes.

What was on your mind?

That detection bringing in fake drugs could cause problems for my safety.

You weren't all that interested in Nicky's services, were you?

No.

If Gina told the police that her client didn't even get it up with Nicky, would that be right?

Exactly. Yeah.

X was taken into custody later that day. Rye and X's driver had already left Rotorua, with the rock salt, and booked in at the Chalet Motel in Mt Maunganui. Another gorgeous summer's day: the motelier hived off at midday to play golf all afternoon, while Rye and the driver lazed by the pool. The police entered their room early that evening. They found the useless salt, and something else, inside Rye's bag — $259,940, plus $35,200 in American dollars, wrapped in clingfilm.

The travelogue was over. All that crystal meth, 79 per cent pure, valued at three-quarters of a million dollars — but it spilled out of a courier's boxer shorts on a slow train in Tokyo, was later nabbed and magically turned into rock salt in Auckland, where it travelled to Room 374 at the Skycity Hotel, up and over the Bombay Hills and through the green and pleasant pastures of the Waikato to Room 24 at the Ascot Motel in Rotorua, then beside the seaside at Mt Maunganui to make its final rest in Unit 9 at the Chalet motel. So much for the foreign intrigue, the international connections; once the P came to New Zealand, the cheap furniture of New Zealand life took over — Park Royal tobacco, $1.50 on tinfoil at Countdown. It was an assignation at The Grumpy Mole, a toilet stop at Te Poi. It was a hooker with a pierced nose, a motelier playing golf in the sun. And it was this, from X's evidence:

Did anyone visit your motel room in Rotorua?
   Yeah, some Maori guy, a big, thick-set Maori guy with a shaved head.
   Why did he come to your room?
   Nicky had phoned him to bring us some McDonald's.

Operation Precious had caught two people red-handed. As well as X, there was the man at the Chalet Motel in Mt Maunganui — he said the drugs were his, pleaded guilty, and was sentenced to seven years' imprisonment. X, who had intended to stay in New Zealand for eight days, was sentenced to six years' jail.

But the evidence against Nobakht and Rye was circumstantial. Why, Nobakht was asked in court, had he changed his flight? Because he wanted to take another look at the car auctions in Japan. Why did he wait so long at the airport arrivals lounge? Because his wife was supposed to pick him up, and he assumed she was late. So why did he leave? He assumed she'd got the wrong date, and was still at home in Napier. After he had sat with his friend at the arrivals lounge, why did he feel it necessary to use his cellphone to call him 19 times that evening, as late as 2am? Because the redial button was faulty …

As for Rye, she said her only role in all of this was as the mama-san who supplied escorts. But what was she doing with so much cash? Rye did not elect to give evidence. Her lawyer, a trim South African woman who wore a pearl necklace, began her closing address by saying to the jury: 'Kia ora.' She emphasised that Rye was one of us. On the subject of Rye's texts (*Luv ya heaps*, etc.) while she was under surveillance at motels in Rotorua and Tauranga: 'She was obviously very involved with the lives of her whanau and her friends … A lot of living and loving was going on.'

What about all that cash? 'It's not illegal to have large amounts of money.' And: 'Money on its own doesn't mean anything.' Also: 'There are any number of reasons why people keep large amounts of cash.'

The lawyer's closing statement clocked in at an economical 57 minutes. Then the judge summed up, and the jury was released to consider its verdict. It was Tuesday afternoon.

4

It was just another P trial. But once I sat in, I had to see it through. My editors said that they'd rather I didn't, but they were indulgent. Yes, they said warily, that sounds like good copy, as I kept them updated by talking up the tension of X's dangerous charade, how it involved hookers and hard cash and 'an international drug cartel' — I probably didn't mention the $1.50 tinfoil. The days and weeks passed; finally, the jury came back with its verdict at 10.16 on Tuesday night. They had gone out for dinner, at the court's expense, at the Hyatt. It was a cold night. The lawyers hung around the courtroom. One or two smokers put on their expensive overcoats to step outside. All the bright overhead lights in the High Court were kept on.

The jury was escorted by a registrar back down the leafy English street from the Hyatt to the court, the judge was alerted, the defendants were called up from their cells. The courtroom was unlocked. 'Silence for Her Honour. All stand.' Justice Winkelmann took her seat, and asked the foreman of the jury whether it had reached a unanimous verdict. It had. The charges were read out. Nobakht was found guilty. Rye was found not guilty. 'You are free to go, Ms Rye,' said the judge, and Rye was all smiles, ready to resume a lot of living and loving, as she stomped out of the courtroom in her Ugg boots without giving Nobakht so much as a backwards glance. He was remanded in custody. The judge said to him, 'A lengthy term of imprisonment is inevitable.'

He appeared for sentencing a month later. The judge said, 'I have received a pre-sentence report in respect of you. At the time that the report was written you continued to deny any involvement in the offending, but this morning I have had placed before me a letter from you in which you admit your involvement.'

And then she said, 'You say, however, that it occurred because of associating with bad people and you assure me that you will never offend again.'

She listed submissions from the prosecution and the defence. Both agreed that there were mitigating factors. Nobakht had no previous offences, 'and you have family who will be affected by your imprisonment'.

And then she said, 'I do not take into account your personal circumstances. In cases involving such serious drug offending, such considerations carry little if any weight. Part of the cost of your offending will be carried by your wife and child. That is inevitable and you must accept responsibility for that.'

She said, 'Mr Nobakht, please stand.' He stood. She read out his sentence. He got 10 years. And then she said, 'Stand down, please.'

The sentence was brutish, ugly and long, and that's the way it goes. All trials are horrible from beginning to end, a meticulous, tormenting re-enactment of alleged wrongs. I had my pick of whatever was happening in the High Court in that spring; I may as well have walked in with a blindfold; it didn't matter that it was the P trial of Nobakht and Rye. It could just as easily have been someone else's terror of their guilt being detected or their innocence being overlooked. Secretly I knew that what I was after was ordinary, run-of-the-mill courtroom misery. This is all that so many P trials ever achieved. From the last, sorry part of Nobakht's evidence to his lawyer:

Mr Nobakht, what do you say is your primary source of income?

I worked in the orchard, and I was trying to expand my business.

Now, do you have anything you wish to say or add in relation to your employment as an apple-picker?

I wanted just simply to show the jury and you that I do work in an orchard and I have got all the equipment here.

When you talk about equipment, Mr Nobakht, what is it that you want to say about that?

Prosecution: Objection. This is a court of law, not an opportunity to give speeches about apple picking. Moving into irrelevance.

Her Honour: It is not relevant.

Defence: *As Your Honour pleases.*

Two boxes of Pacific Rose apples had been placed under a chair outside Courtroom 7. Nobakht's wife had brought them up from their orchard in Napier. The intention was to produce them as evidence. After it was ruled that they were irrelevant, the boxes disappeared. I asked Nobakht's wife where they had gone. She said she gave them away, to friends in Auckland, to a homeless man she had met, and to the Salvation Army. The apples had looked so fresh and delicious. Their absence took away the only goodness to be seen.

Chapter 5

Falling down: Guy Hallwright

1

It would have taken, oh, say maybe three minutes for former Forsyth Barr investment advisor turned New Zealand's most vilified road-rage wretch Guy Hallwright to start showing signs of something resembling a nervous collapse during cross-examination in an upstairs office in downtown Auckland. Employment Court proceedings have a unique kind of dismalness. The worst thing that can happen to you in the criminal courts is that a roll of the judicial dice — a jury's whim, a judge's discretion — will send you directly to jail. Yes, quite bad, but Employment Court offers another misery, and the anguish of it is as personal as if you took your ex-partner to court to say that their decision to dump you was unfair. You tell the judge: they shouldn't have done that. You argue: they broke my heart without, you know, due process. You might also beg: please, for the love of God, make them take me back.

It's a humiliating ordeal, pitiful, almost indecent. I sat next to journalist Matt Nippert during Hallwright's cross-examination at his three-day Employment Court hearing, and after a while — oh, say maybe four minutes — the two of us couldn't look at him any more. We averted our eyes. We whispered to each other: 'Jesus Christ.' The poor devil was torn apart by Peter Churchman QC. He stammered and raved and sweated and reddened, all for want of his job. Churchman rather enjoyed it; a tall, severe character, he turned to Matt and myself at one point, and winked.

Hallwright had driven over an angry Korean, and been sacked. He said it happened outside of work, and wanted his job back. 'There's no impediment that I can see,' he said. Churchman counted the impediments. He told Hallwright that he was remorseless, feckless, useless, more or less a completely hopeless case. 'You're damaged goods,' said Churchman. At least that last remark seemed fair, and when I later met with Hallwright in his old neck of the woods, at a café upstairs in Hotel DeBrett, just around the corner from the Forsyth Barr tower on Shortland Street in downtown Auckland, I asked him, 'Are you a mess?'

Tall, elegant, thin-lipped, he said, 'Am I a mess? No, I don't think I'm a mess. No. But, you know, it is all very upsetting. For everyone involved. Not just me.' He looked like a mess. He was a furtive, gaunt presence, twitchy and bristly — maybe he just needed a shave. But I thought back to a photo of him that is still rattling around online, taken before his public shaming, from when he was in his pomp as a blameless and successful financier. He is at a business function with a man who really is called Paul Hamburger. Hallwright looks overweight, florid, with a glass in his hand while he chews the fat with Hamburger; he's perfectly at ease, untroubled and benign, just another rich Parnell schnook on the after-work drinks circuit. The 61-year-old twitching over his latte in a corner of DeBretts Kitchen was a kind of ghost.

He sometimes took sleeping pills to knock himself out, and also to avoid waking up at whatever dark o'clock of the soul where he would inevitably replay the two or three minutes — a second would have made all the difference, even a quarter of a second —

when his whole life changed and collapsed. Oh, and when someone else's life changed and collapsed, too, and Hallwright's sorry about that, but he never really altered his position from the comment he gave at the time of the 'mishap', of the 'incident', when he told a reporter, 'I did not instigate the incident. The other guy did.'

On a sunny morning in spring in 2010, on a busy intersection in central Auckland, Hallwright got into an argument with another driver, Sung Jin Kim. It ended when Hallwright ran him over in his Saab. Kim suffered terrible physical pain. Hallwright was accused of road rage. Worse, he was accused of never saying sorry, of not showing remorse or contrition or the faintest bit of sympathy. In the media, he was held up as a wealthy and arrogant asshole. In court, a jury found him guilty of reckless driving. In his professional life, Forsyth Barr viewed him with extreme distaste, and got rid of him, wordlessly handing him a letter of termination as he sat at his desk.

He took Forsyth Barr to the Employment Relations Authority. It ruled that his dismissal was fair. He appealed to the Employment Court. It ruled that his dismissal was fair.

At first blush, it felt as though Hallwright didn't have a prayer with his appeal, that he was once again dragging it out — always crashing in the same car. His dispute was an exercise in gall, delusion, greed. His conditions were that he wanted his job, a modest $10,000 for emotional hurt, and his not-very-modest $100,000 bonus. As well, he wanted immediate reimbursement of his salary, $275,000; he tried to make it sound generous, and forgiving, when he said he'd settle for half. Crazy, but he had reasonable grounds to challenge Forsyth Barr's claim that he'd brought them into disrepute.

Much of the court hearing turned on the head of a pin, or not even that; it turned on an abstraction. It was all about perception, the fear of what people might think. Absurdly, Forsyth Barr called on PR trout Bill Ralston to back them up. It reinforced the notion that Hallwright's whole saga was some sort of media game that he had no idea how to play.

Every new scandal in New Zealand public life is treated as a public relations exercise. The right spin can lead to redemption, but a poorly executed strategy will make things worse. Everything Hallwright did made things worse. He blundered this way and that, struck entirely the wrong attitude. He transgressed the social contract by never saying sorry, never entirely accepting fault. As well, he couldn't catch a break the whole way through. He got hung out to dry, pursued by everyone from right-wing blog Whaleoil to the Auckland Council for Civil Liberties. A judge came out in his defence and he really shouldn't have; the comments were provocative, and made things even worser.

Hallwright raved in the Employment Court about that 'quarter of a second', how everything would have been different if only he hadn't had a moment of panic on Mt Eden Road that Wednesday, 8 September 2010. 'A second. Not even that. Half a second. Quarter of a second …' He leaned forward, hunched and neurotic, gabbling, as though he were reaching out to try to reclaim the moment that changed the entire course of his life.

2

Hallwright grew up in Karori, Wellington, a doctor's son. His father was a cardiologist. He left his family when Guy was about six, and remarried. One of the last times I spoke with Hallwright was when he'd arrived in Wellington to visit his stepmother in a rest home. He took the bus; he had been suspended from driving for 18 months.

He said his father was something of an eccentric, collecting 1970s New Zealand pottery, and idly penning persistent, complaining letters to the editor. Sample: 'It amuses me to hear Maori constantly complaining that Pakeha keep using the "race card". Talk about the pot calling the kettle black.' And: 'Am I alone in being fed up to the back teeth with TV advertisements saying, "97 per cent fat-free"? If they mean, "It has only 3 per cent fat", why don't they say just that? Quite simply, it is pseudo-science. It is a con, claptrap.'

Hallwright has a gentler, rather less strident nature. Friends describe him as shy, sensitive, cultured. After boarding at Palmerston North Boys' High School, he studied literature and sociology at Victoria University. Tutor and poet Bill Manhire took him for Old Norse. He said, 'I basically remember Guy as an intelligent and genuinely nice human being. Hard-working, too — you had to be to get by in Old Norse! I was surprised when he turned up in the media a few years later as a business guru, or whatever the term is.'

The term is 'investment analyst'. Hallwright came to finance late in life, at 35. He married radio journalist Juliet Robieson in 1982, and they moved to England. Hallwright studied for an MBA, and later worked for investment firms First NZ Capital in Wellington and Credit Suisse in Sydney. The years in Australia, when he and Juliet raised their son and two daughters in elegant Mosman, were his highest paying, and also the highest pressure.

He took a pay cut to come back to New Zealand and join Forsyth Barr. A former colleague said that the firm headhunted Hallwright. 'There were a number of key appointments made at that time, and he was one of those. It was a fledgling broking business. It's an important player now and it's because of people like Guy, who had a high reputation and standing. He was definitely an important part of the company's growth and consolidation.'

Hallwright dealt with clients from big firms, such as AMP and Guinness Peat Group, and became one of those rent-a-quote experts in the media, relaying his opinion on financial markets to business journalists at *Morning Report, The National Business Review,* and elsewhere. He was an expert in telecommunications, and the retail sector. On top of his salary, he also took home a bonus of about $101,000 every six months.

He bought a big house in Parnell. It was two doors down from the Prime Minister's mansion. It hogged an entire corner, and had a pool, nikau palms, polished wooden floors. The Hallwrights were Friends of the Auckland Art Gallery. Juliet stayed home and wrote fiction. Their younger daughter, Issie, wrote songs, and became close friends with John Key's daughter, Stephie. Hallwright had got to know finance minister Bill English, and attended a music recital given by English's daughter. It was held at a private house; there were about 20 people, and nice sandwiches.

And then the life he knew was taken away. It disappeared, the last seconds of it spent sitting at the lights at the intersection of Symonds Street and Khyber Pass Road, when Sung Jin Kim drove up behind him.

3

Their versions of what happened are very similar. That is, both agree it was about 10am. Otherwise, they're wildly different narratives, and they don't even share the same cast; Hallwright says his teenage daughter, Issie, was in the passenger seat, but Kim believes it was an older woman, that there was something suspicious going on.

It was a Wednesday. Hallwright said he was taking Issie to a studio to record a song she'd written. 'I was going to play a bit of guitar on it.'

The driver behind him honked his horn at him, thinking that he'd waited at a green light. Hallwright claims the driver misunderstood, that the green light was for the bus in the bus lane next to him.

'When I did get the green light, I drove away. This guy followed me around the corner into Mt Eden Road, and kept honking his horn at me. So I pulled into that carpark, the Galbraith's carpark, and he goes past and — and this is the unwise thing that I did, and it's probably a bit of a lesson, I suppose — I gave him the finger.

He screeches to a halt in the middle of the road. I thought, "Oh shit, this is going to be a confrontation of some sort." I didn't want him coming over and trying to attack me, so I went over to his car. I opened his door, and said, "What's your problem?"'

I said, 'That's got to be a mistake.'

He said, 'Well, I don't know what he would have done if I hadn't gone over. I just walked over and approached him. I wouldn't describe it as yelling at him, but I certainly had a raised voice.'

'Why on earth did you open the door?'

'Because he was just sitting in the car with the window up. Otherwise I would have no doubt talked to him through the window.'

This was somehow missing the point. I said, 'That was unwise, wasn't it?'

He said, 'It was unwise, yeah.'

'How were you feeling at this stage?'

'I don't know. The adrenalin was going. I was thinking, "Shit, am I going to have to do something?" He looked like a big guy, as far as I could tell. He just looked at me and his look was very, very chilling. He looked angry, and ... dangerous. And he reached across towards his glovebox, and I suddenly thought, "I've actually walked into something on the dark side. This is really serious, and I need to get out of here as quickly as possible."'

I asked, 'What did you think he was reaching for?'

'A weapon. I don't think he was reaching for his driving licence! A knife, gun, whatever — I actually did think "gun". So I just slammed the door and went back to my car. I don't think I ran, but I certainly went very fast.'

I said, 'Okay, at this point, how do you think you're faring in the story?'

He said, 'The best thing to do would have been to just try to defuse the whole thing. Not done anything at all. Just pulled into the parking space, or actually just driven through and right away. I was rattled.'

I said, 'Are you describing road rage?'

'No. I think road rage is probably what he was feeling. I was feeling under attack. That's what I felt.'

'Under attack?'

'He'd screeched to a halt in the middle of the road, and I thought he was going to attack me. And if that happened, I'd rather it was over there, because of Issie.'

'And then?'

'I saw him advancing rapidly on the car. He gets right in front of it and starts banging his hands on the bonnet and shouting. Very, very angry man.'

'In English?'

'Nothing that I can comprehend. So I sort of ... I nudged the car forward, to indicate that I'm getting out of here. He starts coming around towards the driver's door. And as he was doing that, I pulled forward. And it appears— I don't actually— All I remember is that he wasn't in front of the car when I drove forward. I don't actually quite know still how he got hit. But he got hit. And when he got hit, there was a bump. It sort of felt, when I thought about it afterwards, that we'd run over his foot. Well, we probably did run over his foot, and he got serious injuries, as you know.

'But he didn't get run over in the sense that I ran him over while he was standing in front of the car. The doctor who we got to look at the injuries, the best conclusion he could come to is that his toe — the wheel had got his toe, and he couldn't move out of the way. I was amazed and appalled at the injuries that this guy got, cos it felt just like a little bump.

'So I'm driving down Mt Eden Road, past Galbraith's, and I looked in the rear-vision mirror and I could see he was on the road and people were converging. I turned the corner and stopped. I dialled 111.'

'How were you feeling now?'

'Completely panicked. Well, I was feeling completely panicked when he started coming around to the side of the car. This whole thing was done in shock and panic. Not really thinking. Just reacting. Sometimes I have very fast reactions, especially when my kids are in danger. There was a time in Kings Canyon in Aussie …'

He told a story about a family holiday at the Northern Territory canyon when he saw Issie step back towards the edge: 'Somehow I got to her instantly and grabbed her and got her back from the brink. Juliet said to me afterwards, "I don't know how you covered the distance." This,' he said, 'was like that. Instant reaction.'

I said, 'You mean the driving away?'

'Yep. Yep. This is my chance to get away, he's coming around to the side of the car, things are going to get worse, because I don't know what he's going to do — open the door, drag me out of the car …'

'What should you have done, when you look back?'

'What the prosecution said, which is push the lock-all-the-doors thing. But I didn't even know where in the Saab the thing where you did that was.'

I said, 'But you drove off, and called 111.'

'It took me a minute or two. My hands were shaking. It was a work phone, and you had to put a four-digit code in to open it. I probably spent two minutes trying to unlock it. Then I drove around the block, dropped Issie off at the studio, because there was nothing I could do at the scene, 111 are sending an ambulance, there are plenty of people there, and I didn't want to ruin Issie's big opportunity.'

The police called him, and asked him to return to the scene. Hallwright walked there.

I asked, 'Where was Mr Kim?'

'He was still lying in the road.'

'In agony?'

'Yeah, he was yelling. He was sort of bellowing, actually. He wasn't screaming, but he was yelling.'

'Did you think, "Oh, God, what have I done?"'

'Well, I couldn't tell how serious his injuries were at that stage. Obviously he couldn't get up. I thought he'd broken a leg.'

'What was going through your nervous system?'

'I don't know. I mean ... I guess I thought ... I mean, I knew I would have to go through a few things with the police, and that it was ... um ... you know ... a sort of major deal.'

'What were you thinking about Mr Kim?'

'Well, at that stage, not that much. He was just this guy who'd been trying to attack me and he'd now had his leg broken, which was unfortunate, and I was sorry about that, but people were there to look after him, the ambulance was there, and it was going to be what it was going to be. I had no idea then that the injuries were going to be anything like as severe as they proved to be.'

'Are you taking any responsibility for what happened?'

He said, 'I totally accept that I didn't act as well in those few seconds as I could have. Absolutely. But at the same time, people do need to be reminded I was being attacked by this guy. I felt under extreme threat.'

'You fucked up, didn't you?'

'I think I did, yeah. Absolutely.'

'What is your genuine level of remorse?'

'Oh, high,' he said. 'It's terrible what's happened to Mr Kim. Absolutely terrible. Who would wish that on anyone?'

Even now, after everything, his account lacked genuine remorse. Kim, an 'angry man', was 'bellowing', his injuries were 'unfortunate', and let it be known poor Hallwright was 'under attack'. I asked if he went to the studio afterwards, and played on Issie's song. 'Yes. I was a bit shaky, though.' The song, a sad, pretty ballad, is titled 'Pendulum'.

4

Panic on the streets of Auckland. Scooting out of his Saab ('a gay convertible', in Whaleoil's parlance) to take on a complete stranger, opening the driver's door and giving him a piece of his mind, then scooting back to his car because the idea has formed in his mind that the man had a gun — if that's what happened, then Hallwright fucked up and freaked out, spooked by an angry Asian driver, deciding on the option of fight and then switching it to flight, blundering this way and that on Mt Eden Road, finally oblivious to the fact he'd just run someone over as he left the scene of the crime.

He was plainly incandescent, but was it with rage, or fear? What was he playing at, going over to Kim and opening the driver's door? What was that bullshit with thinking Kim was reaching for a gun? Was it cowardice that drove him out of his wits?

But what about Kim's actions? According to Hallwright, Kim was furious as he leaned on the horn at the lights, wouldn't let it go and kept honking after the lights changed; screeching to a halt in the middle of the road was bound to give Hallwright the creeps, or at least make him apprehensive; and what was on Kim's mind when he approached Hallwright's car, banging on the bonnet, then coming around to the driver's side?

Who's the bad guy, Hallwright or Kim?

'He try murder me!' shouted Kim. He did a fair bit of shouting when I interviewed him at a warehouse in East Tamaki. It was his workplace and his home. He slept in a room on the upstairs mezzanine; four pairs of socks were hung out to dry on the staircase, a bowl and a pair of chopsticks were in the downstairs sink. The warehouse was stocked with crates of Coke, Dr Pepper, Chupa Chups.

Kim, 60, had a large face and a wide, compact body. He was in bad shape. He could barely walk. He rolled up his pants; there were metal rods in one lower leg, and ugly, livid skin grafts on the other lower leg.

He started complaining about an incompetent surgeon, and then complained about a Fijian nurse with a needle. His English was hard to follow. He giggled, flew into rages, shouted, spoke sadly about his parents — they died when he was very young, and he left school at 10. He became a civil engineer, and worked in Saudi Arabia and Papua New Guinea. His wife left him when he was surveying in Indonesia. He came to Auckland 15 years ago, and was renting in Mt Eden with a new partner at the time of the accident.

'She gone,' he said. 'She doesn't like me any more. She say, "You got a stupid leg." I say okay. I just left. I never took anything, no moneys, nothing. Because I'm a Christian. My God always protects me. He always helps me. He gives me all the things.'

He mentioned he was a Christian several more times. I asked him which church he attended. 'I don't know name,' he said.

He told his story about what happened on Wednesday, 8 September 2010. Hallwright was at the lights, he pulled up behind him. 'The light changed to green but he never move. He sit there with lady. The lady looks like 30, 35. She's very sexy. Looks very sexy. Other cars, they shout at him and they make horn. WAAH! WAAH! At the time my horn is broken. It not work. It not me. In car behind me, there's a Kiwi young guy. Oh, he's very, very crazy, very angry, honking the horn. WAAH! WAAH! Hallwright turn and look at me and he give me the finger! I say, "No me! I never make that honk! Please, just go!"'

He said Hallwright finally drove through the lights, and then braked to a halt on Mt Eden Road. 'He came out from his car. He came to me. He open my door, and smash it shut. BAM!'

I asked if he reached into his glovebox. He said, 'What?' I asked again. He shook his head, and continued his story.

'At this time I'm angry. Before, I'm not angry. So I come out my car. I go to his car. When I standing in front of his car, he start driving. Drive over me! Not stop! Fuck!'

I asked if he went to the driver's side, and he said, 'No. Last thing I see, the lady grab his arm. She angry with him.'

I said the passenger was Hallwright's daughter, who was 16.

'No!' he shouted. 'Lie! One hundred per cent lie! He talked to the judges, he say his daughter there. They say, "Okay." But the lady almost 40 years. Not his daughter. Lie!'

Why lie?

'I don't know! He's very popular guy. I think it's his girlfriend or something like that. I think so.'

He mentioned Hallwright talking to the judge; did he think the judge was in on it, that he and Hallwright knew each other?

'I think so. They seem to. But we don't have any evidence … Police, judges, he give to them, I think!' He mimed passing money under the table. 'I don't trust this fucken country! No justice! No honest peoples!'

At such times he was infantile, a loose unit. His injuries made him a pitiful sight, but he was belligerent, unstable. He said he'd had nine operations in New Zealand, and cursed his surgeons; the tenth operation was in Korea, and he claimed it cost a staggering $100,000.

I spoke with Korean lawyer Ken Oh, from Kenton Chambers, who dealt with Kim. He said, 'Mr Kim wanted to have surgery in Korea because so many people there have car accidents and medical people there have more practical experience than in New Zealand. So many people, so many cars, so many accidents! The surgeons are much, much better than in your country. So Mr Kim come to see me and talk about how to recover at least that amount.'

How?

'He wanted to sue.'

5

Everything that Hallwright did after he hit Kim was a tactical mistake of some sort. He made no mention of it to Forsyth Barr.

He regarded it as a matter outside of work, and a minor matter at that: 'A policeman at the scene said there'd probably have to be charges under the Transport Act.'

But even when the police laid serious criminal charges — reckless driving, and intent to injure — Hallwright remained silent. He fought hard for name suppression, taking it to the High Court, but that only inspired the wrath of Whaleoil, Cameron Slater's fulminating blog, which has made a crusade of taunting those who try to hide behind gagging orders.

Forsyth Barr's managing director, Neil Paviour-Smith, first heard that one of his employees was facing serious criminal charges when he was shown a post on Whaleoil.

'Neil was so angry that he'd had to find out through the blog,' said a former colleague. 'He was pissed off about that, big time. Guy needed to come clean. He needed to get it out in the open.'

But the company took no immediate action, and viewed him as innocent until proven otherwise. If the jury had reached a verdict of not guilty at his criminal trial, it was 'entirely possible' that he'd have kept his job, the Employment Court heard. Hallwright assured the firm that he would be acquitted, and carried on with his duties all throughout 2011.

PR trout Tina Symmans, a director at Forsyth Barr, told the Employment Relations Authority hearing that she had met Hallwright at a social function around that time, and tried to offer her advice. He waved it away, saying he was confident of acquittal.

'I was astounded by … his arrogance in thinking that this really didn't matter … He insisted that it wasn't his fault and that the Asian man was to blame. Given his approach, it's unsurprising the media gave the matter the prominence they did.'

In fact, his 'approach' was to tell her exactly what he thought, and to present the facts as he saw them. But was he really so blasé? The stress of waiting for the trial led him to begin counselling.

I asked if he was living in dread back then, and he said, 'Oh yeah. It was a big thing to have hanging over your head. A huge strain.'

Hallwright engaged the services of Paul Davison QC. 'He said I had a very strong chance of beating the intent to injure thing, and the other one, reckless driving, was kind of each way.'

The trial finally took place in March 2012. The judge dropped the charges of intent to injure, but the jury found Hallwright guilty of reckless driving causing grievous bodily harm.

'I was shocked. Very shocked. That felt terrible. Absolutely terrible.'

The hits just kept coming. Forsyth Barr began termination proceedings; Davison, as his lawyer, urged them to hold off until sentencing. That was another bombshell.

Hallwright's sentence, 250 hours' community work, was lenient. But the real offence was caused by the judge, Raoul Neave, when he took it into his head to excoriate the media for their 'puerile' coverage of Hallwright's saga. He got that right. But he was buying a fight that only served to get Hallwright beat up on all over again.

Neave said, 'When it became apparent you had come into contact with Mr Kim, you called the police and in every sense seem to have behaved in a responsible fashion.' It wasn't what anyone wanted to hear; with friends like Neave, Hallwright attracted even more enemies. A witness to the incident, pizza-maker Giampiero De Falco, ran to the *Weekend Herald* and gave them a great quote for the front page: 'If it's not hit-and-run, what the hell is it?'

Neave also described Hallwright as someone with an 'impeccable reputation'. He got that right, too, but it led to howls of outrage, and was perceived as old-boy cronyism at its worst — one law for the poor, one for the rich.

The Auckland Council for Civil Liberties jumped on the bandwagon. Council president Barry Wilson wrote to the solicitor-general, asking for the sentence to be appealed.

Why? The council's interest in the affair was almost frivolous, certainly unbalanced. Wilson took a statement from Kim, but didn't read the court transcripts, just the press reports. He told me, 'I think I looked at the press reports in some detail. There were some pretty detailed press reports.'

That's all?

'Well, what else can I rely on at the time? Are you suggesting that I shouldn't have taken up this issue on the basis of the information available to me, that I should have waited some considerable time before I made any comment?'

If that were the question, what's the answer?

'When one is asked to comment on issues, one comments without full information. Everybody does that.'

Amazing. I asked him what he wrote in his letter to the solicitor-general.

'I suggested the sentence was inadequate, and he should appeal.'

What kind of sentence did he think was more appropriate?

'I'd need to think about that.'

Had he been thinking in terms of imprisonment?

After a long pause, he said, 'I'd need to think about it.'

Did he think about it at the time?

'Yes, I did.'

And what did he think?

'Oh, look, I'm not prepared to be cross-examined about it. I'm not here to be cross-examined by you. I've got a day's work to get on with. If you want to go into it in more detail, the weekend's better for me.'

But it's not a detailed question. Was he recommending that Hallwright go to jail?

'I'd need to think about it. It was a year ago. Over a year ago. I've got to go, okay?'

The solicitor-general's office refused to appeal the sentence. Crown Law spokesperson Jan Fulstow told *The National Business*

Review that the sentence wasn't 'manifestly inadequate'. She said, 'We can't take appeals to the Court to Appeal that we know we shouldn't be taking. It's just wasting the court's time.'

6

Hallwright, foolishly, hoped that the judge's comments might help save his skin at Forsyth Barr. Neave had expressed dismay that the conviction could lead to Hallwright's termination. But the train had already left the station. He was let go when the company's managing director handed him an A4 envelope.

It gave two reasons. Forsyth Barr argued that Hallwright had committed 'serious misconduct'. It also insisted that his crime had brought the company into disrepute. But the firm didn't offer much proof at the Employment Court.

Asked to quantify what losses they might have suffered as a result of the scandal, Paviour-Smith gabbled, 'You don't know what you don't know.'

He sat on one side of the court; Hallwright and his wife, Juliet, on the other. They didn't make eye contact. Paviour-Smith gritted his teeth at having to confront him at all. 'This is just the latest chapter,' he said, exasperated, in cross-examination. 'He always blames others, and never accepts responsibility.'

Before her husband's termination, Juliet Hallwright wrote emails and left phone messages dumping on Paviour-Smith — he was 'slippery', 'a pompous twat', etc. In court, she wailed, 'I'm sorry, Neil!' It was a horrible, pained cry, but Paviour-Smith folded his arms, and turned his head. He'd plainly had it up to here with the pathetic Hallwrights.

Paviour-Smith fell apart in cross-examination. He talked too much, gulped, gasped for breath. In one exchange, he tried to dignify emails sent to Forsyth Barr by 'nutters', as Hallwright's employment lawyer, Harry Waalkens, called them.

The emails were sent after Hallwright was found guilty.

'Some of them were ... uh ... blatantly inappropriate,' Paviour-Smith stumbled.

Waalkens: 'There's no need to be guarded. They're plainly from nutters.'

Paviour-Smith: 'I ... um ... I think that ... These emails are indicative of a depth of feeling in the wider public domain.'

Sample email, from someone called Terry: 'serves you right you talentless loser. what are you going to do? run me over? Bwahahahaha. kill yourself you moron.'

Other emails were read out in court. They all had the familiar, bitter tone of Stuff Comments, of trolls, of nutters. Lame of Forsyth Barr to grasp at such straws; lame, also, to call on the services of Bill Ralston, who brought the gobbledegook of media strategies to the courtroom.

The hearing opened with Waalkens objecting to Ralston appearing as a witness: 'How is this ever going to help you determine?' he shouted at Judge Inglis, who had a heavy cold, and held her head in her hands. Churchman dropped his voice and spoke to her soothingly. 'Mr Rawls-ton,' he drawled, 'is an expert in reputation management, Your Honour.'

They described two Ralstons. Waalkens profiled him as one of the lower forms, a blathering media bullshitter and corporate lackey; Churchman presented the wise and venerable 'Rawl-ston' as a lord of the crisis management manor. 'I accept he is qualified as an expert,' ruled Inglis, and allowed him to appear.

But it didn't make much difference. Ralston began by explaining the principles of a holy paradigm used extensively in crisis management known as CAP, which stands for Concern, Action and Perspective. This wonderful snake oil and hair restorative had worked wonders for many satisfied clients, he said. If only Hallwright had gone to Ralston, instead of wasting his money on Paul Davison QC! 'He should have stated he was

Concerned,' said Ralston, sadly. 'If he had demonstrated remorse, if he had apologised and taken responsibility, the media attention would have substantially decreased.' He spelled out the rest of the advanced theorem of CAP — 'Hallwright should have taken Action', and done something or other about 'Perspective' — as the court enjoyed a free lesson in mod comms.

His central message in his prepared statement to the court was that Hallwright had caused Forsyth Barr reputational damage. Back up, said Waalkens. He wanted to know whether Ralston's statement was an original work, or merely a photocopy of the statement given to the Employment Relations Authority by his close friend and Forsyth Barr director, Tina Symmans.

'You've lifted great parts of Tina's own statement,' he said.

'Some parts,' said Ralston.

'You've lifted whole paragraphs word for word. They are identical.'

'Yes, they mostly are,' said Ralston.

'No, they're not "mostly", they're identical.'

'Some of it,' said Ralston, 'is because I've agreed with it.'

'It'd be plagiarism if it were journalism.'

'It would be if it were,' said Ralston.

'Do you think courts are less rigorous than journalism?'

'No,' said Ralston.

'You're not impartial at all, are you? You're plagiarising the work of your friend Tina.'

'Well,' said Ralston, 'there was a lot of material I didn't use …'

Judge Inglis, in her ruling, made only passing reference to Ralston. She wrote, 'In the final analysis I did not gain much assistance from his evidence.'

Her 35-page report found against Hallwright. It concluded that the firm had suffered reputational damage, and that Hallwright's dismissal was justifiable. It was impossible that he could have stayed on after his criminal conviction. Hallwright had blustered that it didn't impair his ability to do his job. It was as though he were asking, what's driving over an angry Korean got to do with investment advice? But there was another, stronger question at stake. Who would want to do business with someone who drove over an angry Korean? Hallwright wore that cloth of shame: a scarlet letter.

7

After everything — the botched getaway on Mt Eden Road, the trial, the sacking, the doomed appeals to get his job back — what was left of Guy Hallwright's life? He estimated he spent about $400,000 on legal fees, but wasn't poor. He said he lived off interest on his investments. Was he budgeting? He said, 'I'm not in a position where I have to be that careful.'

No one had offered work. All he had was spare time. He bicycled about 30 kilometres a day. He repaired a couple of guitars. He listened to music — he was a fan of King Crimson, Small Faces, Them, Gram Parsons, John Mayer, The White Stripes. He read the classics — *Anna Karenina, The Great Gatsby* ('which confirms my belief it's his finest work'), and had taken on Proust. He meditated. The pile in Parnell was sold, and he moved into his sister's house in Pakuranga.

Had his life collapsed?

'I'm an optimistic kind of guy. But from the outside you might say that. Yeah. But it's that old Chinese thing, isn't it? In every crisis there's an opportunity. I'm not sure what the opportunity is yet. I live in hope.'

Juliet's evidence at Employment Court was revealing of his psychological state. She talked of someone who was 'short-tempered', 'shattered', receiving counselling, 'falling apart'. She, too, was broken. Her pretty face hinted at someone who had once been animated and vivacious. But now she breathed hard, and wept. She said, 'Guy pops off into his study and doesn't tell me what he's done all day, and I don't question him about it.'

After Peter Churchman almost reluctantly tore her to shreds in cross-examination, she sat beside her husband, who stroked her arm for a brief second. It was the touch of a stranger. Afterwards, she left alone, and walked across the road to St Patrick's Cathedral.

I spoke to her for a minute. She looked as though she was going to cry.

Hallwright said, 'There's long-standing stuff that's got nothing to do with this. Tensions.'

Was he happy?

'No. No.'

Was he depressed?

'I'm pretty knocked about. It's been a shattering process. There's been days when it's been difficult to summon the energy to get out of bed.'

I'd heard Hallwright described by someone who knew him as a person who didn't know who or what he was any more.

'Hmm. Someone who probably doesn't know where he is would be more accurate.'

Had his life become a tragedy?

'It's terrible to think of applying a word like that to your own life. But yeah. It probably is tragic. And traumatic. For everyone involved. I deeply regret what happened to Mr Kim. I could have done better. But I didn't, so that's the breaks.

'I also very much regret the effect on the family. It's put them through a hell of a lot of stress, and that was my fault. And Forsyth Barr, too — we argue about who should have done what, and we find ourselves in court on opposite sides, but I'm sure it's been a very unhappy thing for them to have to deal with as well. And I regret that. Lots of regrets.'

What did he have to say to Sung Jin Kim?

'Just … I'm sorry about his injuries and I hope he's recovering from them as well as he can. It was an unfortunate day for both of us. He knows that both of us had a hand in it. I wish him well.' It was said in such a dead voice.

Tina Symmans, in her statement to the Employment Relations Authority, said her advice to Hallwright would have been for him to visit Kim in hospital, 'and show real concern'. Kim shouted at me, 'He must come here and say sorry!'

That wasn't going to happen. Perhaps it wasn't lack of concern so much as some deep and entrenched gormlessness. Hallwright was at once sensitive and dense.

We talked again about 8 September 2010, when Hallwright and Kim crossed paths. Could he see the scene? 'Yep. Absolutely. His car screeching to a halt in the middle of the road is etched into my memory.'

What else?

'His face when he turned to look at me. It was chilling. It was chilling because it was … it was menacing in a deadpan, impassive kind of way. I was very apprehensive at that stage that he was involved in some … that he was part of something, he was some kind of godfather figure, some kind of mafia. That's what I thought. It scared the hell out of me. It was a sudden realisation that I had gone into something way too deep.'

I asked him, 'Are you a racist?'

'I don't think so,' he laughed. 'No. I've worked with people of Asian descent. When I go on holiday, I often go to Asia.'

What a hopeless reply. I said to him, 'Instead of only saying "I am so sorry!", you insist on saying all these other things. Why?'

'Well, I am sorry. But you're asking me how it all happened, and I'm explaining it. There was blame on both sides. He knows, if he's honest with himself, that he shouldn't have done what he did that day. I shouldn't have done what I did. I reacted badly. But it takes two to make this thing.'

I said, 'But is it unwise for you to say so? Are you making the same mistake over and over?'

'Maybe. Maybe.'

I said, 'The whole thing between you and Kim that day at the lights — many people will say to themselves, "What would I have done?" It's like a test, that you can never anticipate.'

He said, 'Yes. In the fraction of the second you have, you don't know until you get there what's going to happen. The path you take through life is a random walk, unfortunately.'

'If it was a test, did you fail it?'

He said, 'Yeah. Yeah.'

'Do you also think you failed your family?'

He said, 'Yes, probably.'

I liked Hallwright. He lacked imagination, and empathy, and compassion, but he had a kind of poise, and there was a suspicion of wit. I remembered the speech he gave when he described how he saved Issie from stepping too close to the edge at Kings Canyon; on that occasion, he protected his family. He achieved the opposite when something inside him broke on Mt Eden Road five years ago. A moment in traffic, at one of Auckland's busiest intersections — the French Café on one side of the street, Duchess Home Bakery on the other, a shoe store, a toyshop, something called Asia Works …

I said, 'It'd be dreadful if the scene on Mt Eden Road was the last thing that ever crossed your mind before you died.'

He said, 'It would. It would.'

'Your whole life compressed to one stupid moment.'

'Yes. Then again,' he said, attempting a smile, 'you wouldn't be around to worry about it.'

Chapter 6

The lair of the white worm: Derek King

1

Monday night was art gallery night, and he'd always dress for the occasion. He favoured big aviator sunglasses. He wore cream pants and grey shoes. He'd spruce up his haircut of tight little blond ringlets, that 'baffling perm', as photographer Patrick Reynolds described it, that 'mad hair' as remembered by gallery owner Gary Langsford. His skin was very pale. He carried a damp flannel in his pocket.

He'd walk. He lived in downtown Auckland, on the pretty green hump of Constitution Hill, in an ivy-covered Edwardian townhouse, bought when he was about 32, in 1978. He rented out the top floor. He kept his yellow Ferrari Dino and his burgundy Jaguar in the downstairs garage. He lived in-between. The front door was gated, and the windows were barred; visitors knew to come around the side.

He attended Monday night openings at the Anna Bibby Gallery on the corner of Kitchener Street and Victoria Street, and the Gow Langsford Gallery in Lorne Street. 'He used to show up to every bloody opening,' said Langsford. 'Just there for the free wine. Never bought anything. Even when we took him off the invite list, he turned up! Always in the same clothes. Crumpled linen jackets. And that mad hair.'

The last time he saw Derek King, he thought, was at the exhibition opening of Karl Maughan's vast, luscious botanical paintings in May 2011. The beautiful painted flowers, the excellent conversation — and King, who looked like no one else, looking on, observing, evidently deranged. Anna Bibby emailed from her home in France: 'He was quite aloof and never spoke to me, actually come to think of it he never spoke with anyone but rather used the room as his private catwalk, did a few circuits, just to make sure that everyone was aware of him and left. Who was he?'

He would sip, he claimed in the High Court, 'only a little half-glass of wine'. It sent his blood pressure 'through the roof'; his health was delicate, due to his coeliac disease, an extreme intolerance to gluten.

He arrived alone and left alone. He'd walk back home, take off his clothes, and put on a robe. He owned three terry-towel robes. They were all he ever wore inside the townhouse. He was naked underneath. He continually wiped his hands with a flannel — he was afraid of germs from the outside world, but he lived in chaos and filth. A friend recalled the incredible layer of grease that had built up on the stove: 'It was at least an inch thick. I mentioned it to Derek and he said it must never be cleaned, he wanted to keep it that way as he wanted to see what happened to dirt like that as time wore on.' The house was a tip, 'a hovel', said Detective Sergeant Andrew Saunders of the Auckland police. He couldn't believe the smell. 'It stunk of, like, rotten vegetables,' said Nikita Jones, a lively 30-year-old former street-kid.

She first visited him when she was 13. Her best friend took her. They were both runaways, sleeping in the gazebo in Albert Park, and 'the hole in the wall' in Myers Park.

The what?

'You know, the hole in the wall,' said Nikita. 'It's like a hole in the wall, and you can lie down in it.'

We met at her flat on a treeless street in Onehunga. It was the middle of the day in the middle of the week, and there were three other adults smoking on the deck, and four kids, aged between one and 10, playing on the trampoline. It was welfare and wagging, the usual hopeless cycle — 'I've missed 18 days of school,' said a pretty seven-year-old with something like pride. But love fell in a light, steady rain on the kids, who were hugged, stroked, kissed; it was a happy home. Nikita remembered back to 1997, and said, 'Me and my mate knew one or two people whose houses we would go and stay at. Older street bums that had a flat in town. My mate said, "I'll introduce you to Derek."'

Air-raid tunnels were dug beneath Constitution Hill in 1941. They connected to Albert Park, and provided sanctuary for an estimated 24,000 people, in case Auckland was attacked. The entrances were filled in after the war. King's townhouse on the hill was another kind of subterranean escape.

'I hesitate to describe Mr King's living quarters as "underground",' a police officer told the High Court at King's trial, but that's exactly what it was: an underworld, created and maintained by King, swanning around in his robes and his slippers, pale, diseased, a social outcast, once an important Auckland architect, clever and successful, with peculiar interests in punk rock and obvious interests in young girls, now paying desperate Maori street-kids — Nikita, her mate, runaways beyond number — to fuck him in exchange for money, shelter, and cheese on toast.

It carried on for nearly 30 years. All the Monday nights, snubbed at Gow Langsford; the plane trees on Constitution Hill dropped their leaves in autumn, sweet fruit fell from the Moreton Bay fig trees in summer; underground, in King's grotto, six generations ('waves', as King put it) of street-kids came and went.

All girls, under 18, some as young as 12. They crashed the night, tagged the walls, smoked his pot; one girl lived with him for five years; another miscarried his baby. 'I'm trying to help a whole bunch of people,' he told the court. He looked after them, he said. Fed them, gave them 'allowances', formed relationships. They were, he said, 'The Family'.

As head of the household, King was a paedophile. He was found guilty of 16 charges of sex offending — mostly, 'receiving commercial sexual services from persons under 18'. Who was this creature? 'Oh God,' he told the court, 'I had a charmed life.'

2

He'd brushed out the corkscrew curls, and wore his white hair long and straight in court. At the verdict, he dressed in moccasins, baggy olive trousers, and a wool jacket with a button missing at the stomach; he had a faded elegance about him, a sense of style, although the fashion belonged to the 1980s. He contemplated the jury coming in, and yawned. He looked medicated.

His lawyer, Nick Wintour, passed on to him my request for an interview. King was eager, but the Corrections Department refused. Prison guidelines state: 'The department has a policy to facilitate media access when the resulting exposure will provide a positive focus on rehabilitation.' King wasn't interested in rehab, remorse, and all the rest of it; he'd had his day in court, when he took the stand in his own defence, and seized the opportunity to rave.

He was like some sort of Humbert Humbert, the cultured paedophile from Nabokov's *Lolita*, with his courtly manner and archaic little pleasantries: 'Oh boy! Goodness gracious me!' It was a manic performance. The judge later complimented Wintour for the way he handled his 'difficult client'. No one believed much of what King said, but a lot of it was factual.

He told people who knew him in the 1980s that he came from a privileged background in Christchurch. They believed that, but were dubious when he claimed he designed the School of Architecture building at the University of Auckland. It was hard to reconcile — King had already gone to seed.

He raved in the High Court: 'I graduated with design honours and they asked if I would design the School of Architecture, I know it sounds like some sort of fantasy that any young architect would love to get involved, but that's amazing how that came about but I don't think we've got time to go into all that sort of thing but anyway I ended up designing it, and suddenly it's published around the world and I'm a famous architect ...'

Auckland University has no record of King graduating with honours. And, although there is no record that his design was published anywhere in the world, it's true that King was responsible for the impressive and ambitious School of Architecture conference centre, in 1978, when he joined top Auckland firm Kingston Reynolds Thom and Allardice (KRTA) as a staff architect.

KRTA were at the height of their fame. They'd designed Selwyn Village in Pt Chevalier, the Pakuranga town centre, and the Holy Family Catholic Church in Te Atatu out of massive precast concrete panels, a torture chamber which continues to freeze the congregation to death in winter, and boil them like lobsters in summer.

Professor Mike Austin, who taught King at the architecture school, was surprised that KRTA offered him a job. 'He was a difficult, noisy and hopeless student. Voluble. Full of bullshit.'

He laughed, and said, 'We were extra surprised when he got to design the school! We felt it was a mean and cruel trick that the profession played on us. It was like KRTA's way of saying, "Well, if you're going to pass buggers like this, then you can put up with the result."'

How did he regard the building that King designed?

'You'd have to say it was competent. There's something quite good about it, but ...' We'd met in Austin's home on the King Edward Parade waterfront in Devonport. I loathed him on sight. A small, intense sort of rooster, he writhed and grimaced as he conceded that the conference centre had qualities. 'The lighting's good. There's a big staircase, which is quite interesting.' He relaxed as he arrived at a patronising thought: 'It's a little folksy building.'

Around the corner, at his pretty home on the edge of mangroves, retired KRTA architect Denys Oldham, 80, had kinder words about his former colleague. He said of King, 'A lively lad. He had curly hair and a genial expression. He was vivacious. Attractive, one could say. You warmed to him. There's plenty of architects you don't remember a thing about. But I do remember Derek. He had a strong personality, aligned with considerable design ability.'

His review of King's design for the conference centre? As he remembered, the project architect had left, 'and Derek stepped into the breach. And really, apart from being a little contrived, he did a very good job. He designed the whole of that conference centre, which involved two lecture rooms, the admin block, the library, two major conference rooms — it was quite a tricky design. And it's a fine piece of work.'

King, in court: 'I only had three months to put that together and it was the third design attempt and, oh boy, it was a tricky one but we got it, I got it sorted, and I got a bonus, enough to put a deposit on my house.' A property search confirmed that King was listed as the owner. The blinds were pulled up on one window in Courtroom 15 at King's trial; it allowed the jury an intimate view of the lovely exotic trees across the road on Constitution Hill.

3

The good job, the house on the hill — the late 1970s were King's halcyon years. He bought a yellow Ferrari Dino, so low that you practically had to lie down to drive it. 'He was anal about that car,' said radio announcer Bryan Staff, who used to see King around town. 'I remember him screaming at a gas station attendant for daring to touch the windscreen — "Do you realise how much this fucking thing is worth, you moron?", that sort of thing.'

A friend said, 'When I first met Derek and got talking, he told me he had two ambitions and he had fulfilled them before his mother died. One was to design the School of Architecture and the other was to own a Ferrari.' He told her that he couldn't afford to insure it, and stored it in the garage like a prized jewel. Once, though, he took another woman for a drive in it to Hamilton; King floored it, drove at insane speeds, until the woman begged him to stop at Mercer. She got out, and never spoke to him again.

He liked danger, excitement. King, soft and cuddly in his denim jumpsuits, became an unlikely player in the cultural explosion of punk rock. In fact, he was an impressario of punk. He put on concerts, and famously hired a bus to take six bands, including the Suburban Reptiles and The Scavengers, to play the New Wave Special concert in Wellington. A 1979 *Eyewitness* documentary on punk rock — it's online at *NZ On Screen* — includes startling footage of King sitting at the front of the bus, giving a long-winded philosophical treatise on the meaning of punk. 'Any extreme movement in society is generally misunderstood,' he instructs. The passengers are spotty youth, 19, 20, cool in their leathers and mohair. There's Johnny Volume, there's Zero. And there's King, 'the famous young architect', a groover in his light beard and ringleted haircut.

The silver Newmans bus is filmed coming into Wellington down Ngauranga Gorge on a cold, drab winter's morning. *Eyewitness* presenter Neil Roberts says in the voice-over, 'Auckland is the centre of punk in New Zealand, and a young Auckland promoter decided to spread the good word south. Derek King gathered about him the crème de la crème of Auckland punkdom, hired a bus, and set off for the Wellington Town Hall. His mission — to bring the punk experience to the capital, a sort of 1978 punk odyssey.'

The show went off, and Wellington took to punk with flair and energy. Strange that it's thanks in large part to King, whose name also features in the credits of another landmark moment in New Zealand punk — the Ripper Records album *AK 79*, then received with awe and as a kind of manifesto of punk, with classic tracks such as 'I Am A Rabbit' by Proud Scum and Toy Love's 'Squeeze'. King was right in the middle of that 'extreme movement', making things happen. Respect or some kind of acknowledgement was surely due from survivors of the punk wars. None was forthcoming.

Paul Rose, who managed punk bands including The Newmatics, remembered King at venues such as the Windsor Castle in Parnell, and the Rhumba Bar on Victoria Street. 'He'd bring his camera and stand at the back and just watch. He was always observing. He was a crowd watcher, not a band watcher. Always on the outside.'

'Always on the outside looking in,' echoed the great society queen Judith Baragwanath, who was also on the punk scene. 'A bit shady. Secretive. Furtive.'

'We used to call him Fish Fingers for the way he chased young girls,' said a former bootboy made good, too respectable for his name to be used in King's company. 'An odious character. His demeanour was just sleazy. He was always your best friend! It was a mix of all that plus his fast-growing reputation as predator. Girls knew to keep away.'

The last time he saw him was a couple of years ago, at the Auckland Film Festival: 'He made my skin crawl. I disliked him intensely.'

Paul Rose said the last time he saw King was at the 2011 Laneways concert in Aotea Square. 'There he was with his camera again. By himself. Watching the crowd. Same old dirty Derek.'

4

After designing the conference centre, King lived in Singapore for three years, as an architectural consultant. He returned to his home on the hill in 1982, and set himself up as a photographer — he approached pretty young girls, and offered to shoot their modelling portfolios.

One such sweet thing was novelist Charlotte Grimshaw. 'He got me into his house once and took Polaroids,' she said. 'I was 15 or 16. He spoke of modelling jobs, then suggested we adjourn to the bedroom. I fought him off, and fled, laughing.' She thinks she may have stolen something on her way out. 'Could it have been a Walkman? Surely not a toaster.'

How many other girls did he try it on with? How many submitted? The answer to both idle speculations might be any number, including zero. Maybe he just liked to watch. Bruce Jarvis, who managed the film-processing lab Prism, developed King's photos throughout that decade. 'They were only ever of young girls,' he said.

Jarvis found an envelope containing negatives of one of King's shoots in 1990. They were head-and-shoulder photos of a teenager who had taken her shirt off. She's gorgeous, but the power of the photos isn't her beauty: it's her apprehensiveness, her look of fear. What was going on with the creature behind the camera? Who was she looking at?

'He was funny, also very intelligent,' said a woman who knew him in the 1990s, 'and completely mad.' She tolerated his eccentricities — the grimy stove, the robes — and was amused by his rabid way of talking. 'He always banged on about discovering all the models who did well in the '80s. According to Derek, it was him who discovered Rachel Hunter. I was sure he wasn't lying as he told everyone.'

Rachel Hunter's agent, Andy Haden, rejected the claim. On holiday in Fiji, he emailed, 'We have a letter and a series of photos that

Rachel has authenticated as the first shots taken of her as a model, and the photographer wasn't Derek King … I've never heard of the guy.'

5

King went on a sickness benefit in the late 1980s. He couldn't find work as an architect. He was fading from view, retreating, going underground. All the wretched Mondays at art openings — he didn't stand a chance. He couldn't claim the same pretensions, was lost in their maze of put-downs and snobbery. Over thick espresso coffee served in china thimbles at a Ponsonby villa, painter John Reynolds and his brother Patrick, who photographs sliding doors and such for magazines, recreated King's agony.

John said, 'I thought he was a tremendously opaque individual. Hard to read. And most people who met him had this sense of — you just backed away a little bit. There was a disquiet about him, because—'

Patrick interrupted, 'Why was he at the art openings? There was no engagement with the work on the walls.'

John said, 'Derek was someone you didn't want to spend time with. Not because he was odious or malevolent; you just had the sense that—'

Patrick interrupted, 'He was slightly slippery, though.'

John said, 'Well, you just had this feeling—'

Patrick interrupted, 'He was all wrong.'

John completed his previous sentence, 'That he was out of alignment.'

'Very bad sunglasses,' said Patrick. 'Too big and too flashy, and wearing them at night! And also the baffling perm.'

John said, 'He needed to get out in the sun a bit more.'

Patrick said, 'The pale, pale skin and the tight hair. And there was a sponginess to him; he wasn't a coiled spring, he was the reverse to a coiled spring.'

'Dissolute,' said John. 'He was dissolute. And conversations didn't actually advance with him. He didn't have anything to say.'

'He'd make these sly asides,' said Patrick. 'Non sequiturs. And you get this feeling of being trapped with him.'

'All of us have that social antennae where you pick up some sense of a person's chemistry, or you get a sense of their social animus,' said John, 'and there was a palpable sense there was never any Mrs Derek.'

6

But he had another, better life, full of lissome young Maori girls, back at his townhouse, in that sealed dark zone of fantasy and grime. He said in court that he first came across street-kids in 1986 — a couple of glue-sniffers, in Albert Park, homeless, 'living in the sewer', runaways from foster homes and abusive families. Then he discovered 40 more, hanging around Karangahape Road. Hardly anyone lived in the city back then; King had downtown Auckland almost all to himself, it was his patch; the arrival of street-kids, frightened and tough, offered him company, society, purpose.

He was asked in court, 'Your house was made available to young people. How did that happen?'

He said, 'Living in the city, when I go out, I'm in Queen Street, that's my patch, that's my suburb, you know. And there they were. It never occurred to me that that would happen in a first-world economy. After the stock-market crash, it really went off then. And they got to know me as somebody who helps them out. There was a huge problem and the community wasn't handling it. I suddenly realised, "I have to do something. I can't just walk away from it." That's when I made the decision that there was no net for them, there was nothing for them. Goodness me, it — it just took you over really, it's quite amazing …'

King rented out the top floor of his townhouse to TV production company Cinco Cine. A friend remembered, 'He used to drop blankets and food left over from film shoots to the street-kids over Grafton Bridge at night …We were seriously under the impression that he was being compassionate towards them with no other motives.'

Another woman who knew him said, 'He used to go on about how they were on the street as they were being abused at home, and that's why he also had some of them to stay, sometimes for months at a time. He probably imagined himself as some kind of hero.'

Well, wasn't he operating at some level of goodness? As well as providing blankets and food for street-kids living rough under Grafton Bridge, there were many other acts of kindness, or patronage, over the years. He bought tampons and make-up, offered shelter, warmth, food; he did nice things. 'I suppose so,' said Nikita Jones, who showed up at his door in 1997. 'Everyone would leave their dirty clothes there, and he'd wash them all with the Lux flakes. He fed us his famous cheese and onion on toast. But he was a cunt.'

She meant the time he found her when she tried to slash her wrists, and responded by throwing her out of the house. 'He shooed me out the door, going "Fuck off, fuck off!", and I was pissing blood everywhere. That's when I turned on him.'

Nikita was a 'fourth wave' street-kid when she met King. She was born in Grey Lynn, 'back when it was just coconuts'. She was abandoned, and made a ward of the state at four; at 13, when she met King, 'I'd been in like 22 placements in 18 months. I kept running away. I'd get picked up probably once a week by the cops and taken back to a foster home and run away again. They ran out of suburbs to put me in, so they sent me to Dunedin. But I made it back. I was on the street for three years.'

How did she eat?

'I stole chocolates from Deka.'

The friend who took her to meet King was 'doing jobs' with him — street slang for prostituting herself. 'We went there, and a couple of other street-kids were sitting around and they were like, "Give us a fucken cigarette, Derek, you fucken prick." That's how they all spoke to him.' She remembers an outing in the Jaguar to smoke dope in the Domain; the girls in the back seat burnt his hair with their cigarettes.

Nikita began prostituting herself to him, too. She was just his type: a thin, lost child. The rate was $60 for 30 minutes. 'After I did a job with him, he was like, "Oh, come and live with The Family, darling. You'll get an allowance."'

Eight other ex-street-kids gave evidence against King. They were grown-ups, just, with kids of their own, several each; they were defensive, bewildered, aggressive. One girl accused another girl of stealing her cellphone at King's townhouse, and said, 'It was kind of obvious that she would of tooken it.' Some of them told wicked lies, like the girl who claimed King paid her a staggering $200 each time they had sex, which was sometimes four times a day. His lawyer protested he didn't have that sort of money. He could also have said that it was out of character, because King was a shocking cheapskate. Several other girls said he welched on the $60 fee, and paid them $40, sometimes only $20.

They were runaways from Blockhouse Bay, Glen Innes, Papakura. They revealed their Auckland — sex work in city backstreets (Turner Street, Cross Street), sitting for hours in internet cafés on Facebook, drinking in Myers Park, starving, stealing, everyone ending up at 'Derek's place'. They were 12, 13, 14, but were told by friends to lie about their age, and say they were older. They told much the same story — a friend would introduce them, they'd smoke pot, and King would say, 'You're a pretty young girl.' Then: 'Would you fuck me for $60?' One girl demurred, so King upped the price: 'Would you fuck me for $60 and a bottle of whiskey?' No, she said. He went all out: 'Would you fuck me for $60, a bottle of whiskey, and some weed?' Still she said no, and punched him in the jaw when he tried to kiss her.

Most girls took the money and did the job. No one was innocent, and everyone was damaged. Morality lay outside the door. Inside that rancid den, everything was consensual, force was never applied, there was demand and supply. 'The Family' were a kind of family. Generations of girls found a place to sleep, and were safe from beatings, starvation, bad weather, loneliness. Operation Elephant, the police investigation, succeeded in locking up King, but it also took away a rare offer of warmth.

I spoke to a youth worker, Faith Atkins, who knew all about King and his 'Family', and asked her whether she conceded that King had done the girls some good. 'Shelter and food are a very kind gesture,' she said, 'but the bottom line is they're kids and it's against the law.'

What use was the law to the girls? They hated their CYFS homes in Pakuranga, Blockhouse Bay, Otahahu, Manurewa and Te Atatu; they really hated the 20-bed 'protection residency', Whakatakapokai. They all ran away to 'Derek's place'. It can't have been too bad. Some of it must have been pretty good. King was eccentric, funny, an enthusiastic stoner ('I'm very precious about my beautiful outdoor cannabis,' he said in court). There were daily allowances, bus fares, snacks, outings — the court heard about a day drinking Steinlager in a park near the airport, and the time he took two girls to visit his sister in Taupo. What did he say? Family, this is family?

There were sometimes glimpses of logic and a kind of decency when he delivered speeches in court, viz: 'I resent the implication I'm hiring the girls as prostitutes, I mean, prostitutes are someone you pick up and dump back on the street when you've used them, I mean, how bizarre to make, that comparison, it's just ridiculous.' One girl talked about visiting King for the first time with two friends who had known him for years. She described the scene: 'Derek was just having a brief catch-up with them, just seeing how they were, where they had come from, how they'd been.'

But as head of The Family, King held the purse strings. A girl who lived with him for five years told the court, 'I did form a relationship with him, but you can tell where he was coming from, because as soon as I had kids and put on weight I was straight out the door. I couldn't even get $5 off of him. He'd tell me, "You're out of The Family." He does it with everyone. He does it over generations.'

Police found a stack of porno DVDs at King's house — *Once Upon a Girl*, *Innocent Bystanders*, *Private Gladiator*. They also found a CD by Maria Callas. King made fleeting references in court to attending poetry nights and folk clubs, to people from the outside world, adults — 'an architect mate' from Christchurch, 'a famous violinist'. But he was most himself with little girls. In bed, he asked them to remove their pants, and kneel in front of him 'like a dog kind of thing', as one girl told the court. Nikita said she was always stoned 'doing a job' with King. 'It made it easier. You'd just sort of buzz out. Sometimes it made it worse. It made it intense, and you'd be thinking, "Oh God, when is this going to be over?" He used to take ages. Ages.'

Priapic, mad, nostalgic, King said in court, 'They used to love having sex with me … I mean, it's weird, I know, it's kind of difficult to explain to people, why would a young girl have sex with an old man? I mean, goddammit, I don't think I would if I was a young girl, but …'

7

King's central defence was that he didn't know the girls were under the legal age of 18 when he paid them for sex. It wasn't an argument that went very far.

The cross-examination was fairly routine — except for one moment when prosecutor June Jelas lost her patience, and squashed King like a bug.

She asked him, 'The reality is you weren't asking these girls their age, were you?'

King said, 'You're out of your mind. Of course I was. It never occurred to me these poor girls could be labelled as prostitutes; what did concern me was the fact that if someone came around searching the place and found girls under 18, I'm going to bloody jail. I come first in this whole situation. I'm no use to anybody if I'm in jail, I'm trying to help a whole bunch of people here and what — I'm going to be disappeared — Jesus, woman—'

Jelas interrupted, 'Yeah, that's right, Mr King. You come first, because your first need seems to be having sex with young girls, that's your big need, isn't it?'

King said, 'Look, that's insulting to me, but it's more insulting to these girls. They're not the kind of girls that you can take advantage of.'

Jelas said, 'But that's exactly what you were doing, wasn't it? You know many of them have no home to go, you know most of them have zero money, and here you are saying, "Have sex with me and I'll give you money."'

'No, no …'

'They're your personal prostitutes, aren't they?'

'What happens when you build up a relationship is that they—'

Jelas interrupted, 'What sort of relationship, Mr King? Let's talk about it. What sort of relationship? It's only a sexual relationship.'

King raved, 'They're my family, they're in my care, this idea that somehow I've turned this place into a massage parlour where I turn up and have sex with them — it's bizarre.

'They may get additional money. I'm more likely to buy someone a cellphone if we're having an intimate relationship than someone who's, you know, just getting their basic survival allowance. They get $20 a week minimum. They get $5 every time they come to the door. They need to be able to catch a bus, they've got to go home, if they've got a home to go to.

'They've got to have money to buy food, if I'm not cooking for them. I try and cook for them cos it saves me money. I've got a deep-fryer now. I just throw chips and sausages in there and they love it. I used to melt cheese on things, I could melt cheese on left-over food, cardboard, polyurethane, anything, and they seem to love it …'

8

You can view the School of Architecture conference centre at Auckland University as a monument to a sleazebag, or assess it as an attractive example of late-modern design. 'It's an illustrious start to someone's career,' said Paul Litterick, a PhD candidate in the School of Architecture, who made many and varied approving noises as he conducted a tour of King's one and only building.

It nestles below the curves of the so-called 'banana building' of the school's design block. A courtyard, with two stately oaks, marks it off as School of Architecture territory, an enclosed space, cloistered. Inside, Litterick liked the light, the spaces, the playful features. There was a spiral staircase winding towards a glass turret, or 'crystal tower', as King's former KRTA colleague Denys Oldham had called it. Litterick noted the use of different textures (fair-faced concrete, smoked glass), and said, 'The design is very much of its time, but it's adapted remarkably well.'

Everywhere, King's hand, his vision, his brief promise. What happened? What madness and collapse brought him to the hell he made for himself inside the house on the hill? A pleasant 10-minute stroll separated the School of Architecture conference centre from his Constitution Hill townhouse; one building had paid for the other, where he created his true masterpiece.

Police photos reveal a house that was no longer a house. King deconstructed it. It was a tip, a cavern — 'It was kind of a dark place,' one girl remembered in court. An entire wall in the lounge was covered in tagging. Six generations of tags, of street names, of hearts and arrows and shout-outs, in felt and pen and pencil, the whole monstrous thing like a giant, genuinely shocking canvas, an artwork more savage and primal than anything dreamed up by painter John Reynolds, the espresso sipper of Ponsonby who wisely avoided King all those years at gallery openings. The couch with the stuffing coming out of it, the tarpaulins and mattresses in the back yard — it was so extreme, more genuinely anarchic than anything recorded by the punk bands King was drawn to in the 1970s. It was a lair, with King as its white worm, gorging on child sex. He had no use for civilisation. He was an outsider, a stately ruin. He was Kurtz who had travelled too far into a heart of darkness. He was probably happy. He had company. Girls knew to visit. They arrived in waves. They smoked his pot and scoffed his cheese on toast, they got on their hands and knees, they had somewhere to sleep. 'Brats,' he called them in court, indulgently, with something resembling love.

Chapter 7

A naked male riding his bike: Timaru

A naked male riding his bike on High St at 3.30pm was given a ticket for not wearing a bicycle helmet.

On and on it goes, a crime wave like nowhere else, washing up on the shore of a pretty harbour city in south Canterbury. 'A Timaru woman, 25, was served a trespass notice at New World in Wai-iti Rd.' And: 'A 25-year-old Timaru man was arrested for shoplifting from Pak'nSave.' Is any supermarket safe in Timaru? No. 'A supermarket trolley was stolen from Countdown in Church St.'

The bulletins are courtesy of the *Timaru Herald*'s wonderful series, 'Police Notebook'. No other newspaper reports its petty crimes with such style. The journalism I love the most reads like sentences spoken in a dream — strange images, disconnected thoughts, random happenings and weird occurrences which may or may not be packed with hidden meaning. 'A Marston Rd resident reported someone threw a wooden rolling pin at his window.' Who walks around with a wooden rolling pin? One moment, a kitchen utensil describing an arc as it flies through the air; the next, the world tipped on its axis. 'A Wilson St resident reported his vehicle had been tipped sideways.'

Every crime, a sentence; every sentence, a little masterpiece of brevity and accuracy, at once banal and surreal. Most journalism is either too long or leaves out too much. 'Police Notebook' is exact. It leaves out almost everything. You can only guess at the rest, and view it with wild surmise. 'A 50-year-old woman lost control of her 2013 Mercedes, crashing it into a fence on Treneglos St.' The expensive new motor, the boring street in an industrial estate — was she running from something? At 50, will she ever escape?

> A naked male riding his bike on High St at 3.30pm has been given a ticket for not wearing a bicycle helmet.

Crime often reads like a map of the human heart. It's a scarred landscape, a smoking ruin. 'A Timaru youth, 18, was arrested for assault after a domestic incident outside Timaru Hospital.' That sounds ugly — the bash, young love gone bad, patients shuffling in their gowns. This sounds worse: 'A 14-year-old Timaru girl was arrested for assaulting her mother.' This sounds common, pathetic, heartbreaking: 'A Timaru boy, 16, was arrested for wilful damage after he went to the address of his ex-girlfriend's new boyfriend and smashed the door.'

Every reporter writes these kinds of stories when they're assigned to ring around the local police stations and ask for a record of the latest incidents. I wrote those kinds of stories for newspapers in Te Aroha and Greymouth, and a Palmerston North radio station. But they weren't in the same class as the *Timaru Herald*'s 'Police Notebook'. When I was doing it, I only selected the most dramatic, the most uncommon. It was a kind of snobbery. 'Police Notebook' publishes everything. It's epic, a complete register. It walks the length of Stafford Street. Thus: 'Police arrested a Timaru woman, 37, for shoplifting jeans from a Stafford St store.' And: 'A Timaru man, 22, will be given a pre-charge warning for urinating in Stafford St.' Also: 'Police are looking for a woman who allegedly vomited into a Crusaders hat yesterday afternoon in a shop on Stafford St.'

The latter incident prompted a rare additional sentence — the woman put the hat back on the shelf, and left the store. It was written with the usual economy of style. The weight and length of the lines often resemble verse. I once compiled a few sentences from the Notebook, and sent them as a poem to Wellington poet Bill Manhire for his appreciation. The repetitions, the dying fall, the echo of his own work (everyone knows his great opening line, 'The naked cyclist came into the room') — he gave it high marks.

A handbag and chocolates were taken from a
Chalmers St address.

A 24-year-old man was warned for breaching the
liquor ban in Stafford St.

A 30-year-old woman was warned for breaching the
liquor ban in Stafford St.

A bicycle was reported stolen from a garage on Rathmore St.

A Baker St property was entered
but nothing was taken.

*

Timaru, Timaru. You have to be careful what you say about Timaru. It's a sensitive place. There were two alarming instances when the townspeople rose up and took umbrage at the *Listener*. In 1964, Timaru was the answer to a clue in the magazine's cryptic crossword: 'You may call it a rum city.' Rum! What the devil was the *Listener* trying to say? The magazine was accused of blackening the city's name, and suggesting it was awash in grog. The matter was raised in Parliament, where all umbrages go to die. And in 2003, journalist and photographer Jane Ussher created a photo-essay for the *Listener* on the sad, tender charms of Timaru's Caroline Bay; Timaruvians hated it so much that they staged a mass bonfire of the magazine. I recall a photo of leering faces in the glow of the flames.

I come in peace. My ode to the 'Police Notebook' is sincere, admiring. Irony only takes you so far — barely across the road — and there are so many other things going on in the Notebook beyond the merely ironic. 'A two-year-old girl was found wandering around King St in the weekend.' God almighty. And what to make of this creepy little message: 'A house in Thomas St was entered overnight on Saturday and two candles lit in the hot water cupboard'?

I'm very fond of Timaru. I visited a number of times with my father when he lived in nearby Fairlie. We'd come to town to do the shopping, to see friends, to have a drink, to have a stroll and see the sights. It's a good place; you'd have to describe it as peaceful. It's not every day that women fill a Crusaders hat with sick and stick it back on the shelf.

Every city has its crimes, its petty incidents, its inexplicable minor events. It's just that they're written better in the *Timaru Herald* than anywhere else.

> A naked male riding his bike on High St at 3.30pm was ticketed for not wearing a bicycle helmet.

One of the great appeals of practising journalism is that you're constantly writing sentences no one has ever written before. It barely seems credible that this should be so, because journalists are among the least creative and original people in modern society. They're taught to write like each other. If you picked up the paper and someone had snipped out the bylines, it wouldn't make the slightest difference. The identity of the author is an irrelevance. And yet the least talented of journalists routinely write the most amazing sentences; sentences that have never occurred to the poetic sensibilities of Shakespeare, Nabokov, Austen, Kafka, Larkin, even Ayers.

The naked cyclist sentence ('Police Notebook', 2014) contains the essence and mystery of journalism. It's only 21 words, and yet its arrangement is unique in the annals of world literature. Incredible that these works in miniature, which make up journalism, should be unique. Fantastic that the infinite variety of human experience, which journalism reports, should form sentences that no one had ever thought of writing before.

The thing that makes these sentences unique is the existence and order of facts. Bores of all ages say to journalists, 'Don't let the facts spoil a good story.' It's a nonsense, because a good story demands the facts; the accumulation of facts is the story. The job of the journalist is to carry the facts in a pleasing and possibly even artful manner — or simply to get out of the way, and tip the facts out onto the road.

> A male riding his bike on High St at 3.30pm would have been given a ticket for not wearing a bicycle helmet if he was naked.

Who was he? Part of the Notebook's elliptical charm is its namelessness — it records the actions of phantoms, and is light on clues. Thus: 'There was an attempted burglary at an Oxford St address. An occupant made the discovery after finding a shoe print on the toilet cistern.' At most, we learn of gender, age and residence. And: 'A Temuka man, 18, was warned for setting fire to a paper cup outside a fast food restaurant in Theodosia St.'

On and on it goes, the Notebook noting all. Greed and probably poverty: 'A woman was arrested after stealing oysters and lollies from Countdown.' Bored youth and broken glass: 'A front bedroom window in a Selwyn St house was smashed when a water balloon was thrown at it.' Odd that a water balloon would prove more effective than a wooden rolling pin. We cross live to St Andrews: 'A car was found on fire in St Andrews. A 35-year-old Tinwald man was located nearby. It appeared he had accidentally set the vehicle on fire.' What?

A kind of melancholy sets in when you read older entries in the Notebook. This, from May 2011: 'A boy, aged about 15, stole two pouches of tobacco from a dairy in North St. The owner chased the boy but lost him when he turned into an alleyway.' The thief will be 19 this year. Is he okay? Or is he further along the road to ruin? October 2009: 'A 29-year-old Timaru man was arrested for offensive behaviour after he was found urinating outside Cheng's Restaurant.' Six years on, what does he feel whenever he walks past Cheng's on Stafford St? Shame? The urge to piddle? March 2009: 'A dining table was stolen from a Browne St address.' Six years on, did they ever replace the table, or do they just walk around the corner to Cheng's and take advantage of its marvellous $5 lunch special with free soup?

The online archive only goes back as far as 2009. But a version of the Notebook existed in the very first edition of the *Timaru Herald*, in 1864. A court report includes a single-sentence entry that records the name of the ancestor of everyone who breaches the liquor ban on Stafford St: 'William Young was fined for being drunk and incapable in Timaru on Saturday evening.' A paper cup in flames, a hat full of sick, the incapable William Young — misdemeanour and literature, riding naked through Timaru for over 150 merry years.

Chapter 8

Mark Lundy: Killing Christine and Amber

1

She phoned for the driver to pick her up. He said he wasn't far away, probably five minutes.

'Any problems?'

'No,' she said.

'Okay. Bye.'

She picked up her handbag, checked the $140 was inside. The client got off the bed and put on his green tracksuit pants. He said his name was Mark.

She said, 'So, what do you do, Mark?'

He said, 'Sell kitchen sinks and taps.'

She said, 'Really.'

He said, 'I fax the orders to my wife, and she does all the paperwork. It's a very successful business — I'm the number-one salesman in the Lower North Island!'

She said, 'Uh-huh.'

It was nearly 1am. She looked around the small motel room. There wasn't much to look at — a photo of the Petone wharf on the wall, a 1.125-litre bottle of rum on the kitchen table. He'd polished off most of it. In fact, he stank of booze, but she didn't think he was drunk, although her heart nearly sank when she met him an hour ago. She was small, and delicate; he was huge, his stomach rolling out of his XXL polo shirt. Well, she thought, she'd seen worse. Some of them were pigs, no better than animals. This guy was actually quite pleasant.

The driver from the nearby Quarry Inn escort agency in Seaview finally arrived. 'Well, good night,' she said at the door.

'Good night,' he said.

After she left, he got ready. The hooker had cleared his mind. He could focus on the job at hand. It was going to be a long night, and required courage, audacity, nerve. Above all, it demanded careful planning. He moved around the small room. He got out overalls, gloves, a paper hairnet and paper shoes from the bulging suitcase. He wore a polo shirt beneath the overalls, which he buttoned up to his neck. He put on a spare pair of glasses. He reached back into the suitcase and brought out a sack, and a jemmy bar. He double-checked he had everything he needed. It hadn't taken him long. Don't rush, he said to himself. Just be careful. He took a deep breath. It was time to go. Let's fucking do this.

He locked the door of Unit 10 and walked softly across the carpark. The motel had its NO VACANCY sign up. Among the guests were a woman on a week-long weight-watching course at Jenny Craig, a cigar salesman from Ponsonby Road in Auckland, a man from Firestone in Palmerston North, a watercress grower from Te Puke who was staying with his father, and Phil, a long-term tenant.

He'd moved the car from outside his motel room to over the road earlier that evening. It was all about thinking ahead, not leaving anything to chance. He might have woken a guest if he'd started up his Ford Fairmont in the motel carpark. But now he could make a clean getaway, undetected, unnoticed, a fugitive in the night.

A new moon had appeared in the sky at 10.20pm. There was low cloud, but visibility was good. A light southerly had died out in the afternoon. It had rained now and then during the day, but not heavily, and the roads were dry.

He got in the car. The bright green light on the Petone wharf glowed in the dark. Oystercatchers marched along the line of the tide, stabbing at food. Their soft, nagging cries were the only sound to be heard. It was after midnight. Petone had gone to bed; the lights were off in the charming cottages with their small front porches. Orange sodium streetlights burned all along the foreshore of the pretty seaside town.

He closed the car door, taking care not to slam it. Wellington's hills formed a ring around the harbour. To the left were the gorsey slopes above Days Bay and Eastbourne; to his right, the shore curved towards the city. The Cook Strait ferry was in dock.

He'd stayed at the Foreshore Motor Lodge before. It was a good base for his travels around Wellington and the Hutt Valley, where he called in to see his customers. 'Gidday, Mark,' they said. 'How's Christine?' Everyone liked Christine. 'And how's Amber?' Their daughter was seven. They had a trampoline and a set of swings for her on the front lawn of their home at 30 Karamea Crescent in Palmerston North.

He started the engine. He drove along The Esplanade. The cigar salesman, who'd watched his daughter perform in a choir at the Wellington Town Hall that night, slept on. The watercress grower, who ate with his father at Valentine's in Petone that night, slept on. The weight-watcher, who may or may not have counted calories when she ate dinner with a friend at her home in Mt Victoria that night, slept on.

He turned onto Hutt Road, opposite the welcome sign for Petone spelled out in flowers, and drove alongside the harbour towards the city. The lights were on in the Beehive. Perhaps Prime Minister Helen Clark was up late, plotting. The railway tracks were to his left, the hills to his right. He drove past a BP service station. Dust from the Horokiwi quarry floated in the air. The black water of the harbour was darker than the moonless night.

It had to be done. It had to be fucking done. He needed the money. Tomorrow was the deadline to settle with those cocksuckers who'd sold him the land for his vineyard in Hawke's Bay. He could make it happen. He had dreams, aspirations; he couldn't let Christine hold him back. Amber was young. She'd get through it. They'd move away, start a new life. He'd spoil her. The vineyard would pay for their future. He could fuck who he wanted when he owned a vineyard. Christine didn't want to have sex any more. Fine. There were whores in every town. The one tonight was good. What was her name? He couldn't remember. Well, he'd get a new one next time he was down.

He turned right into Ngauranga Gorge, heading inland, and left behind the beautiful harbour with its lighthouses and piers, its islands and reefs. He drove 150.2 kilometres carefully, not too fast, nothing erratic, past Otaki, Levin, Shannon, across the Manawatu plains to the killing field at 30 Karamea Crescent. He got the weapon from the garage, he crept inside, he put his knee on the side of the bed, he didn't hesitate.

And then: 'Daddy?'

God almighty. Don't think about that. Don't. And then he stripped off and put his outfit in the sack with the jemmy bar and Christine's jewellery box and got rid of the stuff and got back to his motel room at about 5am. He sat on the bed. He'd done it. He'd done the hard part. Now he just had to get away with it.

The next anyone heard from him was at 8.09am, when he checked out. 'We had a chat,' said motel manager Bruce Sloane, 'about nothing in particular.'

2

Everything in this lurid version of events — well, apart from some of the dialogue, travelogue, and various assorted details pertaining to the small matter of the double homicide — was taken from witness statements and prosecution speeches made during the opening weeks of the murder trial of Mark Lundy at the Wellington High Court in 2015. Was this how he did it? Was this where it started that night? The killings were in Palmerston North, but Petone held the key to whether or not the killer was Christine's husband and Amber's father. He either left the motel room after the escort left and set out on his so-called 'killing journey', or he fell asleep.

Now and then during the trial I would leg it from the courtroom, cross the road to the Wellington railway station, and travel up the line to Petone. It was so nice to be beside that seaside. Grandparents played with children on the long, scruffy beach. Oystercatchers marched along the tide. The door to Unit 10 at the Foreshore Motor Lodge was open. There was a photo of the Petone wharf on the wall.

Chapter 9

Mark Lundy: Sleeping

1

Everything in the following version of events of an unsolved family tragedy — well, apart from some of the dialogue, travelogue, and various assorted details pertaining to sleep — was taken from witness statements and police interviews presented during the murder trial of Mark Lundy at the Wellington High Court in 2015. Does it most resemble the truth? Does it get closest to what happened in Petone that night?

I puzzled over these questions whenever I fled from court and took the train to Petone. I walked the length of the main road, Jackson Street, from the railway station to the vaguely terrifying other end, with its broken windows and wasted dudes in hoodies. It worked up an appetite. I filled my face with biscuits from the Girl Guides office, cheese from The Dutch Shop, and shortbread biscuits filled with raspberry jam from The German Bakery. I considered the menus at Magic Wok and Mr Ji's, and settled for the shredded pork lunchbox and black glutinous rice with coconut milk at Foo Wah. Its shredded and glutinous delights barely touched the sides.

I needed something else. I needed the kind of food a fat man would eat, and I made my way to the tuck shop where Lundy always used to eat whenever he came to Petone. It's now called the Shoreline, a small, narrow shop, and there was a queue outside the door at lunchtimes. Punters chose from waffle dogs and scotch eggs and yoyos. I went for the healthy option: a bun topped with tinned spaghetti and melted cheese. Lundy had ordered a bacon and egg sandwich that morning of the deaths, and had eaten it in his car. I took my feed and ate sitting on the sand. Black-backed seagulls floated on the gentle tide. On the wharf, a fisherman marked his line with an orange balloon. He was after kahawai. I ambled over for a chat. He'd heard that someone caught a kingfish earlier that week. It was a beautiful summer's day. 'If it wasn't for this breeze,' he said, 'we'd cook.'

The drab, grey beach, the inelegant lump of Somes Island in the harbour, the dark surrounding hills … Petone held the answer to the crime. This is where it started with Lundy that night, or where it ended. Petone, the gateway to the teeming bogan savages of the Hutt Valley; Petone, where the first colonists arrived on 22 January 1840, on the *Aurora*, and were taken ashore on small boats. Maori gave them fish and potatoes. It was a day in summer, but the scene would have looked miserable — a tatty shoreline, a swamp. 'A wild and stern reality,' as early settler John Plimmer put it. Petone's settlement and its emergence as an industrial kind of Hell was recorded at the Settlers Museum, across the road from the Shoreline tuck shop. For years, blood and offal ran red into the harbour from the Gear Meats slaughterhouse, and the satanic mills of Colgate, Rinso and Lux created Petone's working-class foundations. There was a small Maori urupa, with its water tap to cleanse the hands of visitors to the cemetery, squeezed in a depressing rectangle of land in between factories.

What happened in Petone on the night of the dead on 29/30 August 2000? Something? Nothing? The more time I spent in Petone, the more I was convinced that the jury — that everyone in the courtroom — needed to be taken there on an outing, to peer into his motel room (Petone locals referred to the Foreshore as 'Lundy's Motel'), to queue for a yoyo or some such treat at the Shoreline, to perambulate The Esplanade where he said he had parked under a streetlight in the early evening to read *The Icarus Agenda* by Robert Ludlum ('Readers will be hooked' — *New York Times*), and to try to picture the Crown's lurid, possibly fantastically improbable version of events, which had him driving under cloak of darkness along The Esplanade and the Hutt motorway to execute his family and thence return to the Hutt motorway and The Esplanade at, oh, say, 5am.

They could stand on the beach and look out to the waters of the Cook Strait, then turn, and look at the Foreshore Motor Lodge on the corner of The Esplanade and Nelson Street, where an escort arrived at Unit 10 on that cold night nearly 15 years ago. She gave evidence via videolink. She was shown sitting at a boardroom table. She wore a white blouse, as though she were playing the role of a secretary. Her sad, battered face indicated a hard life, suggesting the usual misery of men and methamphetamine. It wouldn't be accurate to describe her behaviour as tense or anxious. It was more like she was showing signs of a fast-approaching panic attack. Each question nailed her to a cross.

'Did you knock on the door?'

She took a long drink of water, and whispered, 'Yes.'

'Then?'

She breathed in and out rapidly, and croaked, 'I was let into the room.'

'Did you have to get the paperwork out of the way?'

She stared at the camera, and said in fright, 'What?'

'Did you ask for the money?'

She took slower breaths, and said, 'Oh. Yes.'

She told the court she was in the room for about an hour.

2

She phoned for the driver to pick her up. He said he wasn't far away, probably five minutes.

'Any problems?'

'No,' she said.

'Okay. Bye.'

She picked up her handbag, checked the $140 was inside. The client got off the bed and put on his green tracksuit pants. He said his name was Mark.

She said, 'So, what do you do, Mark?'

He said, 'Sell kitchen sinks and taps.'

She said, 'Really.'

He said, 'I fax the orders to my wife, and she does all the paperwork. It's a very successful business — I'm the number-one salesman in the Lower North Island!'

She said, 'Uh-huh.'

It was nearly 1am. He wanted her to leave. She wasn't what you'd call beautiful, and already he couldn't remember what name she gave. In any case, he'd got from her what he wanted. It was late; he had a busy morning ahead of him. He had people to see in Seaview, in Johnsonville, in Mt Cook. One customer owed him money, but he couldn't remember the address. He'd ask Christine for it in the morning.

The driver from the nearby Quarry Inn escort agency in Seaview finally arrived. 'Well, good night,' she said at the door.

'Good night,' he said.

After she left, Mark went outside to his car. He'd left it on the street earlier that night, when he'd parked under a streetlight to read a novel by one of his favourite authors, Robert Ludlum, until it got too dark. He thought he'd better move the Fairmont into the motel carpark. He felt a bit boozed and couldn't be bothered angling it directly in front of his room, Unit 10, so he left it in front of Unit 1.

It was a cold, still night in late August. There wasn't a moon out, and the sky and the water of Wellington harbour were as black as each other. He could see across from Petone to the city and the streetlights glowing high in the Hutt hills. To his left, a lighthouse flickered at the entrance to the Cook Strait. He shivered, and went inside.

He got back into bed. The rum, the sex … He felt relaxed, content. Life was good. A new laminate product had arrived that week; orders were going to go through the roof. The wine venture wasn't dead in the water yet, not by a long shot. In fact, he was going to call his designer first thing in the morning and get her to mock up an advertisement for a magazine aimed at retired police officers. He was bound to attract a few investors to back the land deal he had going in the Hawke's Bay.

But even if it fell through, no worries. They'd survive. You just had to work hard, and neither he nor Christine were afraid of that. They were a good team. He was away from their Palmerston North home a lot, on the road, selling the sinks from The Netherlands and the taps made in Taiwan; Christine stayed at home and did the books. Actually she was probably doing her brother's GST that night. Glenn had come over that morning to see if she'd finished it. He was at the house yesterday morning, too, asking about it.

Christine's family were always at the house. Her mum came for lunch every Wednesday, and popped in most days for a cup of tea and to see Amber. He smiled in the darkness. Amber. He was crazy about Amber, loved her with all his heart. She'd phoned that afternoon to ask if it was all right to have McDonald's for dinner. When he was away, Christine and Amber always ate takeaway. Christine probably only cooked twice a year anyway. Of course you can, he said. Thanks, Daddy, she said.

She was such a good little girl. There were never any problems with Amber. She had her routines: she'd go to bed at 7.30, read, and have lights out by 8.30, nine at the latest. Christine made Amber's nighties. She'd be wearing one tonight — probably with socks. She often forgot to take them off when she got into bed.

Christine always slept naked. She'd have heated up her side of the waterbed. She might even still be awake; she was a real night owl, reading her mother's subscription to Mills & Boon, playing Solitaire and Patience on the computer, watching TV. He felt a twinge of guilt about the escort. She wasn't the only one he'd gone to. But a man had his needs. Sex just wasn't a thing with him and Christine any more, but he still loved her. In fact, he couldn't wait to see her again. He was in love with her, always would be.

He nodded off. He got up once in the night to go to the bathroom, but otherwise slept soundly. He was up just after seven and went over to the motel office to see if the manager had batteries for his electric razor. The guy didn't have any. They talked about nothing in particular. Mark went back to his room, dressed, and checked out. He drove along The Esplanade to his favourite tuck shop, and bought a bacon and egg sandwich for breakfast. He also bought batteries. He shaved in the car, and ate his scoff, parked on the foreshore looking out to the harbour.

He went about his rounds, and phoned Christine for the address of the client who owed them money. She didn't pick up, and didn't return his calls. He continued to phone. He started to get worried. Then a friend phoned and said get your arse home now, there's police tape outside your house. He set off. It came on the radio that there had been a death in Palmerston North and police were treating it as suspicious. He drove, fast, and howled.

Chapter 10

Made in Australia: Rolf Harris

1

Every New Zealander overseas is aware of the phenomenon of the letter Z, the way it reaches out from newspaper reports or even the casual literature of menus and shop signs — we immediately think it's a reference to New Zealand. Z, that last and loveliest letter of the alphabet, is our trademark. Z is charged with the voltage of home; Z waves out from our obscure archipelago tucked away at the end of the Earth. Once you leave New Zealand, New Zealand disappears. It has no place in the world. No one mentions it, no one cares about it. Good. It's almost a reason to leave New Zealand — finally, an end to that shrill, obsessive conversation we have about ourselves and our 'national identity'. Wandering some foreign turf, we become stateless, free. But then the Z zings into view, and zaps us back. It's always shocking to see it; strange and unsettling, too, to overhear our island nation spoken out loud. It feels like you're the keeper of a secret. *I know that place. I know its ways.* Something similar extends to mentions of Australia. It's as though they've brought up the name of an old friend. *Oh, I know Australia. They live next door.* And you sit there in whatever foreign territory and listen to the names — New Zealand, Australia — like a spy.

Spy, tourist, unable to think of anywhere I'd rather be during a few days to kill in London, I got the last vacant seat in the public gallery at Southwark Crown Court where I attended the trial of Rolf Harris. It was a media sensation. But there was something else going on, something with a deeper resonance — a narrative about Australia and the colonies. England had given Australia its convicts; now Australia was returning the favour.

I pondered such shifts of history as I legged it from London Bridge Underground station towards the courthouse. I expected something with an Old Bailey vibe, but Southwark was modern and large, a tremendously ugly fortress. Inside, the place was a dump. There were torn vinyl chairs, notices drooping on boards because they'd run out of drawing pins, holes in the carpet.

Harris's jury trial was upstairs. I took my seat, looked around, and felt at home. The layout of the courtroom was identical to the lower order of criminal courts in New Zealand. There were the rows of tables for counsel, and there were the press benches. I smiled at the sight of the British press — they looked just like Kiwi journos, nicely dressed young men and women with narrow eyes and thin lips, dying to do away with the word 'alleged' whenever they wrote of Harris as a paedophile.

Eventually, I realised that the old man with white hair, sitting by himself in a glass cage in front of the public gallery, was Rolf Harris. He was dressed in a blue suit. He stood up. He wore his pants high around his waist; he was trim, dapper, with pink skin and a thin mouth. He walked to the door. He tried the door handle. It was locked. He bowed his head, and stood there, trapped, nowhere to go, an exhibit for everyone to look upon and question their childhood. People loved him when they were children. How could they have been so deceived? And now they knew, what ruin did his crimes visit on their innocence? Harris was found guilty, sentenced to five years and nine months' jail. He was stripped of his CBE, his name 'erased from the Register'. In his *Trews* commentary 'Rolf Harris: What should we think?', Russell Brand mused, 'You have to revise your own childhood. You have to go, "Oh, right, so what was going on then when I was enjoying that stuff?"'

As an Australian, Harris's success and genius as a children's entertainer was received with a special kind of enthusiasm in New Zealand. He wasn't an exotic, like he was thought of in Britain; he was just an Aussie joker, our familiar neighbour. We spoke the same not-Queen's-English language. We knew him. We knew his ways ... We didn't know anything.

The usual crackle of celebrity that snaps around the silhouette of the famous had a different, weirder feel to it when I watched Harris in his glass cage that Wednesday in May. It was a damp summer's morning, five to 10. He tried the door handle again. It was locked. Eventually, he walked back to his seat, and sat down. The glass cage; the eyes watching his hopeless little journey to the door and back; the small, blonde prosecutor Sasha Wass QC ('Cool as ice', *The Times*) all set to stab him and stab him and stab him with her latest accusations — Rolf Harris, 84, in hell, in public.

The spectators wore raincoats, corduroy, big woolly jumpers. One old character changed into a pair of slippers. The two men next to me struck up a conversation.

'Never smoked or drank in my life,' said the older man, about 70, who was in superb physical shape.

'A drink's all right,' said his neighbour, who rested his hands on his large stomach.

They fell silent.

'What's in there, then?' asked the younger man, pointing at the plastic bag that the teetotaler had taken out of his raincoat pocket.

'A hat.'

'A hat?'

'A wet hat.'

'This rain.'

'Terrible.'

'All stand,' said the court clerk. The judge entered. Harris was released from his glass cage, and led to the witness box. It was his second day on the stand. He was accused of 12 counts of indecently assaulting four underage girls in the UK between 1968 and 1986 — there were also similar allegations involving two girls in New Zealand. The court would hear about that, in particular about a day in Hamilton; it would also hear about a day at the beach in Australia.

New Zealand and Australia, like remote, bright backdrops to the miserable business of Harris in court. Across town, at King's College on The Strand, was the first Australia and New Zealand Festival of Literature and Arts ever staged in London. I was a guest speaker at three events, and also got roped in at the last minute by Witi Ihimaera to play a role in an excerpt from his play set in World War I. It was performed in a beautiful chapel. There was a haka. I enjoyed myself tremendously, but it was such small beer. The forlorn hope was that New Zealand and Australian writers might attract a new market of English readers; in fact, the three-day festival mostly played to small gatherings of expatriates. I asked the audience at one event if anyone was English. There was a show of hand. Only one! The truly spectacular — and more popular — festival of antipodean culture was at the packed upstairs courtroom, near the splashing Thames.

Harris, the Australian made good in England; Harris, a national treasure with his paintbrushes and his extra leg; Harris, harmless and asexual, chortling and whimsical, the light entertainer who had actually operated in darkness. Now, in court, was his Rick Rubin moment. Rubin produced the last, great records by Johnny Cash, turning his songs into high gothic. He had done the same with Neil Diamond. Harris, though, went further. His life was turned into high gothic, and the producer was Sasha Wass. Rubin made Cash and Diamond sound like their voices came from somewhere deep beneath the earth; Wass made Harris talk in frightened whispers.

She said, 'You're pretty good, Mr. Harris, aren't you, at disguising the dark side of your character.'

'Yes,' he said. His voice was quiet and hoarse.

Wass said, 'This case is about whether, under your friendly and loveable exterior, there is a dark side lurking. You know that, don't you?'

The old, thin voice gasped, 'I suppose so.'

2

It was his standard response: 'I suppose so.' It aimed for diffidence, but it didn't quite get there; it was weak, lacking. I sat in court for two days and heard it over and over.

Much was made of a holiday to Australia in the 1970s. Harris travelled with his wife, Alwen, their daughter, Bindi, and Bindi's best friend. The girls were 13. They went to the beach. Bindi's friend had a swim, and came out of the water. She was wearing a flesh-coloured bikini. Harris came towards her with a towel. He put it around her. Also, according to Wass, he molested her.

A photo of the girl wearing the bikini was produced in court. Harris studied it. Wass said he had complimented the girl on the holiday, told her that she looked 'lovely'.

'Do you accept that when a man tells a woman or a girl they look lovely in a bikini, they are not actually admiring the clothing, they are admiring the person's body?'

'Possibly.'

'You weren't talking about the bikini,' Wass said. 'You didn't mean the fabric. There's not much of it. What you were saying was, "You have a great body."'

The low gasp: 'I suppose so.'

'You suppose so.'

'I suppose so, yes.'

'To a 13-year-old. "You have a great body." That's what you were telling a 13-year-old.'

'I suppose so …'

He denied there was any touching. Wass kept at it. She held out her hand, palm up. She said, 'You digitally penetrated her.'

'That didn't happen.'

Her hand stayed where it was. 'She says you put your hand inside her bikini pants, and digitally penetrated her.'

'No.'

She continued to hold out her hand as she confronted Harris a third time, but this time she moved her middle fingers, thrust them forward, and said, 'You fingered her.'

'No.'

The obscene hand stayed where it was. Harris looked away. He started talking about how he wouldn't have gone to her with a towel, that he didn't spend much time at the beach, that he didn't even like the beach. Photos were produced of the beach. You could see bright blue skies, golden sand, a jetty stretching out to sea — you could see all the beauty of Australia, the lucky country, its sun and surf and glowing light.

Another wildly successful expatriate, Clive James, talked about that light when he spoke at the Australia–New Zealand festival. James was giving what was billed as his farewell performance. He had leukaemia. He was dying, on the way out. He played to a full crowd who cheered and wept for the great prose stylist in his final hour of memoir, gags, and poetry. He said he was too unwell to return to Australia. It was a profound regret. He longed to see it one more time, to 'bask in the light I never left behind'.

But Harris didn't want to know about the light. He was a creature of shadows. 'I hate sunbathing … I hate the sea … I don't like the beach.' His great distaste for spending any time there, he said, ruled out any possibility of molesting schoolgirls.

Wass ignored the logic of his argument, and said to the jury,

'He would do this whether or not there were family members nearby. You will hear other instances in this case where Mr Harris touched children and women alike in quite brazen circumstances. Maybe that was part of the excitement for him, knowing that he could get away with it.'

Harris, said Wass, was 'a sinister pervert'. How the old man with white hair would have envied James, his compatriot and near contemporary, not only because he was playing on the other side of the river to an audience who loved him. James was merely dying. Harris had it worse. He was being shamed in full view of the media.

The press sat in rows behind his wife and daughter. I approached Alwen Harris during an adjournment. The old dear was led to a ripped orange vinyl couch in a kind of lounge outside the courtroom. She was left by herself. It was a heartbreaking sight. I thought she could do with a friendly voice. I figured: we have a bond. Alwen was British, but her long marriage to Harris gave her an insight into the special relationship between New Zealand and Australia. She was in on the shared secret of life in the beautiful light of the Antipodes. I went over to her, and said, 'I'm from New Zealand. Just wanted to say hi. Hang in there.'

She looked up and smiled. She was very frail. She didn't seem quite all there.

3

Another Australian accused of serious sex crimes, half Harris's age, was also more or less walking to the door and then sitting back down again in a cage in London. On a Friday morning, I went to the Ecuadorean embassy in Knightsbridge to pay silent tribute to the extraordinary Julian Assange.

Assange took political asylum in the embassy, which meant he had elected to hide inside a converted women's bathroom. He owned a table, chairs, treadmill (a gift from film director Ken

Loach), laptop, phones, and 'safety equipment he keeps close to his bed', according to the *Daily Mail*. He told the paper, 'Of course it's difficult to wake up and see the same walls but on the other hand I am doing good work … While I'm imprisoned here, there's a developing prison where you're living as well.'

The theme and point of his WikiLeaks work was freedom of information. But that right was supposedly taken away from Assange in a strange sub-plot to the Australia–New Zealand literary event.

The first I heard about it was when journalist Steve Kilgallon rang from the *Sunday Star-Times* in Auckland. He said, 'What do you know about the New Zealand embassy getting Julian Assange banned from speaking at the festival?' I knew nuzzink, but it was a thrilling question. I said I'd ask around.

Kilgallon called again on Saturday morning. I'd made my pilgrimage to the Ecuadorean embassy the previous day. I thought: wouldn't it be fantastic if Assange appeared at a window, and waved or something? I was a fan, an admirer. But when I looked into the claims of his expulsion from the festival, and wrote about it in the *Star-Times*, I presented myself to WikiLeaks as just another running dog of the mainstream media, a dunce, a stooge.

It was my own hopeless little journey. It started well. I went to Harrods, which is in front of Assange's gilded cage, and bought a lobster sandwich. I stuffed my face with the sensational feast while mooching around the streets of Knightsbridge. A cherry-red Ferrari was parked outside Prada. Giuseppe Zanotti held an anniversary exhibition of its shoes in the front window; each pair was given a name, and boring history — 'Slim' was inspired by a beach in wintertime, 'Venere' was a fusion of woman and serpent.

There were two Rolls-Royces on Sloane Street, one white, one burgundy. Dolce and Gabbana, Bulgari, Versace. A serf in a top hat unlocked the gates to a private garden for a man with a greyhound. The mutt galloped inside, and shat on the grass. 'Spare a pound, please?' a beggar asked. She was from Brixton. 'I'm a fucking mess.'

I got to the embassy. It was on a quiet street in a handsome red-brick building. All of the curtains were drawn. You could probably see Hyde Park and the Thames from the top two levels. I thought that might at least afford the WikiLeaks savant some pleasure, but the policeman out front said Assange's rooms were on the ground floor. Its only view was the Harrods loading bay.

He worked 17-hour days, according to reports. He had a personal trainer. He watched TV (*The West Wing*, 1960s sci-fi series *The Twilight Zone*), he shredded anything that might leave a paper trail, he waits — for something, anything.

The officer outside the embassy was feeling chatty. He said three cops kept constant watch from the street. A fourth was on a rooftop. A fifth was inside the building, patrolling the stairwell and lobby — the rest of the building are apartments, and the east wing is the Colombian embassy. 'All this for a sex offender,' he said. 'And we're not even here because of WikiLeaks and all that. It's just the sex.'

4

It's just the sex. On the second morning I attended Harris's trial, he was busy inside his glass cage as the clock ticked towards 10am. He was talking to himself. It looked as though he were practising his lines. Was he perfecting the infinite ways he could mutter, 'I suppose so'? On his opening day in the witness stand, he gave an astonishing performance — he mimed his amazing wobble board, he imitated the didgeridoo, he sang verses from 'Jake the Peg', his 1965 smash hit: 'I'm Jake the Peg, diddle, diddle, diddle-dum, with an extra leg …'

There would be no repeat performance. After Harris's strange rehearsal on Thursday morning, he took his seat in the witness box, and Wass said to him, 'You are a brilliant and polished entertainer, Mr Harris. There's no question of that, and the Crown have no wish to challenge that.'

Harris nodded.

'But,' she said, with dreadful scorn, 'this isn't a talent show, is it, Mr Harris?'

The dry, papery voice said, 'No.'

She took away his music. The judge took away his art. Jurors spotted Harris drawing in court; it's against court regulations, and Harris felt the full weight of justice. 'The sketches,' announced Justice Nigel Sweeney, 'have been confiscated and destroyed.'

What did that leave him? He had his dignity and he had his defence — that he didn't molest or abuse anyone. Wass said his victims were groomed, bullied, traumatised. He denied it. 'They're all lying.' His right hand hung over the edge of the witness box. The fingers were splayed. The hand looked like a kind of starfish. Harris, diabetic, with a bad heart, an old man in a damp month, gasped for air.

Wass leafed through his 2001 autobiography *Can You Tell What It Is Yet?* and tried to place him at the scenes of his alleged sex crimes. Malta, Cambridge, Portsmouth, London, Hawaii, Hamilton … She had placed dozens of yellow and red Post-it notes in the pages. I thought: I'd like to read that book. When I got back to Auckland, I looked it up in the library system. The only copy was at Northcote Library, which has stunning views of the harbour; it stopped me in my tracks, all that blue water sparkling in the sun.

I took the book home and prepared for the usual happy narrative of fame. Most showbiz memoirs are cheerful, self-satisfied histories of success and happiness. But Harris's book is a depressing read.

He admits to a terrible relationship with his daughter. He describes poor old Alwen as arthritic, isolated, with alopecia — her hair started falling out in her twenties. The one time he told his mother he loved her was on her deathbed. 'I've never been very good at discussing anything emotional.' He dwells on failures in his career, his limitations as an entertainer — his manager once insisted he sing a cover of Dylan's 'Blowin' in the Wind' on live

TV, but it was a disaster. He couldn't remember the words. He concludes he just wasn't suited to that kind of song.

In his *London Review of Books* essay on the appalling Jimmy Saville, Andrew O'Hagan wrote, 'There's something creepy about British light entertainment and there always has been.' In his book, Harris writes about the backing dancers who appeared on his 1960s TV shows: 'They were dressed in microskirts or hot pants. Whenever they danced you saw a flash of panties, which is why it quickly became known as the Twinkling Crotch Show.'

There are weird recollections. Bindi's birth: 'I gazed at this little naked girl child, marvelling at the minute size of everything. My eyes travelled down from her neck, to her delicate shoulders and the incredibly smooth skin of her stomach. I reached her genitals and skipped that part. My brain was saying, "Don't be ridiculous. Why are you so uptight about nudity?" I couldn't help it.'

The time his mother knitted her own bathing suit, which had tassels: 'I announced, "They look like pubic hairs." She swung her hand around and slapped me across the face. Mum didn't talk to me for two days. I was 30 years old when that happened.'

Harris left out an even weirder memory. He shared it in an interview in 1974: 'I grew up in the belief that sex was dirty. When I was 10 or 11 my mother decided I should see her naked to let me know it was all natural and everything. We had a bath together ...'

The loveless book, the dismal affairs. He talked in court about sleeping with a penniless lodger. As for Bindi's friend, Harris claimed they started having sex only after the girl turned 18, at the girl's prompting: 'She was flirtatious, coquettish.' It went on for 10 years. The court heard a brief history of blow-jobs. 'Sex,' said Harris, 'with no frills.'

Wass: 'Ten years, and the only conversation you can recall is about cleaning your sperm from the sheets. It wasn't a deep relationship, was it?'

His reply: 'I don't suppose it was.'

5

Harris and Assange, the two white-haired Australians; the light entertainer from Perth, the most dangerous man alive from Townsville; both brought low by sex scandals — but the comparison is odious. To reduce Assange to Harris's level is to trivialise him, and distract from his work with WikiLeaks.

Assange and his supporters are wise to such tactics. Among them is the legendary Australian journalist John Pilger, who wrote a superb column in the *New Statesman* taking careful note of the 'lies, spite, jealousy, opportunism and pathetic animus' of Assange's critics.

It was an honour to meet Pilger at the literary festival on The Strand. He was behind a desk, signing a stack of his books for the festival bookseller. A few days before I flew out to the UK, I'd managed to track down a copy of Pilger's very first book, *The Last Day: America's Final Hours in Vietnam*, published in 1976. I took it to London in case I was able to ask Pilger to sign it. The chance arrived.

He was astonished. 'My God,' he said. 'My first book. How did you get it? American edition! My God.'

He picked it up tenderly, turned the pages with delicate fingers. He shook his head. 'My God.' Pilger, 70, was tanned and in good shape, tall and fit, with luxurious hair and an open, lovely smile. He was deeply moved to see a copy of his book, to hold it. I alerted him to the sticker inside the front cover, listing it as the property of the Nazareth Hospital in Philadelphia, and speculated that it may have passed into the hands of a hospitalised US soldier.

'That's right,' he said. 'A Vietnam vet.'

He signed it, and I said, 'Thank you.'

'No,' he said, 'thank you. Thank you so much.'

I should have asked Pilger if he'd heard Assange was pulled from the festival, but I didn't want to risk ruining the moment. Festival director Jon Slack was standing nearby. I asked him about it, and he said, 'It's bollocks.' He described it as laughable. He laughed, not very convincingly.

Paula Morris, a New Zealand novelist who sat on the festival advisory board, also rubbished the claims. She said the board considered the idea of an interview with Assange, but no one was very keen on it. Slack went a bit further, and said Assange would have been 'a distraction'.

All of which was kind of pathetic. Assange appeared via Skype at the South by Southwest festival in Austin, Texas, in March, and discussed the case of Edward Snowden, government surveillance, 'the military occupation' of civilian space, and hinted at WikiLeaks releasing fresh information — important subjects, addressed by a well-known international figure who happens to be Australian, which might have made him a speaker worth having at an otherwise rather obscure festival of Australian and New Zealand culture.

But the point of the rumour wasn't about programming. It was about political interference. WikiLeaks spread the rumour on its Twitter account: 'Assange talk blacklisted after pressure from NZ High Commission. Funding threat was twofold: 1) if Assange spoke; 2) if the threat was leaked.'

It emerged that the source was Australian journalist Andrew Fowler, author of an admiring book on Assange, *The Most Dangerous Man in the World*, and who was keen to conduct the Skype interview. He said the festival had been ordered to pull Assange from the programme — by the wife of Lockwood Smith, the New Zealand High Commissioner to the UK. Lockwood Smith's wife! According to Fowler, the threat was made at a cocktail party. A cocktail party?

It sounded crazy. Closer inquiry suggested it really was crazy. I ran into Fowler at King's College. He said he wasn't actually at the cocktail party, but that's what he'd heard Lockwood Smith's wife had said, and whether her threat was made directly or indirectly to the festival, it was hard to tell, but the fact of the matter is that Assange would not be appearing …

That weekend, I ridiculed the situation in a satirical diary in the *Sunday Star-Times*. I invented a monologue for Assange, fulminating at the power and influence of Lockwood Smith's wife at cocktail parties … I tried to balance the stupid column, make it clear that I admired WikiLeaks, that Assange was heroic and brilliant.

It was all in vain. WikiLeaks on Twitter that day linked to the column with the dismissive comment, 'Today's idiotic op-ed trend: fake journal entries from Julian.' I writhed in shame and betrayal. I was called out as an Assange-hater, a stooge, a dog, a dunce, stuffed to the gills with 'pathetic animus'. I remembered something Fowler had said at the festival. Unlike his other comments, this one might have been accurate. I asked: 'Who writes WikiLeaks stuff on Twitter?' He said: 'Usually it's Julian.'

6

One of the few times Rolf Harris escaped from his gloom and torment at Southwark Crown Court was when he was shown a photograph of the house where he grew up in Bassendean, near Perth. A plain weatherboard house, surrounded by jacarandas, fig trees, almond trees, box trees, draped with wisteria, on the banks of the Swan River — he climbed the trees and gorged on their fruit and nuts, he swam the Swan like a champ. At 16, he was the junior backstroke champion of Australia, competing in Melbourne in a borrowed pair of silk full-length bathers.

You could see how the photo relaxed him. That tight, compact body loosened, his thin lips almost smiled. Was it for his childhood and innocence, or was it for the reminder of home? I thought: I know where you live. I know WA. I thought of Perth, Fremantle, the Swan, Cape Leeuwin, Margaret River, the vast distances and flat, baked plains and the exact point where the Indian Ocean meets the Southern Ocean. I stored the knowledge, held it like a secret; alone among the pale English in the upstairs courtroom,

I was from the same part of the world as Harris. *Hang in there.*

He didn't hang in there. Wass brought her twitching little hand out again when she talked about the similarities in the versions told by Harris's alleged victims. Harris, reaching inside the bikini pants worn by Bindi's friend; Harris, with his hand up the skirt of a girl at a restaurant somewhere in New Zealand; Harris, grabbing a 15-year-old girl's bottom at a hardware store in Hamilton. All hands, wandering, groping, fingering.

Harris: 'They're lying.'

Wass: 'Why is it the same lie?'

Harris: 'I don't know. It didn't happen. I've established that they're lying.'

Wass: 'No, you're just saying they're lying. You haven't established that at all.'

Her hand, grubby and suggestive; his hand, that starfish, hanging on for dear life to the witness stand. In the front row, Alwen Harris, needing help whenever she sat down; two seats along from her, their daughter, Bindi, a tough-looking broad in a leather jacket and a mauve top with butterflies on it. She'd told the court she wasn't close to her father. 'We hardly talk, Dad and I.'

When her friend told her that Harris had started abusing her when she was 13, Bindi phoned her father and challenged him. She banged her head against the wall while holding the receiver. She told him she wanted to stab herself with forks.

Wass to Harris: 'She was beside herself?'

He supposed so, he supposed so, he supposed so. The empty life he described in his mordant book wafted around the upstairs courtroom, Case Number T20130553, where English onlookers with wet hats and warm slippers came to watch the end of the Rolf Harris story. The love of the British people, his good friend the Queen sitting for her portrait — it was all as distant as Perth, as the Swan River, drifting past his house on the edge of that faraway continent glowing in the light of the Antipodes.

Chapter 11

Terra nullius: Brad Murdoch

1

Assigned, with great pleasure, to tropical Darwin, that vivid, farfetched town closer to Timor or Lombok than the nearest city in its own country, to cover the trial in December 2005 of Brad Murdoch, who apparently killed and buried English tourist Peter Falconio somewhere in the Outback, and tried to do the same and worse to Falconio's girlfriend, Joanne Lees, a striking beauty who arrived at and left the court building every day in a black Ford Falcon, I had absolutely no idea what I was talking about when I concluded my newspaper story by writing, 'There is a police crime scene photo taken the day after the murder. The long, straight highway. The red earth, the scrub purple and yellow. Middle of the continent, middle of nowhere; it looks really beautiful, quite hopeless, utterly savage.'

I'd not been to the scene of the crime or set tyre anywhere on the Stuart Highway, including that fatal part of it, north of Alice Springs and near the Outback town of Barrow Creek, which became known as 'the Falconio stretch'. The prosecution's case was that the gigantic Murdoch had signalled for Falconio to pull over his orange Kombi on the moonless night of 14 July 2001, then shot him dead and hid the body. He was also charged with assaulting Lees and 'depriving her of her liberty', a rather chaste phrase which she described in court as an act of terrifying violence. Lees escaped; all trace of Falconio was made to disappear. The awful, frantic event, at night, in the Outback — the iconic Australian setting stirred the imagination, gave it what it wanted. Emptiness. Nature, red in sand and dingo claw; the mysterious and beautiful desert. In court, Lees talked about her last day with Falconio, driving through the Outback. They saw a bushfire. They saw kangaroos. They smoked some dope Falconio had bought in Sydney and stashed underneath the dashboard. Stoned, happy, alone, they watched the sunset.

The point and the appeal of the murder narrative was that the setting was unpeopled. But that wasn't true. I was given an instruction in myth and geography by Paul Toohey, one of the greatest essayists and journalists in Australia. He attended the trial. He stood out: he was cool. I'd see him tooling around the streets of Darwin in his Chev Impala. He later wrote a brilliant book about the Falconio murder, *The Killer Within: Inside the World of Bradley John Murdoch*. The subtitle said it all. Toohey's book was much less any kind of hard-boiled murder inquiry than an intimate and scary guide to the lawless society of the Top End. He said to me, 'Murder is just murder. We like to romanticise death in the north, but we sometimes forget that it's not a great death just because it happened in the north. It's just another murder. But for some reason it interests people. The setting *is* vast, and it *is* empty, but it's not necessarily lonely. It's just that people are able to get away with things easier up here.'

Murdoch ran drugs, hauling kilos of dope on long-distance drives between Broome and Adelaide. He took speed to keep himself awake. He took his dog, Jack, for company. He took a gun.

Toohey wrote in his book, 'Brad Murdoch is not just Brad Murdoch. He's a breed, a type. There are Murdochs all across northern Australia and they run to kind. White or beige Toyota Land

Cruiser HZJ75 utility. Six-pack foam esky for up front of the cab on long drives ... Weapons of various types — revolvers, pistols, rifles.'

I didn't know anyone like that, and I didn't know anything about that whole scene. I doubt I was alone in that among the press at the Supreme Court. There were a lot of Australian journalists, and also a squad sent out, with seemingly little pleasure going by their steady litany of complaints about Darwin life, from England. They kept apart. The twain did not meet between Australia and England. It was a strange, unspoken apartheid. Most of the English were sequestered in a room with CCTV of the court proceedings. They could have chosen to sit in court; there were usually spare seats on the press bench. I went to and fro, stateless, bewildered at the weird division in attitudes. I found it hard to regard the trial as any kind of whodunit, only a wheredunit — Falconio's body has never been found. In general, Australian journalists were confident that Murdoch was guilty as charged. Almost unanimously, the English had it in for Joanne Lees. They suspected her of something. Either Falconio was dead, and she knew more than she let on; or he was alive, and she was complicit in that, too. They hated everything about her — her manner, her clothes. They talked of her as aloof and snooty, a hard-faced bitch. They remained in a state of scorn at her decision a few days after the murder to give a press conference wearing a T-shirt with the words CHEEKY MONKEY.

The powerful dislike, the baseless suspicions ... Darwin's newspaper, *Northern Territory News*, marked a civic anniversary during the trial by running old photos of memorable moments in the Top End. There was one of the biggest crocodile ever captured and killed; kids played in its vast open jaws. There was also a full-page photo of a couple walking up the front steps of the Darwin Supreme Court in 1975. The husband wore a white shirt and tie. The wife wore a thin sundress. The bright light of Darwin burned their black shadows onto the courthouse steps. I still have that photo of Michael and Lindy Chamberlain.

2

Until I got to Darwin, the biggest person I'd ever seen at close quarters was Jonah Lomu. It was over lunch at the All Blacks training headquarters in Palmerston North before the 1999 World Cup. He ate an omelette scrambled from approximately 4000 eggs, and drank milk straight from the cow, draining it in one gulp, and then he said: 'More.' Certainly he was very big. But he was as a will o' the wisp compared to the giant accused of murder in the Darwin Supreme Court. Lees had said of Murdoch's attack that night in 2001: 'He just seemed to be all around me and over me.'

I looked at him a lot in the dock. He was 47 years old and 6' 5" with a large face, broad chest, and enormous hands. The skin was drawn tight over his bones. His mouth was a narrow, bitter slot. His spectacles gave him the plausible appearance of scholarship as he studied maps and underlined transcripts. He listened closely to evidence and filled out exercise books with a ballpoint pen that looked like a toothpick held in his great fist. When he stood, soaring above his two security guards, he picked up a briefcase and would leave the courtroom like a man rushing towards his next appointment.

He had nowhere to go. Only downstairs to the cells, munching on salad rolls for lunch, and then he was escorted to the nearby Berrimah Prison each night. In court, he peered over his spectacles at prosecutor Rex Wild QC, at his defence barrister Grant Althie, at the jury, and sometimes at the public gallery. In the front row, there were Falconio's parents, Luciano and Joan, a small, forlorn couple who trudged the hot pavements of Darwin every afternoon back to their room at the Saville Hotel. Behind them sat Joanne Lees.

She wore white blouses and long cream skirts to court. Her long black hair was bunched in a Lady Jayne band. She had an oval face and an angry mouth. She chewed gum, she crossed her very attractive legs, she sometimes took the opportunity to inspect the creature in the dock. During recess, she sat with Falconio's mum and dad; one afternoon, Luciano patted her shoulder, and kept his hand there for a few seconds.

Murdoch was immense. Lees was voluptuous. Peter Falconio was the man who wasn't there. As the second witness at the trial, Luciano was asked for his son's age. He said, 'It was 28 when he died.' Murdoch's lawyer told the jury, 'Sometimes people disappear.' Crown prosecutor Rex Wild: 'He was made to disappear.'

A couple told the court they saw a man they thought was Falconio call into their shop about a week after the murder to buy a Coke and a Mars Bar. They couldn't get their story straight. The man said he served her, the woman said she did; God knows how they were allowed to give evidence. Police received eight reports of Falconio after 14 July 'all over Australia'. They also received reports of him on dates before he ever arrived in the country.

'I've heard it said as the Peter Falconio mystery,' Wild said to the jury. 'There is no mystery.' Lees said when Falconio got out of the Kombi to talk to the motorist whom she identified as Murdoch, she heard him say, 'Cheers, mate.' His last words. And then she heard a loud sound, like an engine backfiring, like a single gunshot. She screamed his name. 'He didn't come,' said Wild. 'He couldn't have come.'

Police searches at the crime scene unearthed bottle tops and the remains of a kangaroo. All that was left of Falconio was a pool of his blood beneath a little pyramid of dirt. He vanished along with his wallet containing $630 and his St Christopher's necklace.

Murdoch has always maintained the charges were a police stitch-up, that he was going about his illegal business some 600 kilometres away that night. He had the support in court of his girlfriend, Jan Pitman, a big woman who wore three rings on each hand. Sometimes she was joined by true-crime author Robin Bowles, who wore three rings on each finger. Bowles wrote a book about the murder. Slowly, I would expect; whenever she visited the press room, she jabbed at her keyboard with one very long fingernail.

Her book raised the suggestion that Falconio may have been drug-running. Equally, he may have been abducted by aliens. The notion that Falconio was alive and well somewhere — outer space, anywhere — was taken up in two books by two hacks, Roger Maynard and Richard Shears. Maynard's book was called *Where's Peter?* It begged for a subtitle. Something along the lines of *Oh For Christ's Sake He's Most Likely Fucking Dead is Where.*

3

Lees and Falconio were on their way to New Zealand. They had done Nepal, Singapore, Cambodia, Thailand; the plan was to fly out of Brisbane and spend five weeks in the North and South Islands, where they would celebrate their birthdays, his on 20 September, hers five days later. But first, the drive north, through the Outback, towards Darwin.

Murdoch left school at 15. He'd worked as a truck driver and a mechanic. He was a nasty piece of work with form (jailed for shooting at Aborigines after a football match, charged with the rape and abduction of a 12-year-old girl and her mother but found not guilty). He lived in a caravan behind a workshop in Broome. He was fastidious, very particular about things; he said he liked BP service stations: 'They've got clean fuel.' He drove long distances in bare feet, and stepped out wearing either thongs or moccasins. He stayed awake on the big drug runs by taking speed. 'I always have it in a cup of tea.'

On the morning of 14 July, Lees and Falconio called into a Red Rooster fast-food outlet. Murdoch camped overnight, and had Weet-Bix and tea for breakfast. He was on his way from Sedan to Broome with about 11 kilograms of dope hidden in the Toyota. Fussily, again, he'd been looking everywhere for a particular grey colour for a dash mat: 'I was at the end of my tether.' He was with his dog, Jack, a Dalmatian–Blue Heeler cross. He bought chicken at Red Rooster to share with the dog. 'Jack was a bit of a liker on nuggets.'

Lees and Falconio watched a camel-racing event, and left Alice in the late afternoon. Lees drove; Falconio rested in the back, reading *The Catcher in the Rye*. They played The Stone Roses.

By then, said Murdoch, he was nowhere near. He'd turned off Stuart Highway, and into the Tanami Desert, 'rolling along like Tommy Tourist'.

Darkness fell. At about 8pm that night a man in a 4WD indicated for Falconio to pull over, gesturing that there was something wrong with the Kombi's exhaust. Falconio stopped the van. He took his cigarettes; 'Cheers, mate'; and then on a night without a moon in it, an explosive sound, and a stranger coming around to the side of the Kombi and sticking a gun to Lees' head. He ordered her out. He put his knee on her back, and strapped her wrists together with cable ties. He punched her in the head. He threw her in the back of his 4WD. Lees told the court she was more afraid of rape than death. *He just seemed to be all around me and over me.*

Amazingly, she managed to escape. She jumped out of the back of the vehicle, ran into the scrub, and hid there for five hours in shock and fear until she flagged down a truck driver. He took her to the pub at Barrow Creek to call police. Saturday night in the Outback: there was more beer and cheer than usual, because they were having a delayed New Year's Eve celebration. It's too hot in summer to throw a party, so locals wait seven months for the desert to cool.

4

That was exactly the kind of thing I wanted to hear. *Locals wait seven months for the desert to cool.* I wanted the Outback served up as a land of simple contrasts — mysterious and beautiful, hopeless and savage. I'd seen it for myself. The precious year I rode the magnificent *Ghan* train from Adelaide to Darwin. It took three days and two nights to cross two time zones and three deserts — Great Victoria, Simpson and Tanami — where I rolled along like Tommy Tourist. It was a mesmerising journey. Hour after hour, day after day of the desert void. The train disappeared into it. All around was spinifex grass, cassia trees, mulga bush. Thin, sharp, scraggly things, clinging on for dear life out of all that red earth. Once it entered the subtropical Northern Territory as it neared Darwin, there were water buffalo, rosellas, galahs, even the spangled drongo. Most strikingly, and abundantly, there were also termite mounds, which went by the fabulous word 'termitaria'.

The only people I saw were the rabble onboard the train. I was among 25 other journalists on a junket; the party included two Australians who I raised hell with one night until about 1.30am, when I left them breaking in to the train's bar. They spent the rest of the trip under a kind of house arrest, confined to quarters. They were the only people I liked, so I retired to my compartment and stared out the window at the termitaria, at the desert emptiness.

This was the landscape — epic, unpeopled — where I imagined Falconio and Lees experienced terror. As a pampered passenger on *The Ghan*, I was cut off from the sight or knowledge of Brad Murdoch types tooling around in 4WDs with their eskies and their guns; all I saw were birds, lightning, termitaria. I willingly romanticised death in the north. The setting was so overpowering — the red, hard Outback, and the way it softened heading north, towards the subtropics. Darwin itself was a wonderland. The sky at night was lit by silent electrical storms over the Timor Sea. An illegal snake-dealer was caught with two black-headed pythons in a sack. Fishermen were urged to go up the Howard River where barramundi fed on prawns in the mangroves. There were hermit crab races — two heats of 10 on a sandy board — every night at the Fox 'n' Fiddle. It was December, the wet season, 34 fructifying degrees, with fruit bats in the tops of the banyan trees. A 2-metre saltwater crocodile was found prowling the streets. A public meeting was held to discuss methods of waging war on cane toads.

It was so exotic, so removed from prosaic New Zealand. But one day in court I heard a sound I recognised. It was the familiar vowels of a New Zealander. It came from the prosecution's star witness, James Hepi, who led the police to Murdoch, and gave crucial evidence against him. The two men had a brief exchange in court. I felt proud to hear the Australian drawl countered by the musical voice of a Maori.

Murdoch said, 'You're a fucken liar.'

Hepi said, 'Fuck you.'

5

Hepi was Murdoch's partner-in-crime in the dope-smuggling business. The contraband was usually powerful skunk weed. It paid well. But Hepi got busted with about 4.5 kilograms of the stuff on him, and was looking at jail. 'I had an ace up my sleeve called Brad Murdoch,' he said to Paul Toohey, the Darwin journalist, 'and I used it.' Meaning, he suspected Murdoch was Falconio's killer, and gave his name to the police in exchange for a suspended sentence.

Hepi claimed Murdoch had told him that the best place to bury a body was in a spoon drain. He claimed he saw Murdoch making cable-tie handcuffs. Hepi claimed he could definitely identify Murdoch as the man on CCTV at a Shell service station on the night of 14 July, placing him at a time and location near the alleged murder: 'I know exactly who it is. I spent a lot of time around that man. I know how he stands. I know how he walks.'

There was such a New Zealandness to Hepi's heavy, truculent sarcasm at the trial. Yes, he said to Murdoch's lawyer, Grant Althie, he was definitely interested in collecting the police reward of $250,000 that led to the arrest. 'Who do I see about it — you?'

He was also cross-examined on his attempts to collect the Winfield Gold cigarette butts that Murdoch smoked, with the intent of collecting DNA. 'If it matched the Northern Territory murder, good job.'

Althie: 'What did you do about it?'

Hepi: 'It's not as if I've got a DNA lab in my back pocket, mate.'

Hepi said he threw away the butts. There was other circumstantial evidence, independent of Hepi, that pinned Murdoch to the murder. His DNA was matched to the cable ties, and the Kombi's gearstick. Althie said the cops put it there.

A spot of Murdoch's blood was identified on Lees' T-shirt. Rex Wild told the jury: 'It's the most single significant piece of evidence in this case. It ties this man to this woman on this day.' Althie said the cops put it there.

There were discrepancies. Lees told the court that she had tried to release her hand bindings by rubbing them with lip-balm; police found the lid in a search the next day, but only located the tube three months later. You can guess what Althie said about that, but here is the exact quote: 'Maybe a kangaroo took it away and put it back. Perhaps it was a dingo, or a zephyr of wind. Another possibility is that somebody, one of the police officers, put it there.'

Lees said Murdoch punched her in the head. Murdoch said if he punched her in the head then she wouldn't have got up. Lees said the man had a gun with a silver barrel. Murdoch owned two guns — a .357 Magnum, and a Beretta — and neither had a silver barrel. Lees said the man threw her from the front seat of his car into the back tray. Murdoch's Toyota didn't have front to rear access. In 'the agony of the moment', argued Wild, she ought to be allowed the benefit of the doubt.

Althie argued that his client ought to be allowed the benefit of the doubt, too. The national manhunt to find the culprit took over two years; police were desperate to make an arrest; was Murdoch simply convenient? Nearly a whole volume of the six-volume set of court transcripts from the trial was devoted to the murky CCTV image of Murdoch or whoever it was at the Shell station on the night of the murder. 'That man could have come from anywhere,' Althie said. 'It's just a guy at a truckstop with a moustache.' He also denied that the 4WD caught on CCTV was Murdoch's vehicle; one of his most compelling arguments was that it didn't match the bullbar Murdoch bought from someone with the fabulous name of Woggie Minshull.

The jury deliberated for eight hours. I remember strolling around and looking at the artwork in the court building. One showed a former chief justice smoking a pipe in the foreground and a nude peeling her top off in the background. Another was a canvas with white lettering on black paint. It read *Thou shalt not kill*.

Murdoch was given a life sentence with non-parole of 28 years. In 2014, his lawyers withdrew an appeal against his conviction. He'd wanted a retrial, claiming 'a miscarriage of justice'. His appeal was based on the notion that the prosecution had groomed Joanne Lees 'secretly, deliberately and improperly', because they feared the jury would find her resolutely unlikeable.

Well, possibly. Murdoch still has believers, people on his side. It's just that they seemed deranged. Someone called Keith Allan Noble is the author of a 2011 book with a curiously placed exclamation mark in the title. *Find! Falconio* is described as an 'exposition of Australia's strangest disappearance (murder or missing?) and of the associated misinvestigations, cover-ups, and incompetence. Reveals the show trial in which the jury was lied to. Encourages readers to get involved in finding the British visitor (and drug courier?) Peter Falconio — dead or alive.' Noble is also the author of a book which argues the innocence of Port Arthur mass murderer Martin Bryant.

Enough. Good riddance, you would have to think about Murdoch, to bad rubbish. And cheers to the New Zealander who ratted him out. Hepi did it out of self-interest, but not, it seems, for greed. It was thought he'd claim the A$250,000 reward. He talked about it at the trial. A year later, police announced the reward had been withdrawn. They said no one came forward to claim it.

I asked Paul Toohey what he made of Hepi, and he said, 'I liked James a lot. He was pretty straight-up, a good guy to deal with. Some people would say "He's a drug dealer!" and regard him with horror. But half the people I know smoke dope. They've got to get it from somewhere. I sort of look at marijuana dealers as tax-avoiders.

'He's a shambolic-looking guy. But James could drink a carton of beer and you would not be concerned that he had a switch that would kick in and turn him into someone else. He's quite level. He's very practical.'

The prosaic Kiwi, matter-of-fact, not carried away ... Hepi, like Toohey, was providing a lesson. I wanted to think of it as the quintessential Australian murder — Woggie Minshull's bullbar, chicken nuggets from Red Rooster at Alice Springs, a mad dog with a gun driving at speed and on speed in terra nullius — but what was the point of collecting these scraps of national characteristics? *Murder is just murder.*

Chapter 12

Sex and Chocolate: 'Bones'

I don't need no money, fortune or fame.
— 'My Girl', The Temptations

1

Another murder trial in Australia, again in the fructifying heat of December, again with a Maori at the centre of it, except Tony Williams was the murder victim and his death seemed to offer a parable about the perils of following the yellow brick road to Surfers Paradise. Brisbane was preparing for the joys of Christmas 2014: a downtown pub grandly advertised St Stephen's Day, 26 December, when it would open at the festive time of 10am. The talk at the cafés and bars all along downtown George Street (steak and schooner specials for $16, COLD BEER! HOT CHICKS! at Grosvenor's topless bar) was of the recent storm, when large hailstones fell out of the sky with such force that they pulverised cars, tore roofs off houses, and closed the airport — it wasn't safe to fly with Brisbane under attack from meteors of ice.

Things were back to normal by the time I got to the Sunshine State. There were the moaning crows and squealing ibises in the tops of Moreton Bay figs, and a faint breeze chasing away papery scraps of leaves from the plane trees. The fecund botanical gardens — colonists trialled mangoes, custard apples, sugarcane and tobacco in the grounds — was crowded with fruit bats. One night I couldn't sleep and looked out my window at 4am; it was already light, so I went for a long walk, and crossed two bridges over the Brisbane River. A yellow-faced cormorant came out of the water, and stretched its wings to dry. It didn't take long. Joggers and families were out and about in large numbers by 6am. There were mangroves and rainforest, and poetry marking the birth of Brisbane was chiselled in concrete on the banks of the river: *A large tree would make the first wharf here, and a ship cut free.* I liked those lines very much. I repeated them to myself as I walked alongside the river, which blazed in bright dawn sunlight. I imagined the exhilarating sense of a new beginning, a new world opening up for pleasure and profit — it wasn't just the colonists, it was also the exodus of 21st-century Maori making their way out of our narrow islands to a land of opportunity.

Their great migration was recorded in *The GC*, often thought of as the worst reality TV series ever made: tacky, mindless, strangely depressing. It followed the adventures of young Maori on the Gold Coast. But there was something sincere about it, something revealing. Its publicity drivel might have got it right when it treated murder as just one of those things that happen in between singing and a break-up: 'Jade Louise's debut single "Vibrations" shot to. No 1 on iTunesNZ. On a high, Jade Louise was quickly brought back down after the death of her son's father and then having to deal with the tumultuous end to her relationship with fellow cast member Tame …'

Thus the parable and the perils. The death referred to was the murder of showband entertainer and hospital orderly Tony Williams, who grew up in Matapihi in the Bay of Plenty, went to Mt Maunganui College, and took off for Surfers Paradise in about 1996. His battered body was found in his Mermaid Waters unit on

Christmas Eve 2011. He was 37 years old. He was very handsome, a tall, strapping guy, described as shy, charming, humble, into surfing and womanising.

Question to one of his friends, in court: 'He was a bit of a ladies' man, wasn't he?'

'Yep.'

'He wasn't inhibited by loyalty to any of his male friends, was he?'

'Other than sleeping with his friends' girlfriends, he's not too bad.'

He was exporting a tenet of New Zealand life to his new life on the Gold Coast: the extended family. He had a son to *GC* star Jade Louise, and a daughter to another woman, Shardai Kerr. His friends deny it, but he was also apparently the father of a son by a woman called Sarah Davies — it's what she told her boyfriend, ex-soldier Matt Cox. Cox heard quite a lot about Williams, but never met him until the day he paid a visit and cracked open Williams' skull with a hammer.

'We looked at the jealousy angle straightaway,' said Brisbane Detective Sergeant Steve McBryde, 'because of the brutality of what happened.' McBryde was the officer in charge of the investigation. I spoke with him at the Queensland Supreme Court. I had got there early on my first morning and found him in an office on the fifth floor. We talked about the murder inquiry, about Cox, about the moral of the story — about whether the story had a moral. 'It's just a sad, tragic tale,' he said. 'It's wrecked families. Tony's family, Cox's family. And Sarah's, too. One day her son will have to be told that his biological father was killed by his mother's boyfriend.'

2

The security guard at the courthouse said, 'I thought that's what they must be. Maoris. Yeah, they're here every day, mate. They take those seats over there. Usually about 20 of them. Every day! They bring their own esky.'

He meant Tony Williams' whanau, who came over for the trial. You looked at them and saw the mellow blue water and pale green hills of Matapihi, that small settlement on the Tauranga harbour. Sometimes they sat together in the courtroom, and sometimes they waited outside in the shade. They were there for justice, to see Cox put away for as long as possible; their grief and rage came off them in waves, and rebuffed all approaches. 'We will release a statement after the verdict in due course,' said a relative, who looked away when he spoke.

The jury found Cox guilty. The family statement read: 'Today we are grateful that Matthew Cox has been held responsible for murdering to death in a cruel and cowardly manner. We are grateful that the truth has been put forward and that Tony's name has been cleared back to the friendly brother, son and mostly loving father that he was.' It also expressed sympathy for Cox's parents, but added, 'However we cannot forgive. You are still able to visit your son every Xmas whether it be in jail, you still can!'

Cox, 27, looked afraid when I saw him in court. He had large dark eyes set in a pleasant, rather dim face. 'He's very articulate,' said McBryde. 'From a nice family. Normal people. No problems.' He'd been in the army until he busted his knee. He started a relationship with Sarah Davies in late September 2011. Williams was dead less than three months later.

It takes time for an obsession to feed on the brain, to take over. But Cox was quick to form a bond with her son ('They were really close,' said Davies), and fast, too, to spring into deranged action. When he confronted Davies with a bloodied shirt he had found shoved inside a plastic bag in the cupboard, she claimed she'd worn it on the night Williams had raped her — and got her pregnant. She said she kept it as a kind of talisman, or reminder, of a terrible time in her life. She'd never reported the rape to police. In fact, she remained on friendly terms with Williams on Facebook. Was the rape accusation a lie, an invention? As provocation, it worked wonders. She said in court, 'Matt was devastated and disgusted.'

They lived in Port Macquarie, in New South Wales. It took six hours to drive to Mermaid Waters, on the Gold Coast, where Williams lived. Cox got Williams' address by calling from a phone box and saying he worked for Australia Post. Then he called army buddy Joshua Middleton, and asked him to help case Williams' apartment building. As Middleton put it, 'Do a recce. Get a feel for the area.'

Cox mused to Middleton, 'Should I bash him? Put him in a wheelchair?'

Middleton: 'Do you have to do something so drastic?'

Cox: 'Yeah. Something's got to happen.'

Middleton, in court: 'He talked about that he might use a hammer.'

3

I visited Tony Williams' closest friend, Maori entertainer Paul Thompson, at his home in the Brisbane suburb of Sunnybank. His stage name was listed on his website as: 'The Wolfman'. I said, 'Hello, Wolfman.' He laughed, sheepishly. He was a softly spoken man, quite shy, and sad. 'He's heartbroken,' said his wife, Anita. There was red bougainvillea in the front yard, and a screen door at the top of the stairs. A dog howled, and Paul advised against walking back to the local shops at night: 'There was a shooting that way, another guy got shot over there …'

It was a happy household. Paul and Anita sat at the kitchen table and reminisced about Tony, and let their three children stay up in the lounge until the two girls fell asleep on couches, and their son dozed off on the floor. She'd made them mashed potato and sausages for dinner.

Paul had moved to the Gold Coast from Porirua in 1995. He'd sung in bands, and supported himself as a meatworker; Australia marked a new determination to live the dream and make a living from playing music. He met Tony a year later.

'He was a cheeky Maori boy with a little glint in his eye,' he said. 'He had a glow about him. He was quite shy. He talked in a mumble sometimes because of his shyness. But when he talked, it was almost as if he was determined to get to know who you really are, and connect with you. That was Bones all over.

'He had nothing to hide. He'd look you in the face when he talked to you. That's what I loved about Bones,' he said, using Williams' nickname again. 'If there's a word for better than best friends ... We were more than brothers.

'I'd ring him, and say, "Bro, come over! I've got food." Whenever he wanted to get away, or I wanted to get away, we'd be over at each other's houses. We knew what we both wanted, and that was peace. A peace that we didn't get anywhere else. Just knowing that he was there, my right-hand man ...'

He wept, and then he said, 'I'm all right.'

He talked about Tony's love of surfing, of his board painted in Rasta colours with a koru pattern. 'Surfing with his boys from Matapihi and Arataki. That's what he loved. He was proud of where he came from. Proud of his whanau. Loved his mum. He stayed true to his nature; Tauranga boy. He was wearing shorts and a singlet as when I first met him to the last.

'He loved the lifestyle here. Surf. Bikinis! I came over strictly for the music.' Paul formed a band, which really was called Chur Bro, and Tony became the soundman. He formed another group with Tony on vocals ('Bones had such a beautiful high falsetto'), and Kevin Keepa — three funky Maori guys who really did call their new band Sex and Chocolate.

They developed new moves, took on a new attitude, inspired by a movie based on the life and times of The Temptations.

'The band was started in March 1998, and the movie came out in August,' Paul said. 'That's when we started getting serious. It just connected to us. I got Tony over and we watched it every day for like a month. Every detail. We even learned word for word all the lines in the whole movie from start to finish. The dress, the hairstyle. Their mannerisms.'

It worked, and Sex and Chocolate became a smash live attraction at Surfers Paradise. 'Things just took off,' he said. 'It was amazing how fast it grew. We had people packing out our gigs. We literally did every club on the strip. Shooters, The Penthouse, Avenue, Bird and Bar, all four clubs adjacent to each other, and we played all four, daily, constantly.'

They were the good times. They made good money, they had each other, they were on top of their game. Paul met Anita; Tony met everyone. 'He was very honest about who he was,' said Anita. 'He didn't lie to any of the girls about the way he lived his life. He was very upfront, he never deceived anyone.'

What about their husbands and boyfriends?

Paul said, 'I did see his car damaged every now and then — a broken window, a FUCK YOU written on the windscreen. I'd say to him, "You crossed the wrong brother." It was a joke. It was also a warning. I knew someone might step him out and give him a punch on the jaw, knock his lights out, break an arm, poke an eye out, at the very, very worst. But you'd always laugh it off.'

4

Williams was killed in his apartment on Sunshine Boulevard at around midday on 23 December 2011. Less than two hours later, Cox texted his girlfriend: *I love you baby more than life itself and always will baby xoxo.*

Sarah Davies heard the news of the murder on Christmas Day. She was asked in court, 'Were you affected by Tony's death?'

She said, 'I was devastated.'

'Did Matthew Cox say anything about that?'

She said, 'After about a month it was frustrating him.'

'What did he say?'

She said, 'Basically, it was like, get over it.'

It took the police three months to make an arrest. Cox was careful; he hadn't left any DNA, and he got his army buddy Middleton to dispose of the murder weapon — a claw hammer. But he did leave something behind. It remains a mystery how it ever got there. It was a receipt for three dresses one of Davies' previous boyfriends had bought for her. She said in court, 'I'd planned on breaking up with him that day that I got the dresses, but I didn't have the heart to.'

Police tracked the receipt — a 'foreign object', as Detective Sergeant McBryde termed it — to her address. 'That put us in the right direction,' he said. Police next established that Cox was at the Gold Coast on the day of the murder. They were issued warrants to bug his phone, and listened in as Cox admitted to Davies' brother that he had killed Williams — in self-defence, he claimed.

He was arrested in March 2012. Middleton admitted his involvement later that day. The two men had once fantasised about working as mercenaries, in Thailand, where they would shut down illegal brothels and liberate girls forced to work as sex slaves. Heroes, men following a moral code, etc. In dismal reality, Cox gave Middleton his bloodstained clothes, Williams' brown wallet, and the hammer, and Middleton burned them with diesel in an army ration tin.

Cox never told police what happened or why it happened. He told a friend, 'I went there to fucking hit the bloke that knocked up my missus.' But he'd planned it very, very carefully, and the lengths he went to — the six-hour drive, casing the joint, posing as a postman — pointed towards something a lot more than a punch.

Detective Sergeant McBryde doesn't know for sure whether Cox took his own hammer to Williams' place and lay in wait, or whether he knocked on the door and used a hammer belonging to Williams. Before his arrest, Cox told Davies a version of what happened. She didn't go to the police. Why wasn't she charged?

'That's what Tony's family asked,' McBryde said.

'It's a good question,' I said.

'It is a good question,' he agreed. 'She did lie to the police. She did not disclose what Cox told her. But she only found out after Tony had been killed. She wasn't involved in the planning.'

According to Davies in court, this is Cox's version of the attack: 'He told me that Tony opened the door to him, and they shook hands, and then Matthew headbutted him. Tony threw a hammer at him and it missed and somewhere a screwdriver came into it. Tony had a screwdriver, and they ended up on the floor. Matthew was on his back, and he had Tony on top of him, and was fighting for his own life to stop the screwdriver stabbing him, and he remembered the hammer was behind him and reached for it, and swung up once, maybe twice.'

The prosecution told the jury that pretty much everything Cox had said was a lie. Williams was struck on the head and neck 27 times. There were a further 30 blows to the body. But some of what he said sounded accurate.

Davies was asked in court, 'How did he know that Tony had died?'

She said, 'Because he put a hammer through his skull.'

5

I asked 'Wolfman' Paul more about the glory days of Sex and Chocolate, and whether they had even bigger dreams. He said, 'Yeah! We were never satisfied. We wanted to reach higher and higher. We wanted to be in the movies and make the albums. We never reached that pinnacle; we were just under the bar. Just riding along under that bar for the whole journey. I think we possibly could have done it.'

The great ride eventually slowed down, and the band became part-time. Tony found work as an orderly at the Gold Coast Hospital. He made up a room in his Mermaid Waters unit for his two kids. 'They were his heart,' said Paul.

The bachelor pad with the guitars and the surfing pictures, and the kids' bedroom empty most of the week …This wasn't a cautionary tale of what happens when you chase a dream and the dream dies. The yellow brick road had nothing to do with it. This was just the road a man's life can take when none of his relationships work out. He had a raging argument on the morning of his death. The mother of one of his children dropped him home after they'd been Christmas shopping, and neighbours saw him jump on the car when it reversed down the driveway. He threw a stone at the car. It missed, and hit the neighbour's fence. 'You're not taking the presents!' he screamed. And then that term of abuse straight out of Aotearoa, the insult reaching back to his childhood and adolescence in Matapihi, the rallying cry of frustrated men the length of New Zealand: 'You can't do this to me, you fucken mole!'

Cox paid his visit not long after. That night, Paul Thompson went to the apartment. He was furious that Bones had missed their gig at a club.

'It was the first time that'd ever happened. So I went over and looked in the window. Pressed my nose against it. Couldn't see anything. I said, "Bones! Wake up! You in there?" I went to the front door. It was unlocked. All I had to do was turn the front door knob. I actually had my hand on the handle. I could have gone in …'

The body was found the next day by Kevin Keepa from Sex and Chocolate. A neighbour saw him approach the apartment. They were asked in court, 'What did he look like?'

'A New Zealand type of guy.'

'Do you mean Maori?'

'Like Maori, yeah.'

Keepa started screaming to his wife, 'Don't come in! Don't come in!' Emergency services were called, and then he phoned Paul. 'He was just screaming,' Paul said. 'He couldn't talk properly. You couldn't understand what he was saying. I was saying, "What? Did someone hurt Tony?"'

Rigor mortis had set in. There was blood, and vomit. A tap was running. Tony's guitars were still on their stands, but a Christmas tree had fallen over. There was a bubble-blowing toy on the floor, bought that day at Kmart. He'd also got bread and onions, probably to make stuffing for Christmas Day.

Keepa told the court that he knelt beside Tony, and prayed for him. He quit the band not long afterwards.

Paul said, 'I wish it'd been me who found Tony. I wish I'd just turned the handle and opened the door that night. But at the same time I'm thankful that it wasn't me. Because I don't know what kind of person I would be right now.'

It was getting late. Anita made another cup of tea. The three of us sat around the small table in the kitchen; their kids had fallen asleep, and Paul's eyes were red from crying. He said, 'After Tony died I didn't even want to think about music. I remember lying on the floor — this is about a year later — and thinking, "Everything's gone, the group's dead, Kevin's left, it's the end of it. What's the point without Bones?" And then Anita says, "Come on. Don't let it die." And slowly I started again. It was Tony's death that gave me a determination to keep the band going. It's given me more drive, more steel, more inspiration to continue this. Tony is written over everything we do.'

He brought in new musicians, and renamed the band Sex and Chocolate 2.0. They've become a popular live attraction, playing clubs, corporate events, weddings — in 2014, they were voted the best wedding entertainers in Queensland by the Australian Bridal Industry Academy.

Oh yes, he said, the story most definitely had a moral. It was to do with his best friend, that nice guy from the Bay of Plenty who was fiercely loved, who enjoyed his life, who lived the dream. He said, 'Bones came here for the good life. He wanted that dream. This is the place to do it. The Gold Coast. Dreams — they can happen here.'

Chapter 13

The Rotorua Three: Clint Rickards

TVNZ creamed TV3 with the story.

— Phil Kitchin, *Louise Nicholas: My Story*

1

We met a week after Queen's Birthday 2015 at a café around the corner from where I live in Te Atatu. It was good to see him again. I had stayed in touch with Clint Rickards after the Auckland High Court trials of 2006 and 2007, when Louise Nicholas and then another woman accused him of taking part in a horrifying pack-rape with two other brutes, all policemen. The women said that they were violated with scarcely believable instruments of pain — a police baton, and a whiskey bottle. Two juries found the accusations scarcely believable. Rickards, then a figure of supreme authority as assistant commissioner of police and Auckland district commander, was found not guilty of all charges. Of course his life was ruined by the scandal, and he was forced out of the police. We'd meet every now and then at a café in Pt Chevalier frequented by the mentally ill, shambling outpatients from a nearby drug rehab clinic, and a nice old dear who topped up her tea with gin. It was my local and

I liked it there, but I had another reason for choosing the venue to catch up with Rickards: it was clandestine. I wasn't ashamed to be seen with him, but I was wary of someone recognising him and wanting to cause a scene. Rickards didn't exactly travel incognito. He was massive, and distinctive with his shaved head and deep-set eyes. When I emailed to meet, he replied: *Yep just not at that crap café.*

In 2015, Louise Nicholas was made an Officer of the New Zealand Order of Merit in the Queen's Birthday honours list, named Anzac of the Year, and gave a speech at the parade grounds of the Royal New Zealand Police College to the 36 new police officers who graduated from the Louise Nicholas Recruit Wing. She said to media of the Queen's Birthday gong: 'For all the bad crap that's gone on, so much good has come from it.' Human Rights Commissioner Jackie Blue congratulated Nicholas on her Anzac award in a press release: 'All of us are indebted to Louise's staggering courage and refusal to accept injustice.' Governor-General Jerry Mateparae presented the Anzac award, and read from a prepared statement: 'Louise's personal experience of harm and trauma has resulted in an ongoing commitment to help victims of sexual assault and to enable affirmative cultural change.' Constable Shaun Murphy, one of the new police graduates, told reporters of the high regard they held for their patron: 'She's inspirational and has told us to always put the needs of the victims at the heart of what we do.'

Rickards said at the Te Atatu café: 'She'll be made a Dame one day. Telling you now.' He's probably right, and he said it in all due seriousness with a laugh and a shrug. He was a lot less bitter than the last time we spoke, a lot more relaxed. The second we walked inside, a man called out, 'Clint! How's it going, mate?' He was on the board of the Waipareira Trust, which employed Rickards after he was acquitted. Rickards now works as a lawyer. He studied for his degree at Auckland University, and was admitted into the bar at a ceremony held at the Auckland High Court, which he had experienced during his own trials as a circle of hell. He practised criminal law; I'd read the manuscript of his unpublished memoir, which included his account of an unexpected approach: 'I get all sorts ringing me asking for help. One of the most bizarre, and least deserving, was Samurai sword madman Antonie Dixon, who called from prison, wanting to give me $20K for reviewing his file, just so he could get a "police perspective". He was dead two weeks later.'

He worked on Treaty settlements for five years. But the main claims were settled, and he returned to criminal defence work to make ends meet. It was the usual rats-and-mice stuff — assault, burglary, traffic offences — but he stepped away from sexual offences for obvious reasons. In April 2015, one of his clients made the news — a 21-year-old Pacific Islander was accused of beating up a police officer. Rickards said he liked the work, although it didn't pay much. He had begun a PhD, partly as an intellectual challenge, and also to set himself up in Treaty settlement policy work.

I asked after his wife and children. They were good. I asked after Brad Shipton and Bob Schollum, the former cops who were his co-accused in the two trials. Both men were convicted of pack-rape in a separate trial ('You were confident you could commit a serious crime and get away with it because you were policemen,' said the judge) and jailed for a few years. He never really knew Schollum that well, and they'd lost touch. He remained friends with Shipton; they were young cops together, and supported each other emotionally when they attended fatalities. He visited Shipton in Tauranga once or twice a year. The last time he saw him, Shipton's phone had sounded, instructing him to take his daily walk around the mountain at Mt Maunganui. He took off without another word. Shipton was going downhill with early-onset dementia. Maybe it wasn't such a bad thing. Why would he want to remember anything from the past 10 years?

I liked Rickards. I liked the way his mind worked, his sense of humour, his zest for life. True, he took leave of his senses and his poise whenever he talked about Nicholas and the trials; like all obsessives, he talked too fast and too much; like Guy Hallwright, he failed to recognise one of the golden rules of the New Zealand moral code — he never took responsibility for his own behaviour or acknowledged that at the very least he showed poor judgment. But the fact remains that he was acquitted of all charges by two juries, who reached their own conclusions even though both trials were conducted in an atmosphere of public loathing which resembled hysteria; it didn't seem much of a stretch to treat him like a human being.

'Evil monster', Nicholas called him, when I interviewed her a year after the trial. It was at a secluded house in the Hawke's Bay in winter. She glared into the fireplace. She was small and wounded, biting on her Holiday cigarettes and burning her throat with rum and Coke. But she remained determined to have her story believed. Nicholas had taken the unusual decision as a rape complainant to waive her right to name suppression; she used her name and subsequent fame to campaign on behalf of rape 'survivors' — a stronger, more hopeful term than 'victims'. And so began her work as a 'national survivor advocate' for Rape Prevention Education, and her position on the executive committee of Te Ohaakii a Hine — National Network Ending Sexual Violence Together. She will have helped countless people. *For all the bad crap that's gone on, so much good has come from it.*

But was it based on a falsehood? None of her complaints were ever upheld. There was insufficient evidence to convict. Enough, apparently, to accuse. Nicholas's version of events has been accepted by the wider public as the truth. Rickards never stood a chance. He said, 'As soon as the shit hit the fan, the police buried me.' He had served for 28 years and stood a good chance of being made police commissioner. It didn't count for anything. He was suspended the day that Nicholas's accusations were made public. The last time he wore his police uniform — with pride, and also with maximum theatrical impact — was when he turned up to the High Court on the first day of his trial.

2

It caused a sensation. He looked incredible, a hulk in tight-fitting blue (he'd lost 20 kilograms to make a good impression on the jury), with the line of his mouth set firm. 'Not guilty,' he yelled in answer to the charges. Then he took his place alongside fat Shipton and small Schollum, those two mad rooters of old, 49 and 54, respectively, in 2006, who seemed to regard their past engagements in threesome sex as a kind of hobby. Rickards, too, said in court that he was into it. And that was the core of the trial — the casual depravity of threesomes, or 'swapsies', as Nicholas called it. Rickards' lawyer came up with a delicate euphemism: he described it as 'a joint venture'. Whatever, it was debauched, and it drew a crowd. The trial was packed every day for three weeks. There was a tipsy character in a Hawaiian shirt, who took along a red canvas bag clinking with bottles of Japanese plum wine, and there was a crazy lady who got nabbed gossiping about the case to a juror in the court café — she got hauled into the cells for contempt.

It was a gruelling, sordid three weeks. Police laid 20 charges against the three defendants. Nicholas alleged that Rickards and Shipton had showed up uninvited to her 54 Corlett Street flat in Rotorua in 1985–86 on maybe a dozen occasions and abused her in the usual choreographies of group sex. She further claimed that they were joined by Schollum one summer's afternoon at 36 Rutland Street — the nice term used in court for what she said happened was 'the Rutland Street incident'. The actual description she gave was that she was vaginally and anally abused with a police baton. The three defendants denied the use of a baton, and said sex with Nicholas was always consensual. Rickards said he had never met Nicholas at the Rutland Street address.

It subverted the usual innocent image of Rotorua (the smell of sulphur, the glow of neon) and remade it as a kind of Sodom and Gomorrah, with the emphasis on Sodom. The 1980s setting as described by witnesses — rattling old Triumphs and Vauxhalls, drinks at the Cobb & Co bar — evoked that grim period in New Zealand society after the Springbok tour and right at the time that Rogernomics was gaily creating a new underclass.

Justice Tony Randerson began proceedings by instructing the media: 'For the sake of clarity I order that the use of the expression "pack-rape" is prohibited.' Three weeks later, after the verdicts, he had the last word on the pack-rape trial. 'This trial was relatively straightforward,' he said, 'but complicated by outside events swirling around in the world.' He meant the attention, the outrage, the moral climate. Inside the sealed world of Courtroom 12, criminal law was practised at an exceptional standard.

John Haigh QC acted for Rickards. He was tall, grave, lugubrious. He led the defence team, and imposed his intelligence on proceedings. His oratory was compelling. But the star performer was actually Schollum's lawyer, Paul Mabey QC. The only equivocal thing about him was his name. A small, discreet man who made you think of Le Carré's favourite spy, George Smiley, Mabey was meticulous and devastating in cross-examination. Nicholas hated him, as well as Haigh. She said of them when I interviewed her that afternoon by the fire in the Hawke's Bay: 'Nasty bastards. There was no need to be so brutal. They can burn in hell for all I care.' But they were defending their clients, who had been accused of heinous crimes.

Christchurch solicitor Brent Stanaway appeared for the Crown. An aristocratic fellow who walked with a very high step, Stanaway was dressed so fine in a suit tailored from a bolt of beautiful French fabric — black, with a very light red polka-dot. He came across as arch and rather louche, and was no match for Haigh and Mabey. Or Rickards: his cross-examination was poor. They'd once worked together when Rickards was working undercover in Invercargill. Stanaway put it to Rickards that he'd learned to become a 'practised liar' as an undercover cop. But this was absurd. Rickards pointed out that he'd very often given evidence to Stanaway when they worked together on prosecuting drug dealers, and his word had been good enough for him then.

The lawyers framed the narrative, gave it shape. But the most important people in Courtroom 12 were the accused, and their accuser. Louise Nicholas gave evidence on day two of the trial.

3

She didn't look well. She didn't look at all well. She was small, narrow, thin; she looked starved. She later told me that she lived on coffee and cigarettes during the trial.

The judge removed the public, and blinds were put over the courtroom window.

She began by telling Stanaway about her early life in Murupara, and moving to Rotorua as a teenager. She got a job at the BNZ, and found a flat. She talked about buying a bedroom suite on HP from Smith & Brown, playing indoor cricket with the BNZ social team, forking out her share of the $130 weekly rent. A normal life; until one night after work she went to the police bar with friends, and met Shipton.

They talked. She was just his type: she had a pulse. Shipton and Rickards, she said, began coming to her house uninvited.

She said, 'The reason they were coming round was for sex. My heart would just drop. I didn't want them there. I said, "I don't want you to do this." Never at any stage did I consent to anything.'

Stanaway asked, 'What happened?'

She said, 'They would start by undressing me, normally the bottom half, then theirs. They'd put me on the floor on my back. Shipton would hop on first. Rickards would put his penis in my mouth. And they'd swap, or put me in other positions like on all fours. That's just what happened and there was nothing I could do about it.'

Shipton arrived once on his own. Stanaway asked, 'What happened?'

She said, 'It was in the lounge. It was just sex. Sex.' The word sounded flat, emptied out.

Stanaway asked, 'When did these visits occur?'

'When I was off work or sick.'

'Was that pre-arranged?'

'No.'

'How did they know you were home?'

Nicholas said, 'I wouldn't have a clue.' Neither did anyone else.

4

And then she told her harrowing story about 'the Rutland Street incident'. It was listened to in utter silence.

'It was a lovely, hot day in January,' she began. She was wearing the white muslin dress her boyfriend, Ross — later her husband — had bought her that summer in Whangamata. She was walking home from work. Schollum drove by, and offered her a lift home. Instead, he took her to a red-brick house at the end of the cul de sac in Rutland Street. She recognised Shipton and Rickards on the balcony. She said, 'I had grave reservations.'

They went inside. She said she was led into a bedroom. 'I kept saying, "I don't want to do this."'

Stanaway asked, 'What happened?'

What she said happened came out in a long anguished moan sans punctuation, and it sounded like this: 'Schollum laid me on the bed on my back and got on top of me and had sexual intercourse with me and while that was happening Rickards is on my left and he's naked and he puts his penis in my mouth and this went on for some time and then Schollum got off and licked my vagina while I'm still giving Rickards oral sex and then he moved away and then Shipton got on and then Schollum turned up and took Rickards' place and it seemed like it was going on forever and then it was all finished and then I saw Shipton with this police baton in one hand and Vaseline in the other and I said no fucking way mate no fucking way and I'm moving back I can't go any further I'm up against the bedroom wall and he had this dirty smirk on his face and then I was on all fours and then he …'

When she finished her story, collapsing into sobs, Justice Tony Randerson adjourned the court for 15 minutes. I went outside for a cigarette. People who didn't smoke went out for a cigarette. No one talked.

5

Back in court, evidence was read from Nicholas's ex-flatmate. She was 17 when they lived together; Nicholas, 18. She said, 'Louise was a really happy, fun person, and was really pretty.'

The woman said Shipton and Schollum ('Brad and Bob') would visit, usually in the evenings, and have sex with her and Nicholas. She thought she possibly had sex with Rickards as well, but couldn't remember. She said, 'There was always a friendly atmosphere. I don't ever recall Louise being upset or her demeanour changing.'

In her statement to police, she said, 'I recall a time in Louise's room when she was having sex with one of them. I was in a room with one of the others — she certainly wasn't saying no.'

She thought there were three or four visits. She said, 'I was partly in awe of them, and slightly intimidated … I'm not sure why I participated. It was a case of it being easier to go along with it than resist it. I can see now all they came around for was sex. I didn't see that at the time … I wasn't forced into anything, and neither was Louise.'

Half of the prosecution's case — the rape accusations against Rickards and Shipton in the Corlett Street flat — was probably lost then and there. In cross-examination, Haigh asked Nicholas to explain the 'vast discrepancy' in the versions of events told by her and her flatmate.

She said, 'There's no discrepancy. That's her recollection. It's not mine ... I've always stated she was not there when these men called.'

Haigh said, 'Well, I suggest her recollection is correct, and yours is contrived.'

'I do not accept that at all.'

'Have you deliberately set out to destroy Assistant Commissioner Rickards?'

'I've come out and told the truth.'

'I suggest you've enjoyed the media attention in an extraordinary way.'

'That isn't right,' she said. 'I was given an opportunity to tell my story. I didn't instigate it. I was approached about the police investigation. It made me definitely think I had been duped something shocking. It's why I went to the media.'

Haigh allowed a pause, and then said, 'Repeatedly.'

6

Why would she lie? Who would want to go through the whole ordeal, putting their own name out there when they had the option of suppressing it, and make false accusations? What could possibly motivate someone to do something so wicked and harmful and weird? The accepted notion is that Nicholas came forward because she was telling the truth. She was brave. She had endured appalling treatment, and found the courage to bring 'evil monsters' to account. It's possibly the correct version as well, but in court, at the actual trial, she was held up as a damaged soul who was a stranger to the truth.

'She has told a series of calculated lies,' Haigh said to the jury. 'All her evidence is made-up, delusional, utterly false. If it wasn't so tragically serious, one might almost regard it as laughable.'

He said she was in it for the attention, the intoxicating rush of publicity. He said she was a serial accuser; along with Rickards, Shipton and Schollum, she had accused a policeman in Murupara of raping her when she was 13, and three other officers stationed there as well. Much was made of her alleged comment to a schoolteacher that she had also been raped by a group of Maori horsemen. Nicholas denied she ever said it, that it was rubbish. Haigh dared to have fun with that one, timing his pauses to create black comedy. He said to her, 'You also made allegations that five Maori on horseback raped you. After they had presumably dismounted.'

The defence also introduced a witness who said Nicholas had flirted with Schollum years afterwards, at a wedding: 'She lifted up her skirt and showed him the top of her lacy stocking. Quite a way up the thigh.' Nicholas denied it ever happened, that it was rubbish. Mabey asked her about a statement she had given to police about having sex with Schollum — long after the alleged abuse with the baton. 'I must have said it. I signed the statement,' she said in cross-examination. 'But I do not recall it.'

Her credibility was further questioned over claims that she remembered what happened with Rickards, Shipton and Schollum only after counselling sessions led to the phenomenon or gobbledegook of 'recovered memory'. She denied that was the case. 'I didn't have to dredge up what happened,' Nicholas said. 'It happened.'

The most damaging challenge to her story was the statement from her ex-flatmate. Bafflingly, her written evidence — she lived in Australia, and didn't come to the trial in person — was introduced by the prosecution. In essence, though, she was star witness for the defence. After the trial, Nicholas and journalist Phil Kitchin secretly tape-recorded the flatmate at her home in Australia. The woman told a different story. Her recollection was a lot more vague. Kitchin writes in *Louise Nicholas: My Story*, 'She was so flakey, so unreliable that her evidence should have never been allowed in court.' Nicholas writes in their book, 'There was something at work deep down in her life that wouldn't let her tell the truth. What had those bastards done to her?' The answer might be: nothing.

In court, the defence seized on the woman's cheerful, breezy account of early evening threesomes. 'It puts paid to the dark, forbidding atmosphere that Mrs Nicholas has described,' Haigh said. 'People obviously did go in for that sort of thing. People's sexual preferences are startlingly broad.' Startlingly, too, a witness later came forward to say that she had willingly engaged in having a police baton used on her during threesomes with Shipton and Schollum. Her evidence was suppressed during the trial. The journalists weren't allowed to write anything; we sat there and stared at the woman as she shared the intimate details of her enjoyment of a sex toy varnished deep red and measuring 30 centimetres.

A story in *The New Zealand Herald* one morning announced that Rickards was about to take the witness stand. It had the impact of an advertisement. There was standing room only in Courtroom 12. Crowded around the door was a visitor from Brisbane who wore a Lycra bicycling outfit, and a man who used the adjournments to consult his racing guide for the field at Avondale.

Rickards gave his version of events. His face was held together with rage and hate. He said he had sex with Nicholas on two occasions. 'There was laughing and giggling.' He told the court five times, 'It was a happy, jovial occasion.' He said it without a trace of happiness or joviality. That same tone was heard when he said Nicholas was 'lying', was a 'liar', told 'lies', had 'lied'; by my count, he said those words 29 times.

Rickards writes about having sex with Nicholas in his unpublished memoir. Again, he strips it of pleasure. The first time: 'Apart from the fact that Brad came in and watched us, there was nothing out of the ordinary about the sexual act. If at any time she had indicated that she did not wish to continue, I would have stopped. She didn't. After we finished, we spoke to Brad, and a short time later Brad and Nicholas had sex, and I watched them.' The second time: 'She had phoned Brad again and we drove to her place in the early evening. Brad had met her [flatmate], and she had phoned because the friend liked him, and wanted to get to know him better ... Brad and the woman soon left the room, and Nicholas ... gave me oral sex. Afterwards, we chatted away, and a short time later Brad and the flatmate returned. I got on well with her and ended up in a room with her, where we had sex. That's it.'

In 1986, two police officers, aged 24 and 27, met up after work with an 18-year-old secretary at the Bank of New Zealand, and had sex with her. Their visit was brief, less than an hour. When Rickards and Shipton walked through the door that day, they never really left.

7

The wait for the verdict was long and unbearable. The jury deliberated for 74 hours and 55 minutes, three days and two nights, scoffing filled rolls from Pandoro bakery for lunch, and served two evening meals at the Hyatt — would it be the roasted whole prime rack of lamb with pistachio crust, or the beef and shiraz pie with confit shallots?

Co-prosecutor Mark Zarifeh broke out in a terrible red rash. His face looked bad, very bad. John Haigh could be found nursing a whiskey at the Hyatt's bar. Louise Nicholas could be seen on the balcony of a hotel overlooking the High Court, fagging it up on her Holiday cigarettes, usually alongside journalist Phil Kitchin, who had got her to this point — it was Kitchin who got the whole thing rolling, when he found documents suggesting that a senior officer had covered up Nicholas's original police complaint about Rickards, Shipton, and Schollum. He showed them to her at her house. She was shocked, and decided to go public with her accusation. Kitchin's amazing story — unusually, he shared his exclusive with *The Dominion-Post* and TVNZ — remains one of the greatest and most far-reaching scoops in the history of New Zealand journalism. It led to police inquiry Operation Austin, as well as to the Commission of Inquiry into Police Conduct. It led to the Nicholas trial. It led to the two of them awaiting the verdict. Kitchin had long ago given up on boring codes of detachment and objectivity; he believed in Nicholas, and they'd become close friends. It was at Kitchin's adobe house in a Hawke's Bay valley where I'd interviewed Nicholas. That was an uncomfortable, stifling afternoon. Kitchin's wife was there, and Nicholas brought a friend. The four of them were like some kind of cult — the cult of Nicholas, held together by faith in her story.

When the clouds of smoke parted, Kitchin and Nicholas looked anxious on the hotel balcony. In their book, Kitchin wrote that he doubted they'd get a guilty verdict for the Corlett Street charges, but was hopeful the jury would convict the three men for 'the Rutland Street incident'.

Rickards, Shipton and Schollum waited it out downstairs in the cells. Shipton read the seventeenth-century poem by Richard Lovelace that famously and foolishly begins, 'Stone walls do not a prison make, / Nor iron bars a cage.' But that's exactly what the walls and bars make. That's the point of that particular architecture. Rickards swung between fear and loathing. His blackest rage was for the cop who alerted Kitchin to the story in the first place. Kitchin writes in the introduction of his book: 'I'd like to pay tribute to my anonymous police sources.' In his manuscript Rickards writes of 'Kitchin's spies, including a couple of jaundiced officers who had it in for me … [and were] willing to lie just to take me down'. He blames one particular officer. Rickards was his boss. He gave the cop a poor performance rating, and marked him with a score of two, meaning average. The officer insisted that Rickards give him a score of three, which would have qualified him for a pay rise.

Rickards refused. His working title for his manuscript is 'But For Three'.

The wives of the three defendants formed a tight bond of silence as they waited outside Courtroom 12. Tania Rickards walked with her head held high. Karen Schollum was small and contained. Sharon Shipton wore hooped ear-rings, and walked with her bouffant hair held high; you could imagine her, before the agony of the charges, as someone expressive and funny and big-hearted, the life of the party. The problem was that you also imagined her husband rooting someone at the party. Shipton was the numbers man. Shipton, always Shipton, at every threesome; Shipton, saying he watched while Rickards had sex with Nicholas in Corlett Street, saying he and Schollum had sex with her at another address, saying he never had sex with her 'on a one-to-one basis'; Shipton, who gave Nicholas's flatmate 'the creeps', but was 'persistent'.

Shipton, always rooting or talking about rooting. From his police interview, read out in court: 'I put it to Louise a threesome would be good for her … My sexual encounters with Louise have always been group sex. Me and Bob, or me and Clint … She openly expressed her sexuality … I believe she had sex with other officers. She frequented the police canteen, and Cobb & Co, where police drank. She was one of those girls …' He talked and talked and talked; he couldn't shut up; the interview lasted three hours. Asked why he thought Nicholas 'thoroughly enjoyed' their sexual encounters, he said: 'It's the same as when you have sex with your wife. The vibes, the reaction you're getting.' God almighty. Shipton, the priapic blowhard; Shipton, raving about 'vibes' as he equated his conquest of a teenage secretary with sex in the marital bed.

No one other than family was particularly concerned about the lecherous fatty's fate. In any case, Shipton and Schollum were already in jail for their part in the sickening pack-rape of a girl in Mt Maunganui. But Rickards still had his freedom at stake. Haigh had tried to get Rickards a separate trial, to distance his client from the two co-accused jailbirds. He'd also applied to have it heard in Rotorua. He was happy with Auckland as the choice; the city he wanted to avoid was disapproving Wellington.

I joined Haigh now and then for a lunchtime drink during the long wait. He was always warm, lively company, and his death in 2012 at the age of 65 was felt with enormous sadness throughout Auckland's legal profession. A thousand people packed Holy Trinity Cathedral for his funeral. Rickards was among the mourners; he knew he owed Haigh his liberty. When the charges were laid, he called Crown prosecutor Simon Moore to ask who he recommended he should engage. Moore suggested Paul Davison, John Billington, and Haigh. Part of the reason Rickards chose Haigh was because of his speciality as an employment lawyer: at that stage, Rickards wanted to fight for his job. By the time of the trial, he just wanted to stay out of jail.

As soon as the jury retired, the extended Rickards family moved into the courthouse, and it became a Maori thing. There was a sad, mournful prayer in te reo on the first night. But radio broadcaster Willie Jackson turned up the next day in support, and introduced a boisterousness, dispensing wisecracks and good humour. At midday on the Friday, two hours before the verdict, a boil-up in a pot was brought in, along with loaves of Tip-Top bread, paper plates, and a bag of apples. I may be indulging in racist misremembering, but I'm pretty sure someone strummed on a guitar.

All day the tension had swelled, raised itself to boiling point; something had to break. It broke at quarter to three on Friday afternoon when word finally came through that the jury had reached its verdict. Lawyers, defendants, press, court staff and the public were herded into the courtroom. It was filled to capacity. Five minutes passed in complete silence. A silence that long picks up everything around it — hope, fear, anguish, dread. And then the jury came in. The foreperson was a young woman. She read out their 20 unanimous verdicts.

Nicholas fled the court. The three defendants wept for joy. They probably thought it was the last they would ever see of her.

8

To the victor, the spoils. Five days after the verdict, John Haigh could be found loping along the quiet waterfront streets of Picton, and was a picture of health and happiness. He was on holiday with his wife, Sue. 'Let's drive to Mapua this afternoon, Johnny,' she said.

I sat down with him on the shore and we talked about his life and career for a while. I was particularly interested that he was the son of 'Fighting Frank' Haigh, a legendary lawyer of high principle and socialist conviction, who represented the watersiders' union in the 1951 waterfront strike: 'My mother remembers other lawyers refusing to have anything to do with him, or her.'

He remembered that his father took him on a protest march in Queen Street in 1960, in the 'No Maoris, No Tour' Springbok protest. He said: 'I don't have the courage he had.'

His father was 48 when Haigh was born. Were they close? 'He wasn't a great family man. He was focused on the bigger issues. He worked virtually every night, and about 48, 50 weekends every year. He didn't want me to go into law at all. Dead against it. Because he knew what it took out of him, I think.'

But he did go into law; was part of that wanting his father's approval and respect? John replied, 'There's always a desire to please … I wish he'd been alive when I was made a silk.'

And it had come to this: the son defending a policeman charged with raping a young, vulnerable woman. It seemed more likely that his father — champion of the underdog, who waged war on social injustice — would have wanted to represent Nicholas. I asked Haigh the old chestnut about whether he thought his client was innocent.

He said, 'First of all, I don't allow myself the indulgence of determining whether clients are innocent or guilty. Some lawyers do. I don't. I think it removes the necessary detachment. But after we received the majority of police disclosure, I formed the view that he had not committed the offences as charged at all.'

The jury hadn't been told that the co-accused were already in prison or that the three of them would face another rape trial. A group of women who supported Nicholas threatened to make it public. Haigh said, 'They were acting out of ignorance, because they're saying that somehow the truth eluded the jury. That's a fallacy. The jury knew everything that was relative to this trial.'

The police gave it their best shot, he said, but they simply came up short. The accusations didn't stack up. 'The size of the investigation, the resources they put into it ... I can't think of anything that might have equalled it. Well, maybe that tragedy here in the Marlborough Sounds,' he said. We looked out to the deep, green water, where Ben Smart and Olivia Hope had been murdered.

9

The standard happy male fantasy of a threesome is one man, two women. Rickards, Shipton and Schollum acted out another fantasy, travelling in pairs, in pursuit of the mathematic of one woman, two of them. To see them a year after the Nicholas trial, once again sitting in the dock at the Auckland High Court, once again defending charges of sexual offending, was to realise that they were the threesome that endured, that stuck together.

The second trial was a kind of reunion. The three defendants were accused of kidnapping and indecently assaulting a woman, once again in Rotorua, in the 1980s. The same themes of power and sex and abuse, the same denials.

The same lawyers. Brent Stanaway modelled his latest range of groovy ties. John Haigh carried his familiar gloomy air of a man about to attend or more likely conduct a funeral. Paul Mabey had once again climbed into his snug little QC jacket of many buttons, and once again performed his slow, assured, precise craft in cross-examination — it was to his questioning that the woman said, 'I know poor Louise Nicholas lost her case and I am trying damn hard to make sure these guys get done.' The prosecution case wasn't entirely lost then and there, but perhaps it never really recovered.

She said she met Shipton at Cobb & Co. She was 16 and had just left school. She fell in love. She said they would go driving in his car, park up at Sulphur Point, and have sex. But Shipton must have felt lonely, because he soon began asking her to have sex with him and Schollum.

She said she went to visit Shipton at a house one day. She said other cops were drinking in the lounge, passing around whiskey, and Shipton suggested they all go into the bedroom where they would pass her around. No, she said. She said Shipton picked her up and took her into the bedroom where they had group sex, and Shipton — Shipton, always Shipton — assaulted her with what she thought was a whiskey bottle.

Shipton and Schollum gave statements to the police saying that they had had sex with the woman, but that the assault didn't happen. As for Rickards, his defence was simple: he'd no idea who the woman was, had never even heard of her, had never seen or met her until she arrived in court.

In any case, Haigh told the jury, Rickards' leg was in plaster during the time she claimed the offences took place. As hard evidence, that was the leg he had to stand on.

There were other discrepancies, other gaps in the story, and the prosecution's case fizzled out. Shipton and Schollum were free to go back to jail. Rickards was free to go, and to at least try to obey one of the golden rules of the New Zealand way of life — once something is finished, move on.

10

He had and he hadn't, but mostly he basically had. 'Life just sucks sometimes,' he said at the Te Atatu café. 'That's all I can take from what happened.'

He ordered hot chocolate. A toddler waddled past, and gave Rickards a toothless grin. He wiggled his fingers at the little boy, and gave him a lovely smile. He said he still wanted to do something about getting his memoir published. I advised against it. I said he could probably do without the grief. He said he didn't expect it would change anyone's mind about him.

Wasn't he just as inflexible in his own thinking? He wrote in his manuscript: 'Phil Kitchin needs to be held to account, NZ Police need to be held to account, and, more importantly, Louise Nicholas needs to be held to account.' His book details why. But it doesn't hold himself to account. Surely his own behaviour led to his downfall? As Heather Henare from Women's Refuge said after the Nicholas trial, 'As a police officer he and his colleagues took advantage of a young woman in a situation that was beyond her control.' Also, engaging in threesome sex with another cop was never going to be a smart career move; as an ambitious young detective wanting promotion to positions of trust, he must have been aware that he was playing with fire.

Strangely, it didn't occur to me to give him a stern lecture on issues of morality when we met. In fact, the above lines — about his behaviour, playing with fire, etc. — wasn't even what I thought. They were said to me a few days after I met Rickards by another journalist who had covered the Nicholas trial. My own thinking didn't stretch that far; I was more taken with the notion that Rickards had kind of gone rogue after his early experience as an undercover cop. He got assigned to Invercargill at 19. He writes excitingly about those 14 months: 'drinking with the lowest of the low — freezing workers, shearers, pub bouncers and gamblers — in fleapit clubs and hotels all over Southland'. Throughout, he experienced the intensity of living a double life, the constant adrenalin of being discovered. Maybe it was something he craved when he returned to Rotorua. He was never debriefed; he said he came out a changed person, someone a lot less conservative.

We talked a bit about that at the café. We talked for two and a half hours, and inevitably a lot of it was about various aspects of the trials, of the past. I asked him how close he thought he came to being appointed commissioner of police. He said it was always going to be a political decision, and it was possible that he'd have been passed over. But he really wanted the job. He talked with enthusiasm and vigour about the community and grassroots policing methods he had wanted to introduce.

While he talked, I thought about how he and Nicholas actually had a lot in common. Rickards wanted to make things better for people; so did Nicholas. Rickards as a defence lawyer and Nicholas in her various roles were both concerned with matters of justice, with standing up for the vulnerable. They were of the same generation, the same background — both left school early, both came from working-class families in the same North Island catchment. They were both fighters who stood their ground, were staunch, resolute.

Rickards' manuscript, and the book by Nicholas and Kitchin, were both artless tirades. Rickards writes about his feelings after the second trial, and why he wanted to get his side of the story across: 'Like a dog kicked into submission, I had become pliant, begun to lose my bite. But as I cogitated on the hell I had been through, I realised that getting angry wasn't the way to get even. Only the truth would put the magic salve over that festering sore.' Nicholas writes about her feelings after the second trial, and why she wanted to get her side of the story across: 'I needed the New Zealand public to stop taking as gospel what they were reading in the newspapers or hearing on TV.' Mission accomplished: the New Zealand public now believe the gospel according to Nicholas.

The three men were found not guilty, but almost no one regards them as innocent. 'Punishment comes in all forms,' Nicholas said with terrific piousness to a women's magazine in 2014, 'and they're judged every day.' Schollum reportedly had cancer. Shipton had gone ga-ga. Clint Rickards finished his hot chocolate at the café in Te Atatu, and the waitress asked whether he wanted something else. He ordered green tea.

Chapter 14

The killings at Stilwell Road: Chris Wang

Music and food, and also I saw somebody is riding the horse.
— Chinese witness describing a party given by Chis Wang on his rural property

1

The first person I ever met who had been accused of butchering two people with a blade was Cheng Qi 'Chris' Wang, a small, lithe fellow with a shrewd face and thinning hair. I had an appointment. I went around to his house. It was gated. An old Chinese lady was pottering about in the front garden. I called out to her: 'Hello! Is Chris home?'

She said, 'What you want?'

I yelled, 'I'm here to see Chris!'

She said, 'No English!'

She fled indoors. I hung around on the pavement and Wang eventually drove up and invited me inside. He had a kind of manservant who poured cups of tea. We sat at either end of a very long dining table in a dark kitchen with small windows. When the sun went behind a cloud, I could barely see him. He was 53 then, and the last time I saw him he had just turned 56. It had been a curious three years, and it ended when a jury in the Auckland High Court reached a curious verdict in his double-murder trial. He was accused of stabbing two men to death on a summer's morning in the expensive Auckland suburb of Mt Albert. It was his third trial. The first was abandoned very late in the piece. The jury was already down to 11 — a juror realised she had been treated by the police doctor who gave evidence, and had to be excused — when the prosecution called its last witness, a cheerful pathologist from Vermont.

He was asked, 'Did you identify a large number of stab wounds?'

'Yes,' smiled the American.

'Did they in fact total 23?'

'Yes.'

He went on to explain that to accurately measure the length of a wound, you press the edges of the skin together; skin has tremendous elasticity. The jury stared at him, and bent their heads to study a death booklet — images from the autopsy, pale bodies on a white sheet. One of the two dead men had his eyes open. An afternoon tea break was called. Suddenly, the jury was reduced to 10 — an ambulance shrieked to the side entrance of the High Court, and a juror was taken to hospital for emergency surgery on a ruptured bowel.

Court resumed for the judge to announce that it was all over. Wang was free to go. As he made his way past the press bench, I handed him my card — with both hands, something I'd seen in Japan, and thought might convey to Wang, who was born in China, that I was a polite and respectful fellow. He took the card, and bowed. He phoned the next day and I went over for a memorable afternoon.

The second trial went the whole way. And then it got nowhere: the jury was unable to deliver a verdict. They had signalled to the judge that they were 'very close' to reaching a majority verdict of 11–1, but couldn't go any further. It was assumed there were two obstinate jurors. Had they prevented a verdict of guilty? Family of the victims wept bitter tears.

The third trial was held a year later, over three weeks in the middle of winter. It was a kind of re-enactment: the same evidence, most of the same witnesses. It was in a different courtroom, upstairs in Courtroom 14, with views of the museum through the window. Three weeks of rain, and storms; on the opening day of the trial, a bottle of Landscape merlot had been smashed on the front steps, and broken glass lay among wet leaves.

Jury selection, held downstairs next to the criminal office with its soft toys and All Black flags, resulted in a woman foreperson. She wore confident outfits. There was the matching green jacket, skirt and shoes, and a bright red polka-dot top with a large white ribbon around her skirt on the day she announced their verdict. The other jurors included a tired man with a ponytail, and a woman who wore blue-rimmed glasses, her hair in a bun, and an expression of furious distaste.

But there was one person missing that morning: the accused. The proper release forms hadn't been filled out, and Wang remained in his cell. The jury weren't aware that there had been two previous trials, nor could they be told that Wang had recently been sentenced to two years and nine months' imprisonment for money-laundering and fraud.

Calls were made to the prison. The trial finally began after lunch. Wang stood in the dock, once again in his usual tunic — a collarless jacket, with a horizontal pinstripe, its cuffs unbuttoned to reveal a tartan lining. Was it all he owned? His shoes looked old. Wang, too, was worn; in the year since his last appearance in the High Court, his face had lost some of its vitality.

Justice Venning welcomed the jury. Crown prosecutor Kevin Glubb, a thin, stately individual with a throbbing voice, which he kept moist with furtive handfuls of Eclipse mints, gave his opening address. For the third time, a tragedy was told about two men who were chopped up and killed on a summer's morning at one of the most amazing addresses in Auckland.

Police photographs of the crime scene show bright sunlight falling through the upstairs windows at 23 Stilwell Road, a grand old mansion with a glass elevator, an indoor spa pool, chickens out the back, and a trail of blood leading to the body of Zhuo 'Michael' Wu, 44, who collapsed and bled to death at the bottom of the stairs. His friend, Yishan 'Tom' Zhong, 53, had also tried to escape the slaughter. He made it outside. Drops of his blood led past a white fountain and down the front steps onto the driveway; he collapsed and bled to death in a clump of leaves.

'Michael', 'Tom', 'Chris' — the made-up names signal the otherness of Asian life in Auckland. The three men got to know each other through the Chinese community, conducted business in Mandarin and broken English, flew in and out of Beijing. Witnesses talked of yum char and karaoke; Michael Wu's widow quoted an old saying: 'You can get rid of the monk, but you still will not get rid of the temple.'

Wu and Zhong drove to Wang's house on a Friday morning in January. It was 23 degrees, cloudless. They opened the front door and walked straight in. Did the two men — and this was the question which haunted three juries, and became the central riddle they tried to solve — step into the kitchen and grab a knife? Wang was in his bedroom. In a doorway at the top of the stairs in the house on the hill on Stilwell Road, there was a fight to the death.

Wang claimed self-defence. He said the two men had come to kill him. He gave a four-hour interview at the Avondale police station that afternoon — he had changed out of his blood-soaked pyjamas into a white police-issue suit — and demonstrated his miraculous escape. He was, he explained, expert at kung fu.

2

In broad daylight, 23 Stilwell Road is a magnificent sight to behold, as big as the sky. From *The New Zealand Herald*'s homes section, when the mansion was put on the market in 2007: 'You approach the house through an arbour draped with bougainvillea ... The formal dining room ... The elegant leadlighting ... Breathtaking deck views stretching from Waterview, across to the Waitakeres and around to the Chelsea Sugar Refinery ... A ladder pulls down to take you up to a secret door, which leads onto an even higher deck. Here the view widens to include Huia, Rangitoto, the city and Mt Eden.'

All of Stilwell Road has a gentle, soothing quality; the pulse slows, the struggle and narrowness of life is elsewhere. The trees are so pretty. There are the cedars and conifers planted in the 1930s by Reverend Thomas Joughlin, a Methodist minister who lived at 7 Stilwell Road. There are the wonderful palms, grown from seed in the 1970s by botanist Alan Esler, who lives at number 7 to this day.

Stilwell Road is within the 'golden triangle', property-sales blather for the three most expensive and desirable streets in Mt Albert. The other two streets are Sadgrove Terrace and Summit Drive. The swimming pools, the ornamental gardens, the grassy slopes of the volcano ... Anne Duncan of Ray White Real Estate listed three recent sales on Stilwell Road. One went for $1.4 million, another for $1.66 million, and the highest for $2.45 million. 'All,' she said, 'to nice families attending local schools.'

Schools in the immediate zone include Mt Albert Grammar, Marist College and Gladstone Primary, with its vital statistics of decile 8 and 61 per cent white.

The epicentre of this happy, well-educated colony of the rich is 23 Stilwell Road. More from the sales pitch in the *Herald*: 'Hollywood glamour meets genteel colonialism ... Park-like grounds, a colonnade entry, sculpted fountain ...'

It was built in 1929 for a fantasist. The first owner was Maria Cossey, who passed herself off as the Princess Marie-Jeanne de Guise. She claimed direct ancestry with the royal House of Lorraine in France. The family line included Marie de Lorraine, queen of both France and Scotland, and mother of Mary, Queen of Scots.

Maria of Mt Albert's grandson is Andrew Hunter, who lives in France, and demands to be known as the Prince de Guise. *The Baronage Press* reports: 'We have full particulars of Andrew Hunter's ancestry, which show his claims to be a total fantasy ... It is presumably his grandmother's fantasies that he has adopted.'

Her faux palace in the Antipodes sold to a knight. Sir David Henry emigrated from Scotland to New Zealand in 1907 when he was 19. He found work as a farm labourer. Clever and ambitious, he rose to become New Zealand's pre-eminent industrialist as the head of Forestry Products, building Kinleith pulp and paper mill. 'Past-president Auckland Rotary. Past-president Auckland YMCA ... Recreation: bowls and golf.' Former Cabinet minister Michael Bassett, who lived on Stilwell Road for 37 years, read out loud from his copy of *Who's Who in New Zealand*, the sixth edition, published in 1956. He noted of Sir David: 'He probably would have been in the seventh edition, gone by the eighth.'

Sir David put in an elevator for his wife, Mary, a paraplegic. A year after her death, he married her younger sister, Dorothy. He had created fabulous wealth, and made a profound difference to the New Zealand economy, but a cold and joyless rage lingers over his name. In his history of New Zealand forest products, Brian Healy wrote, 'Sir David lacked warmth and humour in his working relations and tended to be abrupt and demanding with his subordinates.' Sydney Shep of Victoria University wrote in a research paper on the Kinleith mill, 'Business contemporaries found him stiff, sombre, intense, driven, and dictatorial.' Michael Roche, writing Sir David's entry in the *New Zealand Dictionary of Biography*, noted his subject's 'erratic behaviour' in later years. 'Many meetings were held in his Mt Albert home, during which he repeatedly lashed out verbally.'

He died in 1963. The house went on the market after Lady Dorothy died in 1979. Historian Michael Bassett attended the auction. He said, 'Every sticky-beak in the neighbourhood had a look at the place. The rooms were large, the kitchen had Terrazzo benches — they were all the rage in the 1930s. We had one at home. The only trouble was that whenever any lemon juice got anywhere near it, your Terrazzo would end up being all pitted. Anyway, it had Terrazzo benches, it had a lift that went up, it was dingy, dark, old. Nonetheless, at the auction, it went for the staggering sum of $155,000, which had everybody gasping and nobody could work out who had actually bought the place. Up steps this guy in short pants and a singlet. He slaps this woman next to him and says, "Meet my de facto!" And then, "Ho-ho-ho, keeps you young!" His name was Barrie Cardon.'

3

The first witness called by the prosecution took the jury on a guided tour through 23 Stilwell Road. It was a strange kind of open home. Jason Barr, a forensic technician at the ESR, who wore a tight black suit and a hipster's full-strength beard, had used specialised camera equipment that allowed viewers to walk through 22 locations. A screen was set up in court. Barr loaded a DVD. It played moving images of the approach to the house — the driveway in sunshine and shadow, Tom Zhong's body with one foot poking out from beneath a sheet, wisteria in the courtyard, a gas barbecue on the front porch.

The house loomed white and wonderful, gleaming in the sun. Inside, Michael Wu's body lay face-down at the foot of the stairs. His white iPhone was nearby. He'd made his last call as he staggered down the stairs, dying. The number he called belonged to Zhong. It went unanswered. Zhong had already staggered down the stairs; his phone probably rang when he was outside, dying. Was it a call for help?

The hipster's groovy ESR film delved into the basement, went up the stairs, looked over the balcony. And throughout, one thing jarred, kept intruding on the guided tour of a beautiful old house with lovely wood panelling and delicate leadlight: a sense of cheapness. It was there in the plastic clotheshorses in the front room and the upstairs lounge. It was there in the full-length mirror merely propped up against a wall in the hallway. It was also there in the absences. There wasn't anything on the walls. There was a glass cabinet, and the only thing in it was a chamber pot. There was a bedroom with a cot, empty bags of potato chips, a flat-screen TV on top of a sideboard. There were cardboard boxes in the hallway. There were wet towels flopped over the bath. It was as though the occupants were passing through; it looked like a hotel which had seen better days.

Auckland businessman Dermot Nottingham discussed property investments with Wang, and visited him at Stilwell Road numerous times. He said Wang claimed to own several properties, and a $2-million duck farm.

He said, 'There was always an undercurrent with Chris that he needed money. He was driving around in a small car, which was quite strange, because most affluent Chinese show off their wealth. The grass wasn't kept; it had different layers of grass in the various gardens. It gave me the feeling there was something wrong financially.

'I'd go around and it wasn't unusual for Chris to be out in his kitchen, because when you live like a pauper, you live in the kitchen. There were hardly any furnishings in the house. The kitchen didn't have a table and chairs in it. It was a large kitchen, and it was a kitchen you'd normally dine in. He did have large knives in the kitchen, very large knives, like cleavers. I put that down to him owning duck farms and maybe taking a couple of ducks home and killing them ...'

It took a full day in court to screen the ESR silent movie. The auteur's cameras moved around Wang's bedroom, showed a telescope on the balcony, $5.50 in change and a knife sheath on a round table. In the next-door lounge, there were two knives in a pool of blood on the carpet, one pointing left, one pointing right.

The knives were the trial's two most significant objects. They contained the meaning to what happened, were at the centre of everything. They were displayed in court on a low table beneath the witness stand. They had remained so sharp that Justice Venning fussed for two days about whether to allow the jury to handle them. The risk of a bad cut was high. 'Not on my watch,' he fretted, before settling on the use of a protective tape.

Crown prosecutor Kevin Glubb picked one up with his long fingers and waved it in the air. It caught the light, and there was a flash of silver in the courtroom. It was the hunting knife that belonged to Wang. 'It's a very beautiful knife,' Wang had said in his police interview.

It was a heavy weapon, with a ridged blade, and an image of a baying wolf on it — it was referred to in court exhibits as WILD WOLF KNIFE. A fingerprint expert, a heavy black man from Durban, said the last person to hold the knife was Chris Wang. Wang kept it in a bedroom drawer. It was plunged with such force into Zhong's back that it broke through two ribs and pierced his right lung. It killed him; he coughed blood on the stairwell walls, and died curled up against a fence, frothing at the mouth.

But all eyes at the trial were fixed on the other knife — a Galaxy knife with a stainless-steel blade. In essence, the trial was about the mystery of the second knife. A tenant at Stilwell Road had bought it for $3 at the Made In Japan bargain shop on Queen Street. (The knife was actually made in China.) It was kept in the kitchen at Stilwell Road. The night before the killings, it was used in the kitchen to slice a pizza.

'How did it get upstairs?' Glubb asked, turning to the jury. His answer was vague. Somehow, he said, it was placed next to the hunting knife. Its presence was staged.

'How did it get upstairs?' Wang's lawyer, Tom Sutcliffe, asked the jury. 'Who put it there, and why?' Sutcliffe, an earnest, thoughtful Mormon from Hamilton, supplied an exact answer. 'Michael brought it. He upped the ante. They had visited before. They knew where the kitchen was. This was a premeditated plan to locate and confront him.'

With the knife came Wang's plea of self-defence. He told police that the two men came at him with the knife, and he did everything he could to protect himself. His actions included scampering into his bedroom and unsheathing his own knife, the WILD WOLF. The three men rolled on the floor. Wang told police that Michael Wu got hold of the hunting knife, but he managed to turn it around, and point it at his attacker. Tom Zhong, he said, pressed Wu onto the knife — in effect impaling his own friend, and causing the fatal wounds. Then, Wang said, he grabbed Zhong and used him as a human shield; as far as he could tell, in the confusion and tumult, Wu stabbed his own friend in the back.

'Ridiculous … Bizarre … Outlandish,' Glubb told the jury. 'If we're to believe this, it's not just one of the most ineffectual attacks ever mounted, it was suicidal.' He said that Wang simply went at Wu, and then stabbed Zhong in the back, while he was trying to run away.

Sutcliffe told the jury: 'Chris Wang believed he was going to die. He used every ounce of his physical strength and mental will to survive.'

The fatal struggle had lasted three or four minutes. Wang walked down the stairs and called 111. The despatcher wanted to know where he lived. The call was played in court.

Wang screeched, 'People want come and kill me!'

She said, 'Can you stop talking when I'm talking? I need your address, mate.'

He shouted, 'Ambah-lance! Hurry up!'

'Tell me,' sighed the despatcher, 'your address.'

4

Barrie Cardon lived at 23 Stilwell Road until his mysterious death in 2005, when he fell off the upstairs balcony. He was a happy, lively property developer who owned a row of buildings at the sex-trade end of Karangahape Road. His tenants ran massage parlours and strip clubs. Cardon collected their rents in cash.

'I was married at Stilwell Road,' said his daughter Deena. 'I got into my bridal dress, came down the front steps and hopped in the Mustang — we had Mustangs for the wedding cars. Dad collected Mustangs. He loved classic cars in general, but he had five Mustangs.'

She said the house was run-down when her father bought it from Sir David Henry's widow. 'I remember a huge renovation going on. He gutted it completely and put in the flash kitchen and the wonderful stairs out the front. Dad just absolutely loved his garden, and he was quite obsessive about his roses. There was a massive garden — most of the property was manicured garden beds, just little circular garden beds.

'And there were servants' quarters! Dad made it into the spa room. It had a tongue-and-groove ceiling like an upturned boat's hull. It had the Axminster carpet as well, and mirrors … It was just beautiful, the spa room.

'He absolutely loved the house. There was no expense spared when he did things to it. He was excited when, for example, the carpet he selected was the same as in Westminster Abbey. It's got a really intricate design woven into it.'

Her memories of the house were of its charm and elegance, and the enjoyment it gave her father. But it ended in tragedy.

In about 2002, her father began to develop Alzheimer's. 'He went downhill very quickly, and we realised he was going to need live-in care.' He'd already hired a Tongan woman to live at the address as his housekeeper. 'Funnily enough, she used to be his tenant many years ago. They bumped into each other at the shops one day. He wasn't sick at the time, but he realised that he was getting older and was looking at getting someone to look after the house. It was becoming too much for him.'

The woman had worked at the mental-health unit at Carrington. With the onset of his Alzheimer's, it was decided that she would become his caregiver.

Deena: 'And then Dad fell off the balcony onto the concrete pavement down below. I use the word "fell" loosely. Nothing was ever proven. Nobody knows for a fact what happened that night because he was found in the early hours of the morning.'

His caregiver discovered him. 'She was sleeping in the bed with him at the time. Apparently, she heard his cries for help.'

He died in hospital about eight weeks later. The day of the funeral, she said, legal papers were filed which excluded his family from the house. The caregiver claimed matrimonial property rights, and asserted that she had been in a relationship with Cardon.

'My sister and I were excluded from the home for 18 months. We weren't even allowed to take a photo or a T-shirt or anything that belonged to Dad. By the time we finally got in, most of his stuff was gone. We did get photos and stuff, but as far as his furniture, his clothing, all his personal belongings were pretty much gone.'

Her father, she said, was an extraordinary man. 'Definitely eccentric. He walked around in a singlet and shorts and bare feet 24 hours a day, summer or winter. You'd see a guy you'd think was homeless step out of a Mustang — that was Dad to a

T. Extremely generous, caring, would often take people into the home that might be going through a rough patch and help them get on their feet.'

The last time she saw 23 Stilwell was on the TV news on the night of the murders. 'The way it was portrayed was like "A house marred with tragedy." It instantly took us back to what happened with Dad. He would've been horrified to know what had happened in his beautiful house.'

5

In his police interview on the afternoon of the killings, Wang drew stick figures to illustrate what happened at the house that morning. He gave them names. His spoken English came and went; his written English was hit and miss. Next to his drawing of Michael Wu, he wrote, *Maccl*. He identified another figure: *Gall*. He meant 'girl' — Soo Jin Ahn, a young Korean woman who had met Wang that week, and was a witness to the killings.

A tall, slender woman with black nail polish, she appeared in court as a prosecution witness. She described a kind of summer romance. It lasted less than a week. Wang took her to a restaurant on a Tuesday night, and she stayed the night at Stilwell Road. He made porridge in the morning and brought it to her in bed. They met again on Thursday night. They ate pizza in his downstairs kitchen. She sliced it with the Galaxy knife.

Wang went night-fishing in Waiwera with friends. She went to bed. He came back at about 4.30am. She woke at 7am, had a shower, and read the paper in the lounge. Wang woke up, and she opened the balcony doors. 'It's my habit,' she told the court. 'When I get up I want to bring fresh air in.'

The gorgeous summer morning, the curtains of the balcony moving in a light breeze. Ahn was barefoot, and wore a pink tracksuit. She sat on a couch and opened her laptop.

Glubb asked her, 'While you were sitting there, what happened?'

She said, 'I felt some indication of human being so I lift my head.'

Michael Wu and Tom Zhong were at the top of the stairs.

They asked for Wang. She went into the bedroom, and said to him, 'You have visitors.'

6

Michael Wu was a friendly, laid-back kind of guy. He'd married a pretty young nurse, who gave birth to their son in 2010. He spoke good English, unlike Tom Zhong. Tom had worked for 30 years in China as a pharmacist, restaurant manager and prison guard, and had qualified for a pension. He took his family to live in Auckland. Like Michael, he became friends with Chris Wang.

Michael and Tom went into business with Wang and got burnt. Both said they'd lent Wang money — $125,000 from Michael, $30,000 from Tom — and he hadn't paid it back.

Their frustrations led them to Wang's ex-wife, Michelle. All three had grievances. The question on their lips was: what do you do with a problem called Chris? She told them that Wang had taken over her four properties in Auckland — 75 College Road in Northcote, 55 and 57 Morningside Drive in St Lukes, and the Stilwell Road mansion — and ordered the tenants to pay rent to him, in cash. Her mortgage payments fell behind. She was under increasing pressure from the banks. In an effort to hold off on mortgagee sales, she engaged Michael to act as her representative. He travelled to see her at her home town in China to discuss a plan of action.

Michael and Tom met with a lawyer, David Snedden, who prepared trespass notices against Wang, and documents authorising them to divert rents back to Michelle's account. The two men went to Stilwell Road that Friday morning to advise the other tenants that their rent had to be paid to Michelle.

They took documents. Police photos show the papers where the men left them: in the back seat of their car. Why didn't they take them to the house? Why did they simply walk in the door and traipse up the stairs? 'Whether they knocked,' Glubb told the jury, 'we will never know.'

What had they discussed when they met at Tom's house the previous night? Or did they decide on a course of action that morning in the car? Sutcliffe reminded the jury that the documents were left in the car, and said, 'They weren't going there to serve papers. There was something else going on here.'

It was a compelling argument. The prosecution felt that the hung jury in the second trial prevented a conviction. But were the two obstinate jurors the only ones, in fact, who voted *for* a murder verdict? Had they prevented Wang from hearing the sweet words 'Not guilty'?

7

Wang's lover, Soo Jin, was the prosecution's star witness. According to her evidence, the fight broke out seconds after she stepped back out onto the balcony. Glubb took this as evidence that Wang simply exploded, saw red, snapped, grabbed his WILD WOLF knife and went berserk.

But her evidence also played in Wang's favour. She said that when Wang saw the two men, one of them silently gestured to him by raising his arm and beckoning him to come closer with his index finger. She told the court, 'I thought the visitors were upset or angry. The reason was because Asian people do not call people like that.'

No one calls people like that unless they want a fight. 'Upset, angry'; were they armed?

8

Detective Sergeant Joe Aumua said, 'During our inquiries, we kept hearing from the Chinese community that they thought this guy Chris Wang was untouchable. And to some extent, he was.'

It may be regarded as incredible that Wang had only ever been held in custody for six weeks after his arrest on two charges of murder. His former lawyer, David Jones, successfully applied for Wang to be released on bail. The police appealed, wanted him kept banged up until he came to trial, but got nowhere.

When the first trial was abandoned, the man accused of butchering two people with a hunting knife left the court with my business card, and went home. I called around the next day.

9

Chris Wang said grandly, 'I live good quality.' We met at his own house on Salisbury Road in St Lukes. 'Here, you can see.' He waved his hand in a broad gesture, taking in the oak table, the faux Victorian chairs, the pompous grandfather clock. They looked very expensive. 'Of course! I never live poor quality. I always live very nice quality.'

He was vain, trim, small, muscled, fit, shrill, and very courteous. A handsome man, with a kind of regal bearing. His hair was cut short. He had a nice smile. He talked a lot. He was likeable, a good host, quite charming. He stayed on the move; there wasn't anything languid about him. It was hard not to stare at his hands.

We drank green tea, and sat at his kitchen table. An old lady who didn't speak a word of English watered a pot plant. The clock bonged. It was a dark house, dimly lit — bizarrely, Wang was arrested four months after the killings, accused of stealing $164.96 of light switches from Bunnings in Mt Roskill. No doubt they were quality switches.

Wang talked about arriving in New Zealand from Shanghai with only $50 in his pocket. 'I do everything. Mow lawn, cut the tree, do the painting, the plumbing, the carpentry. Then I bought a house for $10,000 in Beach Haven and sell it for $150,000. I think I'm very clever! I think, "Oh, I'm rich!" New Zealand give me everything.'

He loved it here, he said. Fishing, and hunting, and bush walks. 'But very bad memories here. I will probably move back to China.'

First, though, there was the matter of his criminal trial for double-murder. Was he worried that he'd be found guilty? He said, 'Worried? Why you think I worried? I tell the truth. The evidence tells the truth.'

The story he told about the killings on Stilwell Road began with his claim that Michael Wu and Tom Zhong had threatened him for months, demanding repayments, and blithely walking in and taking his furniture.

'I say to Michael, "I can get your money back, but give me a bit of time." I scared. I want to keep him away. He play rugby. He very strong. He say, "Chris, you start from nothing to now you have plenty. I can make you nothing again."

'They just come into my home, my gate all broken, it happen all the time. Yes, they take furniture! Of course! All the time! Michael take one container — all the nice furniture. Beautiful, much better than that!' He waved a hand again at the somber grandfather clock. 'I always get nice furniture. The best. I pay millions of dollar. Michael take and say, "Oh, got anything else?" And reach out and grab things. Just like that!'

He told another story. He said he came home one day and found Tom having sex with his wife in the movie room. 'I was quite angry with that. At that time Tom was quite good friends with me. I tell Tom, "We never ever be friends. You just out." I angry with my wife. I say, "You are so bad! Why you do that?" She think she divorce me, she get the lot. She have no money! Poor! She from very poor family. I pay everything. We meet in China. At that time she so nice to me. So nice! Even I put my shoes on, I never need to — she will kneel down and do it. Just like that ...'

But his wife owned four houses in Auckland, including Stilwell Road. They were in her name. Police believed that she had all the money, that Wang was penniless.

As the only one of the three men left alive after the killings at Stilwell Road, he told the same story he gave to police. Michael and Tom appeared at the top of the stairs. Michael attacked him with a knife. 'I push the knife away. Because I learn kung fu a long time ago. No one know.' He ran and grabbed his WILD WOLF. 'I scared. In shock. I in my pyjama.' There was a struggle. Michael was impaled on the knife. 'He get two cuts. He [the pathologist] say 23 cuts. But the others just scratch. Real cuts, just two.'

The maths is false. The postmortem carried out on Michael identified a stab wound above the hip which entered the peritoneal cavity, a stab wound to the back which cut the kidney, a stab wound through the rib cage, and a stab wound cutting the liver. Four 'real cuts'.

Wang said he didn't see Tom being stabbed, just heard him yell 'Fuck!', and run away. 'I thought he was going to get a knife or a gun. I was worried about that.'

Earlier, when he talked about the two men coming to Stilwell Road and taking his furniture, he said, 'Never they take shoes off inside the house. Final time they come into my house, it's with the shoes.'

Why go on about the shoes? Was it really that important?

He said, 'Of course! It my house. People come into my house never with the shoes. No one with the shoes come in. No, no, no. I got a new carpet. Nice house.'

10

To gaze upon 23 Stilwell Road is to see it as a big old luxury-liner, splendid and gleaming, a fantasy of wealth and success. Possible, too, to think of it sailing through a history of Auckland, taking onboard an essence of the city over successive generations. Built by a woman who invented herself as a royal in a young colony making itself up as it went along. Taken over by a bitter capitalist who helped build a nation. Passed into the hands of a gadfly who thrived on the city's long-established sex district. Then, in about 2007, owned by new New Zealanders, an Asian couple (Michael Bassett chuckled when he recalled a neighbour who called Wang 'chop suey'), who kept to themselves.

The house Mr and Mrs Wang bought for $2.3 million was sold by property developer Greer Stevenson. He'd carried out extensive renovations, and employed a neighbour, university student Chris Williams, to do odd jobs around the house. 'Greer paid me really well and, like, bought me heaps of beer, which was awesome,' Williams said.

He remembered an unusual indoor spa. 'It had like a pole, and a mirrored ceiling ... Greer took all that out.'

Williams worked over summer. 'They'd put down a ready-lawn that grows through cardboard, and it has to be kept wet, so I stood out there for like three or four hours a day just watering ... I also chopped heaps of trees down, and I painted the green fence all the way down the driveway. It's quite a big fence.' It was what Tom Zhong had rested against as he died.

After the murders, Wang left the house. The next occupants were a Tongan family. This time, the South Pacific had come onboard Stilwell Road.

Williams said, 'The Rugby World Cup was on. They had this massive bamboo pole, and stuck it right at the top of the house with this huge Tongan flag. There were all these kids running around. There was rubbish outside everywhere, and skateboards and old BMX bikes kind of just like chucked in the garden and left there ...'

Michael Bassett said, 'When the mortgagee sale came up, well, you can imagine a potential buyer of a grand place like this turning up and finding a whole load of bloody Tongans wrapped up in blankets lying around the floor — not exactly being a come-on.

'And they hadn't cleaned the property up properly. The carpet by the front door had great big blood stains over it, and the wallpaper up the sides had splats of blood everywhere. Can you imagine it? It's bizarre.'

Real estate agent Anne Duncan went through the house. 'I was very disappointed at the presentation,' she said. 'It was still like it was at the bloody murder scene. On the front door there was still the fingerprinting dust, there was blood on the front doorstep.'

Police from Operation Otter visited the property and spoke to the tenants. They said their landlord was Chris Wang.

11

The jury took their seats in Courtroom 14 to announce their verdict on a cold Friday afternoon. The sky was already dark. They had been sent out the previous day at 10.40am. It had been a long wait — not just for this trial to end, but all three trials, the years of justice delayed.

Like all left-handed people, the side of Kevin Glubb's palm was smudged with ink. He sat at a bare desk. Court staff and counsel had tidied up. The knives had been taken away.

12

The police hoped for a guilty verdict. I always enjoyed chatting with Detective Sergeant Joe Aumua, one of the first officers at the crime scene, who came to court every day. He was very dignified, quietly spoken. 'He's a dangerous man,' he said of Wang.

He saw the bodies that day. 'We believe that Chris just flew off the handle, that he snapped, and armed himself with a knife and, before there was any discussion, he attacked ... It's the most vicious attack I've ever seen.'

He credited Wang with having the presence of mind to immediately concoct a story to explain why two people had died of multiple stab wounds.

Wang was smart, but was he that smart? To be able to stage two knives and choreograph a fight to the death suggests a kind of criminal mastermind. Was he really able to think on his feet that quickly?

13

The families of the victims hoped for a guilty verdict. Aumua said, 'They've invested all their trust and faith these past three years, not only in the police, but in our justice system.'

But were they mourning two unarmed men, or two men who had made the fatal mistake of choosing to fuck with the wrong guy?

On the day of the verdict, Michael Wu's young widow, Maggie, played outside with their son. She held him in her arms as he reached out and touched a parking meter. He was round and small, fatherless.

14

Ruth Money of the Sensible Sentencing Trust hoped for a guilty verdict. We met at her small office upstairs in the Golf Warehouse. The stacked clubs and golf bags made it difficult to take her seriously, and so did her own flair for loose statements. She said, 'We know Chris Wang walked around with a knife down the back of his pants.'

I said, 'How do you know that?'

She said, 'We were told. There was also talk he killed and skinned a sheep with a hunting knife ... He's a bad, bad man.'

Ruth had dealt with a Chinese couple who had bought Michelle Wang's two houses in St Lukes. They told the tenants to move out. 'But then a big Samoan boy came out of the sleep-out and said, "Fuck off, these are my boss's houses."' He said his boss was Chris Wang.

Money visited, and said, 'He had rented out every room in the house. There was a person sleeping on the floor in a bathroom where there was a toilet. The houses were just disgusting, absolutely filthy. You wouldn't put animals in there.'

She said, 'Be careful. Watch yourself. He'll have his little spies in court.'

15

Private investigator Phil Jones hoped for a guilty verdict. We met in a noisy bar on Auckland's waterfront. He was easy to spot — a tall ex-cop with a severe haircut and a military bearing. Tom and Michael had hired his services during the time they were trying to serve trespass orders on Wang. He spoke with them on the morning they were killed. He said, 'If they went into the house, that's dumb. It wouldn't have taken long for Chris to get inflamed and grab the knife and get into them.'

He gave evidence in court about his stand-off with Wang a month before the killings. He went with Michael and Tom to the house on Stilwell Road. 'It became very confrontational very quickly,' he said. 'Tom and Michael were baiting him. Chris had an evil, mad look in his eye and a horrible smile on his face. Michael was just laughing at him and thought it was all a bit of fun.'

But then someone shouted that Wang had a knife, and Jones saw Wang reach behind his back. He yelled at Tom and Michael to run to their car.

He said, 'I keep myself reasonably fit, but there's no way I would have fancied my chances with Chris. The difference is the fact if he's got that mad adrenalin rush, you're going to come off worse. His eyes were scary. I've dealt with scary people before; I've dealt with terrorists in the IRA. It's where the eyes are going, if they've got relaxed eyes or if they're very focused. His eyes were very focused. That's when it's scary.'

Prosecution tried to play it out as a crucial episode, casting Wang as some kind of knife-wielding psycho. But it fell flat. No one actually saw the knife. Was it another instance of a knife that wasn't there? You could form a sympathetic picture of Wang. There he was, at the house he used to live in with his wife, suddenly approached by three men — one of whom he claimed was sleeping with his wife — who told him that he had to leave the premises. They laughed at him, goaded him. He told them to clear off. He phoned Jones the next day to apologise for losing his temper ... He sounds put upon, blameless.

On 13 January, the day before the deaths, Michael rang Jones and said he was going to go back to Stilwell Road with Tom. Michelle Wang needed to get her rents. The banks were talking about mortgagee sales. Sutcliffe told the jury: 'The pressure was building for action to be taken, the heat was on to do something ... They had to resort to violence.'

Jones tried to talk Michael out of returning to Stilwell Road. He said, 'I'm almost a witness that helped Chris a bit. I've said I warned Michael not to go in, and he does.'

He advised Michael to go to the Avondale police station and ask if they could go to the address with an officer. They spoke again on the phone on the morning of 14 January. 'I told Michael, "Even if you go by yourselves, you get any sniff that Chris is there, even if he's fine, ring 111 and tell them he's aggro and violent and jumping up and down." He obviously didn't do that.'

Tom's daughter Jade dropped him off that morning at 8.30am; it was the last time she saw him. Michael was looking forward to a family holiday in the South Island. The two men went to the Avondale police station, but were told that an officer was unavailable. Michael and Tom were described as cheerful, relaxed. Glubb told the jury, 'You do not go to all that trouble if your sole purpose is calculated violence. It makes absolutely no sense. Their only intent was to reinforce the trespass order.'

Jones said, 'Michael talked about protecting himself, taking a weapon. I said, "Listen, you can't."'

Does he think the two men threatened Wang? 'They could have. Yeah. Possibly.'

Threatened to kill him? 'Absolutely not. No way. There was no inkling of that whatsoever. In my view,' he said, 'he murdered a couple of innocent people.'

16

Chris Wang hoped for freedom to go about his business — collecting rent in cash, fishing for eels, buying 'quality' possessions. No one came to support him in court, despite Ruth Money's predictions he'd have his 'spies'. We nodded at each other when he came in to hear the verdict.

Who was Wang? He had passed through danger, scatheless, on that summer's morning in Mt Albert; sometimes, during the long days of his trial, I wondered whether there really was something supernatural about Wang, the way he had escaped death; but the Chinese demigod of Stilwell Road, nimble and 'untouchable', tensed when the jury arrived.

17

The forewoman wore a bright-red polka-dot top with a large white ribbon around her skirt. She said of the charge of the murder of Michael Wu: 'Not guilty.'

Wang closed his eyes and swayed.

Not guilty, also, of manslaughter.

She said of the charge of the murder of Tom Zhong: 'Not guilty.' But they found him guilty of his manslaughter.

The families of the victims had gone pale with shock. They had to be helped out of the courtroom.

Justice Venning thanked the jury, and told them they could leave. He waited until the door to the jury room closed behind them, and then he said, 'Well.' His smile was bemused.

Kevin Glubb said, 'Remarkable.'

Tom Sutcliffe left to talk with his client.

It was as though the verdicts were a wager each way. *You can get rid of the monk, but you still will not get rid of the temple.* The jury had accepted self-defence in the killing of Michael Wu, that there was a second knife, that Wang was just trying to save his life. But the implication was that they rejected Wang's claim that Michael had accidentally stabbed Tom in the back. Their verdict identified Wang as the killer — but that he had lacked murderous intent when he had plunged the knife 13 centimetres into Tom's back. How you lack murderous intent when you do that is very curious indeed.

What really happened that morning on the house on the hill? The final answer — the legally binding one — was given by Justice Venning at sentencing in a cramped downstairs courtroom. It was the final reunion of the prosecution and defence teams, of the nice old gent from Victim Support, of the petite translator who sat at Wang's side, of that small, blessed survivor, Chis Wang. He appeared in the familiar collarless tunic, the old tan shoes. Jurors from all three trials came, too.

The judge got down to business. He said Michael Wu came to Stilwell Road with a knife. There it was, stated out loud, as fact — the second knife did exist, was taken upstairs in a home invasion. He said he did not accept that Tom Zhong had his back to him and was trying to run away when Wang killed him with the hunting knife. The fatal wound, he said, was most likely inflicted in the confusion of the violent struggle between the three men. 'I accept you acted in self-defence,' he told Wang, 'but that you went too far.'

It felt like a minor chastisement. He then set about the terms of sentencing. He said that he'd observed Wang throughout the trial, and didn't see any evidence of remorse. He noted that Wang had offered to pay $30,000 to the families of the victims, but the offer was rejected. He sentenced him to four years. He should be out around about the time this book is published in late 2015.

18

Partly because there was blood everywhere, the house got snapped up at a mortgagee sale in November 2011 for $1,641,000 — an absolute bargain, $700,000 less than it fetched when the Wangs had bought it.

There is the balcony from where Barrie Cardon plunged to his death; there are the grand front steps where Michael Wu and Tom Zhong walked towards their horrible, bloody end. But the great ship of 23 Stilwell Road has sailed into calm waters, taking onboard a good Catholic family, pillars of Auckland's establishment. It was bought by Kevin Ryan. His father was the celebrated criminal defence lawyer, Kevin Ryan QC; his sister is Judge Claire Ryan. He and his wife, Bernadette, have five children.

'Kevin's done a lot of work on the house,' observed former neighbour Michael Bassett. 'He's very proud of the renovations.'

Chapter 15

Mark Lundy: The trial

> There it was again, the sentimental fantasy of love as a condition of simple benevolence, a tranquil, sunlit region in which we are safe from our destructive urges.
> — Helen Garner, *This House of Grief*

1

Too bad they challenged the guy who looked as though he was about to have a nervous breakdown unless someone gave him his medication, quick. Too bad they challenged the nice old duck who was plainly as deaf as A POST. Too bad they woke up the sleepy individual who came to court wearing his pyjamas, and challenged him. There were even stranger candidates among the 60 potential jurors who showed up at the Wellington High Court on a Monday morning in the summer of 2015, the day after the Waitangi holiday weekend, to see if they would be selected for duty in the trial of Mark Edward Lundy. Their names were pulled out of a green metal box. The nice old deaf duck had her name roared out twice before she got up, but she had barely risen to her feet before she was challenged, and excused. She might have made a difference. Pyjama guy and the dude needing his meds might have made a difference to the verdict reached more than six weeks later by the chosen 12.

I stood among the mob of 60 in a queue outside the courthouse that Monday morning. I thought they were freaks wanting to watch the trial from the public gallery, and that I'd better wait with them for the doors to open. Mike White from *North & South* magazine was inside the court and spotted me through the glass. He raced out and grabbed my arm. 'They're jurors,' he whispered. 'You can't be seen anywhere near them.' He dragged me inside. I walked into Courtroom 1 — Ewen McDonald wuz here, 2012 — for the first time. I liked it at once. It was a portrait gallery, the walls decorated with dark oil paintings of judges of old, who variously expressed states of calm, wisdom, despair, constipation, lasciviousness, prudence, vigour, severity, brutality, kindness and madness. The courtroom was windowless and white-ceilinged. It would be not so much my office for the next two months as my home. It was where I felt happy, where the sum of every moment was precious, where I ate, rested, slept. I liked being there and missed it when I was away at weekends, back in Auckland, with my family in my real home. The courthouse was opposite Parliament, with its smooth green lawn and its pohutukawa in crimson health. I had my routines on the way there (breakfast every morning of honeypuffs and toast with spreads served by Nigel at John's Kitchen, on Lambton Quay) and in the evenings (Chinese at either the Redhill, Shanghai or Regal in the old opium end of town). Court hours, with their set tea breaks and lunch at 1pm, established another pattern.

And then there were the familiar faces of my brethren in the media, most of whom thought Lundy was as guilty as sin, and the officers of the court, and Lundy himself — sometimes I thought of him as the volunteer in some kind of experiment, as though he had been chosen at random to test the memory and knowledge of intimates, acquaintances, strangers and experts. The trial was a character study. It was an examination of how well we can know someone and the traces they leave behind. The trial was also a test of the efficiency and efficacy of itself; the workings of a trial sometimes assume a greater importance than the point of it. The guilty and the innocent share the same reply when they're accused of something: 'Prove it!' The burden of proof provides the context of a trial. It can be a very heavy burden, and it can lead to a robust and lengthy discussion about issues which have no basis in reality. That way lies madness — and, inevitably, the founding document of the nightmare that swirls behind all false accusations.

One day when I was at Kumeu, Geoff Levick said to me, 'Have you ever read a book called *The Trial*?' I had, but it was a long time ago; and so I bought a copy of Kafka's great novel at Unity Books on the way to court one morning, and sometimes even read it in the courtroom. I imagined Levick opening up the book, and relishing its famous opening line: 'Somebody must have made a false accusation against Josef K., for he was arrested one morning without having done anything wrong.' Crazy, of course, to treat the book only as a parallel to Lundy's case. It's a work of art, and its fantastical world was created by Kafka in response to his own crises — a heartbreak, a harsh judgment. In his introduction to his English translation of *The Trial*, Idris Parry writes of Kafka being summoned to face his accusers: 'He remained silent as the words crossed over him like a knife passed from hand to hand.' But that, too, was Lundy's role in the trial. He stood there mute for the six weeks as one witness after another read him like a text, and claimed to interpret examples of wickedness. 'My innocence,' Josef K. broods, 'doesn't simplify the matter. What matters are the many subtleties in which the court gets lost. But in the end it produces great guilt from some point where orginally there was nothing at all.'

K. is never described in *The Trial*, but you imagine him as looking similar to Kafka — someone thin and haunted, bony, pale, a serious figure inside a tight black suit, intense. At least no one accused Lundy of looking like that. Still, it was strange to see him that first day in court in his blue blazer and long pants. He had shambled around in shorts and T-shirts that summer in Kumeu. Now he looked like a professional, and he swung his black briefcase with purpose. The goatee made him look either like an academic, or 1970s whistler Roger Whittaker. 'You did murder,' announced the court clerk, 'Christine Marie Lundy.' Her widower stood in the dock, with his hands behind his back; he wore his wedding ring. 'You did murder,' the clerk also said, 'Amber Grace Lundy.' He answered each charge with the only words he spoke in the entire trial, the two words that meant the most: 'Not guilty.'

The voyage began. Justice Simon France, plump and cheerful, his silver hairdo as high and glistening as anything sported by Little Richard, welcomed the jury. 'There is a rhythm to a trial,' he said. But almost immediately he was out of step, and played a shocker when he tripped over his own tongue. He meant to say, 'The prosecution will try to prove Mr Lundy is guilty.' Instead, he misspoke, and referred to 'Mr Guilty'.

It would be a long trial, he advised, and might even continue past Easter. Much would be said and much would seem strange. 'Things unfold. There is more to come. Be patient.'

And then: 'You may or may not know this is a retrial. Do not concern yourself with the first trial, or why we are here again.' You could see the sense in that, but in essence he was asking everyone to pretend the first trial had never happened. He ventured further into make-believe in a note given to the media. 'I am loathe to create a fiction by ordering there be no reference to a retrial. However ...' Yes, loathsome as it was, he wished to create a fiction. After a bit of hand-wringing, the note declared it was a request, not a formal order, and as such it was roundly ignored.

He introduced the lawyers, and invited them to proceed wih their opening addresses. Philip Morgan QC, a tall, remote, saturnine individual from Hamilton, with a widow's peak and downturned mouth, led for the Crown. He was assisted by Ben Vanderkolk of

Palmerston North, who had prosecuted the first trial. He was slim, affable, handsome, beautifully tailored, and only rarely questioned a witness. In fact, he idled for much of the following six weeks. His relationship with Morgan seemed distant. They seldom shared each other's company during breaks; on the rare occasion that they did, they walked in silence. I said to Vanderkolk one day, 'Are you ever going to, you know, do anything in court?' He had a lovely smile, revealing small, even teeth, and joked, 'I've got battered prosecutor's syndrome.'

Experienced court watchers said that Morgan's trial work in Hamilton was outstanding. In Wellington, though, he was merely nasal and slow on his feet, and his opening address was strangely hesitant. It wasn't as though he didn't have good material. 'The accused,' he said, 'had his wife's brain on his shirt.' But it was as though he were describing a minor traffic incident. Where was the force, the necessary disgust? And if there was something apologetic in his tone, then it was revealed in Morgan's narrative of events on the night of 29/30 August 2000, when he made public for the first time that the police had completely and radically changed their mind about when Christine and Amber were killed. They had abandoned the 7pm theory. They had moved on. They now put it in the small hours of 30 August, when Lundy drove under cloak of darkness from Petone to Palmerston and performed the vile deed with a 'heavy, sharp object'.

Morgan went through the main points. Lundy was sick of his wife. Look at the savagery of the attack: 'You may think the ferocity was carried out by someone with hostility, to put it mildlly, against her.' Lundy used one of his tools as the weapon. The break-in and burglary were staged. A bracelet was found on the front seat of his car; it had fallen out of the jewellery box. He did it for the insurance. He was wearing Christine's brain: 'You will be completely satisfied it was central nervous system tissue from brain or spinal cord.' All of which had been previously stated, more elegantly, by Vanderkolk at the first trial. But Morgan announced that he had something new. He paused. The media looked up, their paws poised above their laptops. An old man in the public gallery gently dozed. The eyes of the insane judge in the portrait gallery seemed to widen, and bulge. Morgan folded his arms. Then he thrust his hands in his pockets, where they could hide from view. He looked down. He said Lundy had confessed to the murders to an inmate: 'He will tell you of their conversation.' A jailhouse snitch! Incredible — as in not credible, a pathetic joke. But there it was. A jailhouse snitch, one of the great stock characters from criminal justice, in the flesh. Were things that desperate?

Ross Burns spoke for the defence. He was a hirsute and distinguished man in his late fifties, and a roguish smile was never far from his lips. His face was surprisingly firm, as though it had been offered a lift. He had such a beautiful voice. It was the voice of a sensualist; it was redolant of strawberries and cream on a summer's evening. But he tended to mutter, and lose his place. It didn't seem as though he'd given his opening address much thought or rehearsal. Like Morgan, he played down his address. He went through the main points. Lundy was wrongfully convicted in 2002. He loved his wife. His finances were solvent. The stain on his shirt may not be human, and why was it that there was no blood splatter on his glasses, watch, shoes, or anywhere in his car? And then he, too, announced that he had something new. Evidence gathered in 2014 showed that DNA of two unknown men had been found beneath Christine's and Amber's fingernails.

I remember sitting in court when Burns made that revelation, and thinking: God almighty. Was it possible that Lundy actually was innocent, that Christine and Amber were killed by brute or brutes unknown? A new horror came to mind — two men, two strangers, two monsters, who broke into their home and went at Christine and Amber in the middle of the night. Burns added that the paint flakes found at the crime scene suggested a second weapon.

But the findings about the mysterious DNA beneath their fingernails was only ever referred to during the trial in passing, as a minor detail, nothing to really concern anyone.

'It was not possible,' Burns concluded, 'that Mark Lundy committed these crimes.' He sat down. Justice France thanked him, and dismissed the jury. It was 1.05pm. 'A short day,' he said with a smile. The first witness would be called the next morning. According to the witness list, it would be the man who had discovered the bodies.

2

She is forever seven years old, always that lovely, silly age — Amber Lundy never grew up, only ever knew life as a child, someone happy, someone adored. 'Amber,' a woman said on day two of the trial, when asked about her parents, Mark and Christine Lundy, 'was the light of their life.'

She was killed, horribly, at least swiftly. Her body was discovered in the doorway of her parents' bedroom. She got out of her own bed because she had heard her mother being killed. She can't have seen very much. It was dark. But she likely saw who was standing by the side of Christine Lundy's bed. A monster, covered in blood, a weapon in his hands. She turned. He followed.

Did she know him? Yes, said the Crown, it was her father. Yes, agreed the defence, Amber knew him. They were family. It was her Uncle Glenn.

Glenn Weggery appeared as the first witness called by the prosecution, and in cross-examination was accused of killing Christine and Amber. It was astonishing to watch. I'd never seen anyone in a court other than the defendant accused of murder. There ought to be a law against it. It was brutal and it gave notice that Lundy's defence team, led by David Hislop QC, was going to be rather more rigorous and vigorous than the team at his first trial.

I spoke with Hislop during the wait for a verdict. I said, 'Did the police warn Weggery you were going to do that?'

'Oh no,' he said. 'He was taken by surprise. That was a completely planned assault.' He laughed, hard, when he arrived at that last word. Hislop wasn't what you'd call a passive individual. He had an intelligent, sarcastic face. A tall man in his fifties, thin of hair, losing the war on plump, he was funny, likeable, and perhaps arrogant, now and then ill-tempered. His law offices were in London. It took a while for the flat vowels of New Zealand to return to his expatriate mouth; in those first couple of weeks in Wellington, he presented himself as some old duffer from the Old Bailey. We talked more about his treatment of Weggery. He said, 'We had to demonstrate that the first investigation was approached with tunnel vision. So he [Weggery] was only an example of someone we didn't think was properly investigated.'

Before his cross-examination, Weggery had told Morgan about driving over to Christine's house in the morning. He'd phoned first, but she didn't pick up. She'd promised to calculate his GST return. The curtains were closed. The sliding door at the back was open. He called out, 'Hello?' He entered the hallway, and saw Amber on the floor. He phoned for the police. The 111 call was played; Weggery sounded very calm. He felt for Amber's pulse. He said in court, 'Her head was cracked open and blood was everywhere.'

Morgan asked, 'What did you see?'

Weggery said, 'Brains.'

Amber was in the doorway of the bedroom. He looked into the room, and saw Christine.

I'd asked Levick one day about the responsibilities he felt as someone campaigning for Lundy's release. It was something that bothered me as a journalist looking into the case; I felt the pressure to act responsibly, and not recklessly, out of respect for Christine and Amber's family. They had suffered enough. Levick talked about a responsibility to the truth. He was impersonal about it. The facts were all that mattered. But that same impersonality had trampled over Weggery, the man who had discovered the mutilated bodies of his sister and niece. He later became convinced Lundy was their killer. Weggery and Levick once exchanged unpleasantries in the letters pages of the *Manawatu Standard*. Weggery wrote, 'Mr Geoff Levick, or should that be simply Levick, as he has never met or spoken to either myself or any member of my family, suggests I have "not spent a minute reviewing anything nor read a single document" … As for the insinuation that I know nothing, believe me I wish I didn't know what I do. That is that I have to look at photos to remind myself what my sister and niece even looked like, as without them all I remember is as they appeared in the crime scene photos.'

Weggery was a solidly built, tough-faced customer. He wore his hair in a crewcut, and could be seen during the trial down the road on Molesworth Street enjoying a Guinness for lunch. He was a truck driver. At the time of the killings, he flatted with a lesbian solo mother. Hislop said to him, 'Do you remember being interviewed for three hours or more by the police? Do you remember the police suggesting you knew Amber was dead before you called 111, and that's why you didn't check to see she was alive, because you had killed her?'

Weggery: 'They incorrectly suggested that.'

Hislop kept at it, and later introduced something else.

'Were you ever alone with Amber?'

'No.'

'Did you ever babysit her?'

'No.'

'Was there a particular reason why you weren't allowed to babysit Amber?'

'Not that I know of.'

Hislop then implied Weggery had form as a child abuser, and referred to an alleged incident with a 10-year-old girl. Weggery angrily said that was false. (The court later heard that the allegation was made when Weggery was about 12.) Hislop said, 'Would you describe Amber as big for her age?'

'I suppose so.'

'About the size of a 10-year-old, wouldn't you agree?'

Hislop moved on to the outrageous punchline of his vile implication — that Weggery killed Christine because she'd found out he'd been doing something to Amber. 'Your sister was asleep when you struck her, wasn't she?'

'No, I did not, and I'm not going to sit here and be accused of it!'

But that's exactly what he had to do. He sat there and was accused of it, over and over. Justice France instructed Weggery, 'If Mr Hislop suggests you have done something unlawful, feel free to ask me if you need to answer it. You are entitled not to give an answer.'

Weggery took him up on it.

Hislop: 'I suggest you were the one who hit Amber on the head.'

Weggery: 'I don't want to answer that.'

The rest of the time he straight-out denied Hislop's accusations, with rage and scorn, nailing shut the end of his sentences with an angry, over-pronounced consonant: 'No, I did not-ah ... No, that didn't happen-ah ... I know nothing about that-ah.' The latter denial was in reply to Hislop's revelation that two spots of blood were found at Weggery's house. The DNA of one spot had an 83 per cent match with Christine; the other had an 88 per cent match with Amber.

Hislop also questioned a fresh scratch on Weggery's nose at the time of the killings, and requested that the jury see a police photograph taken of Weggery. It was magnified 200 per cent and put on a flat-screen in the courtroom. Weggery's large, implacable face stared out, and the scratch looked very red, very livid. He said it was from scratching a pimple.

'It must have been a big pimple?'

'Have you never had one?'

Hislop seemed lost in thought for a moment, as though he were trying to remember whether he ever had a big pimple on his nose. Then he said, 'You changed your mind, didn't you, and told the police a cat scratched you?'

'It could have been either.'

Hislop pointed at the screen, at Weggery's giant face with the large red scratch on his snoot. He said, 'It looks fresh, do you agree?'

'At 200 per cent magnification, anything would look fresh.'

Hislop's accusation was that the scratch on his nose was caused by Christine as she tried to fend off her younger brother in the seconds before she was annihilated. It felt shocking to hear it the first time Hislop said it, and it felt no less shocking as the cross-examination wore on. On and on it went and, throughout, Hislop's manner suggested he was merely passing the time of day. Now and then he roared at Weggery, but he kept it to a minimum. He also asked about blood found on one of Weggery's towels; he'd cut himself shaving, Weggery said. 'That was careless, wasn't it?' said Hislop, not quite smiling.

After accusing the Crown's first witness of double murder and insinuating sexual abuse, you wondered what he was going to do for an encore, but he merely suggested to the next witnesses — two St John ambulance officers — that they accidentally tampered with the crime scene, galumphing here and there, transferring blood and brain tissue from one place to another like a couple of fools who should be taken out and shot.

His job done, Hislop handed over to Burns for the remaining cross-examination of Crown witnesses that day. There wasn't much to challenge. Friends of the Lundy family talked about a loving household, busy, active, normal.

The nice middle-aged woman who said Amber was the light of her parents' lives was only on the witness stand for about

10 minutes. She used to live on the same street as the Lundy family. Her son was in Amber's class, and her daughter was in Pippins with Amber.

She entered the courtroom with a young woman, who sat by herself in the public gallery: her daughter. She stood up when her mother walked back through the court after giving evidence. She touched her arm, briefly, and they left together. She had long, straight hair, and wore a summery dress. She looked about 22 or 23.

3

A metaphor for the Crown case that first week seemed to present itself on a wall outside Courtroom 1. The strict policy that dictates that New Zealand courtrooms must only exhibit really terrible works of art was maintained at the Wellington High Court in the shape of two big painted oars fastened onto the walls on the ground floor. One was on top of the other, and one went one way and the other one went the other way. The artist was identified as someone called Denis O'Connor — possibly a joke, a sly reference to America's Cup buffoon Dennis Conner — and the oar-inspiring caption blathered that his artwork 'creates an embracing, calming quality'. My feeling was that the artwork created a mocking, not especially subtle commentary on the Crown case. It felt stuck up a faecal creek without a paddle; held fast, unmoving, oarless.

The defence made the early running with Hislop's 'carefully planned assault' on the seething Weggery, and then with his even less civil treatment of former police computer 'expert' Maarten Kleintjes. Outside, it was a hot, bright day; inside Courtroom 1, with its colour scheme of dark chocolate and creamy vanilla, Hislop hoped to make Kleintjes melt. He sort of did, but mostly he didn't, and at the end of it you wondered what it had achieved, other than making the 2002 conviction look like an absolute disgrace.

Back then, the Crown alleged that Lundy had fiendishly, and also rather brilliantly, managed to manipulate the clock on his home computer. They said he had killed his wife and daughter at about 7pm, but made it look as though the computer had shut down at 10.52pm, when he had an alibi. Kleintjes was very helpful with his support of that crackpot theory. He demonstrated how it could have been done, stated there had been 'extensive manipulation of the time and date'. It created the impression that the cunning Lundy had rehearsed for the killing by fiddling with the computer on at least five occasions. The notion was rejected by the Privy Council, and formed one of the chief reasons why Lundy's conviction was quashed. The theory was a nonsense. The clock showed 10.52pm as when the computer was closed down because that was when it happened. It's also the last known time that Christine and Amber were alive.

What, then, would Kleintjes say now? He had since retired from the police; a lanky Dutchman, he had the possibly charming habit of saying 'd' instead of 'th'.

Hislop: 'You must have known that if the clock was accurate, Mark Lundy could not have carried out the murders?'

Kleintjes: 'Dat's not for me to decide.'

'No, no, no. I'm not asking you about any decisions. I'm asking about what you knew. You're not telling me you didn't know the consequences that would have on the investigation?'

'Oh, I knew de consequences.'

But he maintained that he never at any time actually stated that Lundy had manipulated the shut-down time on the computer. 'I said it was possible to change it, but I didn't say it happened. It was given as a possibility.'

'Let's see,' said Hislop, 'if the word "possibility" occurs in your conclusions in 2002.' He leafed through a document. 'There's no reference to "possibilities" in here.'

'Dere's also nothing in dere dat says it actually happened.'

'The prosecution said the computer clock was altered, and it was from your evidence.'

'It's not my evidence. I said it was possible to change it, but I didn't say it happened.'

'Sir, your evidence has changed.'

'No, it hasn't.'

After a bit more related back and forth, Hislop asked, 'Are you deliberately dancing on the end of a pin, or are you telling the truth?'

'I'm sorry,' smiled Kleintjes, 'you are getting so confused.'

He danced on de end of his pin until Hislop had finished with him, and there was a spring in his lanky step as he left the witness stand. Court adjourned, and Hislop said as we left to enjoy the summer's evening, 'Would you buy a used car from that man?'

4

What would your family and friends and people who you work with do if your back was up against the wall? Who would remain loyal, who would turn against you? And what would you do in their shoes? Yes, yes, obviously it depends; the devil is in the variabilities; but it could be that those whom you depended on would be the first to desert you, and those whom you barely knew would give you a chance. There were glimpses of the life Mark Lundy no longer knows — blameless, employed, suburban, free, loved — during the opening fortnight of his trial, when people who used to know him made their way to the witness stand.

Evidence presented in 2002 was also read out from Lundy's father, Bill, and Christine's mother, Helen, who had both since died. 'Mark and Christine live for each other,' said Bill. Helen also talked of a happy marriage. She was close to Christine; she visited every Wednesday for lunch. She wasn't aware of any problems. The biggest issue confronting the Lundy household that week was choosing a lightshade for the spare room. 'They lived,' as prosecutor Morgan said, 'in a modest little home in a blue-collar suburb.' Life was about managing time — Pippins, scouting, guiding, dance lessons, seeing friends, work. The weekend before the killings, the Durhams had gone around for dinner. Lundy cooked a barbecue. The two families played cards until after midnight. In fact, the Lundys often hosted dinners, soirées, get-togethers; they led social, busy lives.

But two friends talked about how worried Christine was about her husband's vineyard plan. The interest, she told Karen Keenan, was $600 a day. Keenan told the court, 'I said, "How the hell do you sleep at night?"' Caroline Durham told the court, 'I knew they were paying a lot of interest. I'm sure she wasn't very happy with the financial burden … It wasn't a pretty picture.' Neither woman looked at Lundy. Their instinct in cross-examination was to give short, grudging replies; hatred for the person who they believed had killed Christine and Amber filled the courtroom.

They were also the first signs that the prosecution's case was getting somewhere. Their witness list was ordered, in part, to give their case a narrative shape; it was going to be a long story.

I made myself comfortable in the public gallery. I had plenty of leg-room and occasional company. There was a pretty ex-criminologist, whose thesis was apposite: parents who kill their children. There was a woman named Mary from Epsom, in Auckland. She commuted to Wellington especially for the trial, and took a room at the YWCA during the week. The rest of the media sat squeezed in the exact same places at two long tables, behind the two rows of lawyers; on day four, Ben Vanderkolk finally broke his silence when he was given the task of questioning parking officers. For the defence, Julie-Anne Kincade brought the pleasing vowels of Belfast into the room. It almost enlivened the questioning of the parking officers.

The jury elected their foreperson at the end of the first week. Slender, with long, straight, blonde hair, she wore expensive clothes, and smoked with her left hand, holding the cigarette out at arm's length. An old courtroom saw has it that the juror who sits next to the foreperson is the one who really wanted the job. I could believe that at the Lundy trial. There was a pomposity to the Indian woman next to the forewoman; she looked as though she was used to taking charge. The faces of the jury had become familiar. There was the callow youth. There was the old boy with a limp. There were the two grey men in their fifties who came and went in a greyish fog. There was a small young woman in glasses, and a thin, worried woman of uncertain age. There was the dude with the shaved head who had the shrewd, ruthless features of someone who worked in advertising — worse, he looked like a hipster. There was the comical munter with the rubbery and really expressive face who wore talkative T-shirts. IF IT AIN'T BEAM, spoke one shirt, IT AIN'T BOURBON.

More witnesses who knew the Lundys were called to the stand. Lundy was given a conspicuously warm smile by family friend Bronwyn Neal.

Ross Burns asked, 'Did you think Mark and Christine were very much in love?'

'Oh, yes,' she said.

'Very tender and affectionate towards each other?'

'Yes. Very.'

'Argumentative, would you say?'

'Never.'

'And Amber? Was she the apple of Mark's eye?'

'Ridiculously so.'

Milvia Hannah knew Lundy through work. He had come to her showroom in Mt Cook on the day the bodies were found. She said his behaviour was 'odd'.

Hislop said, 'But when you spoke to police at the time, you said, "He was happy, smiley, like he always was."'

'I was a bit like a possum in the headlights,' she explained.

'It wasn't until after he was arrested, wasn't it, that you described his beheaviour that day as "odd"?'

'Yes, but I thought it on the day.' She ignored Lundy on her way out of the courtroom.

Brent Potter knew Lundy as a sink salesman. He invited him for morning tea in his Lower Hutt joinery business on the day the bodies were found. He had an open, relaxed face, and looked like the archetypal good joker. When he left the courtroom, the two men gave each other the familiar New Zealand male greeting of raising their eyebrows at each other.

'I bought a sink tap off of him that day,' Potter remembered. 'It was an impulse buy.' He said Lundy and his staff sat down for smoko. 'He was cheerful, the same as ever.'

Smiling, laughing; a cup of tea in the smoko room; the buying of a tap … All while Christine and Amber lay dead in their home, blood all over the walls, 'brains' as Glenn Weggery said, with the ranchslider open and the curtains closed and the phone ringing, and Christine's mother about to drive over to her daughter's house for lunch.

Maybe loyalty — and sympathy, and support — is like water. It finds its own level. If you deprive someone you know in a difficult situation of those qualities, you're as likely to place it elsewhere, with someone else who deserves it.

When Helen Weggery turned into the street, she was stopped by two police officers. Christine's house was taped off.

She said, 'That's my daughter's house. What's happened?'

They wouldn't give her a straight answer, but Helen said, 'You may as well tell me.'

One of the officers said, 'There's a body in the house.'

Helen said, 'What about Amber?'

The officer said, 'She's dead, too.'

5

Auckland, I realised during the second week of the trial, should pack up and move to Wellington. Every single summer's day was stunning and shimmering, cloudless and windless, and the Cook Strait ferry rolled along Wellington like a ball on a billiard table. At lunchtimes at the nearby waterfront, I would see jurors, lawyers, even Justice France, denuded from his black robes and scoffing an apple in the bright sunlight. The fabulous excitement and sense of national well-being stirred by the New Zealand team at the Cricket World Cup that summer added to the general happiness. Something like joy filtered inside Courtroom 1. There was an optimism that the trial might finish early, certainly before Easter. Things moved at great pace, and with the steady drip of evidence.

Over half of the 144 witnesses were called in that opening fortnight. We heard about the discovery of the bodies, Lundy's stay at the motel, the escort, morning tea, Kleintjes and his nonsense, and the 'killing journey' — Morgan's tabloid expression for Lundy's alleged drive to murder his family. Police Sergeant Danny Johanson talked of simulating the drive to and from Palmerston North. Johanson had done it six times, occasionally at great speed. That mythical journey — back then, police were in thrall to the notion of Lundy racing to and fro to commit the murders at 7pm — had become part of New Zealand motoring folklore. One day during the trial I took lunch with a barrister who told a possibly apocryphal story about Lundy's lawyer at the 2002 trial, Mike Behrens, arriving late for a meeting, apologising, and saying: 'I got here as quick as I could. I drove like a Lundy!'

Across a crowded courtroom, Johanson looked a bit like Dan Carter. At closer range, his enormous face made him look like two Dan Carters. The oversized All Black simulacrum's evidence about petrol use would assume particular importance towards the end of the trial.

Most of week two was devoted to the root of the trial's evil. The prosecution teased out their narrative that Lundy was under intolerable financial pressure, and regarded Christine's $200,000 life insurance as the answer to his woes. Enter the beancounters. Lundy's two accountants were asked about his ambitious wine venture. They described a flop. They talked of investors who never materialised, bridging finances that weren't approved, and outstanding debts that had to be written off. Lundy made an unconditional offer ('we tried to warn him') of $2 million for two parcels of land in the Hawke's Bay, where he would establish a vineyard. Lundy's stake: around about precisely zero. He registered a prospectus to raise money. He reckoned an investor in Britain would go in for £500,000. Beancounter: 'Nothing came of it.'

Actually, something sort of came of it: the mystery investor appeared in court. She was given name suppression. She said how shocked she was to receive an email from Lundy setting out the terms of her generous investment.

Morgan: 'Did you have that sort of money?'

'No.'

'Did you know anyone with that sort of money?'

'No. And I still don't.'

She was a family friend of someone who knew Lundy. The man sent her the prospectus. She was thinking of maybe making an investment of £2000. She was so stunned by Lundy's email, which breezily assumed she was good for half a million pounds, that she switched off the computer in horror.

'I couldn't even begin to respond to the email,' she said. 'It was so far out of my reality.'

What was Lundy's reality? Mike Porter, who had put together the land deal, shared his knowledge of Lundy's apparently loaded investor. He'd told Lundy, on 28 August 2000, that he had two days to make good his $2 million offer, or the deal was off. 'He said he needed more time. He had someone coming with the money. He said it was an English person. He was fairly vague …'

One parcel of land was owned by Chris Morrison, from Havelock North, who advertised that he was a landowner from Havelock North with his excellent tan, his open-necked white shirt, his cowboy boots, and his insistence on chewing gum with his mouth open. He sat next to Porter in the public gallery. They made an interesting pair, whispering and snickering; Morrison, the lord of the manor, and Porter, the ex-con who got jailed for his part in bringing in illegal immigrants to New Zealand to pick fruit and harvest grapes, and paying them peanuts. Morrison told the court that the land he sold Lundy was worth $700,000, and had asked Lundy for a 10 per cent deposit. 'He preferred zero.' They agreed on $10,000.

Lundy was supposed to pay the balance in February 2000. He missed that deadline, and the one after that. Morrison: 'I thought I'd better call him myself rather than hear second-hand his various excuses. I wanted to get to the bottom of it. He said there was no problem, apart from the excess of investors — he had such a surplus of them that he'd have to scale them back …'

He gave Lundy a final settlement date of 30 August. The bodies of Christine and Amber were found that morning.

I half-expected a gasp when the court was told about that coincidence. Things were starting to look bad for Lundy. Quietly, steadily, the case against him had made considerable ground; it was as though Morgan's prosecution was conducted in stealth. And yet there was nothing really new in any of it since the first trial. Once again, we heard the certain truth that Lundy was useless at trying to create some kind of vineyard empire; once again, we heard the argued claim that he wasn't even very good at running his kitchen sink business.

Lundy was in constant debt to sink wholesaler Robert McLachlan. 'It never seemed to go below $100,000,' said McLachlan. He rather reluctantly conceded that Lundy's sales figures were excellent. He didn't speak with anger about Lundy. It sounded more like disappointment. It sounded unforgiving and final. 'He came to stay in our Hamilton home for meals and good times,' he said, with disbelief. The last time was a fortnight before the killings. McLachlan had held a seminar for all his sales reps; he'd brought in a clinical psychologist to conduct role-play with the cream of the North Island's sellers of sinks crop. A shame the sink shrink wasn't called to give evidence about his assessment of Lundy. It was the closest anyone with actual training ever got to inspecting his character. 'You snapped, and ... became mentally ill,' said Justice Ellis, at his first trial. It was a baseless observation.

McLachlan, who was effectively Lundy's boss, said that he was concerned about the debt level of his man in Palmerston North. But his testimony also included revelations of vice and greed that were at once evil, loathsome and completely irrelevant to Lundy's murder charges. It concerned a man who wanted a good deal on a sink. McLachlan — a decent, frail man who mentioned that he had suffered four strokes — sometimes forgot small details. But his memory was vivid about a call he received when he drove to Palmerston North shortly after Christine and Amber were killed.

One of Lundy's customers was phoning. He asked — in all seriousness — if the price of a sink would still stand in light of the deaths, or if he could now get a better deal.

McLachlan searched for words. He said, 'That's the level of ... how do I put it ... ? That was human nature at its worst.'

God almighty. The want of a sink is the root of all evil. Who was that guy? Are you out there, you sonofabitch?

6

Lundy was in sinks. His failed scheme to buy and develop a Hawke's Bay vineyard suggested he should have stayed in sinks. Morgan sketched a portrait of Lundy as someone who had got in way over his head. He was facing insolvency and the threat of bankruptcy. To a murderer, life insurance is an income stream.

Phillip Sunderland, who acted as Lundy's solicitor, said he remembered meeting his former client to first discuss his plans to buy land in Hawke's Bay to grow grapes.

Morgan: 'Did Mr Lundy have any money to make the purchase?'

Sunderland: 'No.'

He said Lundy's plan was to raise the money through shares offered to investors. Lundy, he said, impressed him with his close knowledge of public subscriptions. That meeting went well, but Sunderland expressed some dismay when Lundy subsequently told him he'd made an unconditional offer to buy land valued at $2 million.

Morgan: 'Did you explain the consequences?'

Sunderland: 'Yes ... What I said to him would have been relatively robust, given that he was an adult in full control of his faculties.'

However, Lundy kept missing the settlement dates, and owed about $140,000 in penalty interest.

David Gaynor, Lundy's business advisor, described his level of encouragement when he heard about the vineyard scheme. It wasn't a very high level. 'I told him it was high-risk, and if it didn't work out it would have serious consequences.' He said he spoke with Christine Lundy about six weeks before she was murdered. 'I encouraged her to relay my very serious concerns to Mark ... She said she was very worried about the project, and would talk to Mark.'

Ross Burns took to his feet and said, 'What you haven't done is include the other side of the ledger.' Gaynor conceded that Lundy's sink business was growing, and he wasn't particularly worried about its debt levels. Burns also ferreted out similar admissions from Reginald Murphy, a police forensic accountant. Murphy had a dry cough, and presented his evidence in a kind of croak. To Morgan, he said Lundy was more or less insolvent at the time of the murders. But to Burns, Murphy croaked that Lundy's business was 'viable, and looking to the future'.

Levick gave me the impression during my visits to Kumeu that the question of Lundy's finances was the least of his concerns. He said the debts were normal for a small business, and that Lundy's income was steady. The court heard evidence that Lundy's sink business was ticking over, and a new laminate product was expected to boost sales. As for the wine enterprise, Levick admitted that was a total disaster. 'He [Lundy] really thought that pig would fly,' he said. The threat of bankruptcy, though, was fanciful. The owners of the vineyard simply had a better offer. Lundy signed up for $24,000 per acre; an American buyer offered $36,000 (and ultimately bought it). They were keen for Lundy to walk away from the deal so they could sell it for a lot more than Lundy was offering, and wouldn't bother chasing up Lundy for penalties.

What about the curious incident of Lundy's mystery investor? Her evidence was that Lundy got it into his head that she was good for half a million pounds. Why would he think that? Did he simply pull the £500,000 figure out of thin air? Was he really such a fantasist? Or was it based on some kind of information? Did someone say something to him? The woman was a family friend of one of Lundy's business acquaintances — a man who sent the woman Lundy's prospectus. A man who stood to make personal gain in the deal — he was in the root stock business — and who was a person of considerable interest during the first police investigation. Police accused him of being involved in the clean-up of the crime, and offered him immunity if he testified against Lundy. On the day of the murders, two men came to his house wanting money they were owed. Their demands frightened the man's wife and she called the police … The man was given name suppression, and provided only fairly sketchy written evidence to the court. He was too ill to appear in person. He had cancer. A month later, he died.

7

'Oh,' said Mary from Epsom, 'you missed a good week last week!' We ran into each other on a Sunday night at Auckland domestic airport. We were both headed for Wellington to attend the trial. I was going there because it was my livelihood; she was commuting because she couldn't bear to miss a second. 'I just find the whole thing,' she said, 'so deeply moving.'

I had skipped the trial for a week. Every day I longed to be in the courtroom. The thing I most wished I'd seen was the police video taken at the crime scene. I wanted to look inside the house where Christine and Amber were killed.

It felt strange to be away from court; strange, too, to return, to once again sup on honeypuffs and filter coffee at John's Kitchen, to study the progress of the brand-new paving at the Cenotaph war memorial beside Parliament, to look around the familiar faces in court. There was Lundy, his intellectual gravitas perhaps undermined by his habit of sitting with his mouth open like a door left ajar. There was Glenn Weggery, sitting in the back row of the public gallery, an intense, sardonic presence. There was Justice France, who had trimmed a metre or two off the top of his bouffant. There was Ben Vanderkolk, whose magnificent tan seemed less varnished. He'd looked Greek the last time I'd seen him, maybe Syrian. Now he looked like a guy from Palmerston North. There was Ross Burns, snug in his buttoned waistcoat, staring deeply into the screen-saver on his laptop: the blue waters of the swimming pool at his new home in Tauranga. There was Radio New Zealand reporter Sharon Lundy, whose excellent online reports were always asterixed with the note she was not related to the accused 'for avoidance of doubt'.

The subject of the morning was paint flakes. As entertainment it was about as exciting as watching paint flakes dry, but as information it was crucial to the police case. At the first trial, the jury were told that nine orange and nine light-blue flakes of paint found in Christine's hair and at the crime scene were 'indistinguishable' from the paint Lundy had used to mark his tools. The exact match — based on colour, and chemical composition — meant he had surely used one of his tools as the murder weapon. But the colour-matching was made by eye only, and there's a broad range of about 80 varieties of that paint shade. The colour was not 'indistinguishable'. The ESR's tests revealed that the paint in Lundy's garage and the chips found in Christine's hair were both alkyds, meaning they were both enamels diluted with turpentine. Meaning ... nothing much, because that's an extremely broad category of paint. The chemical composition was not 'indistinguishable'. In 2015, the paint evidence was rather less emphatic. The theory that the flakes matched the paint on Lundy's tools 'could not be excluded' as a possibility. As for the source of dark-blue paint flakes found at the crime scene, that remained a mystery. Did they come off a second weapon? Levick speculates that there were two tools — a jemmy bar, and the murder weapon — taken to the house that night by two men.

When I returned to court that Monday morning, ESR forensic scientist Bjorn Sutherland was giving evidence about the possible movement of the paint flakes. He had been on the witness stand for four days — Bjorn again — and the final hours of his epic appearance concerned the subject of whether there might have been an innocent explanation for the flakes in Christine's hair.

Hislop, in cross-examination: 'Can you discount the possibility she may have had paint fragments in her hair beforehand?' He suggested — painted, you could say — a scenario where Christine had picked up one of the tools when she was mucking about in the garage, got paint flakes on her hands, and transferred them by running her hands through her hair. Sutherland said he could not discount the possibility, but in his opinion the transfer of the paint flakes found in her cracked skull required a 'vigorous activity'.

Gillian Leak, a stout, rather humourless blood-splatter expert from Kent in England, was called to give evidence. It was startling to hear that one of the cases she'd worked on was that of the Yorkshire Ripper. She talked about the likelihood of contamination at the Lundy crime scene. In her considered opinion, it was highly likely that blood and brain tissue was accidentally transferred by officers and other people handling the bodies. She drew a kind of diagram, with arrows. Christine's brain tissue transfers to Glenn Weggery when he discovers the bodies. The tissue follows him to the back seat of a police car. The tissue transfers to police officer Brent Amas, who inspects Lundy's car — where it arrives at its final, incriminating destination, as a stain on Lundy's polo shirt.

If that was a long bow, she had another quiver to deliver. It concerned the likely movements of paint. Leak had written a report based on a theory. It actually only came to her the previous week when she was sitting in court and saw photos of Lundy's tools in his garage. Leak appeared as a defence witness. In cross-examination, Morgan said to her, 'You write a report based on something you heard in this court. Is this how it works? That's how you came up with this theory?'

'You can't rule it out,' she said.

'And are you also seriously suggesting the paint flakes in Christine's hair were transferred to Amber's head when they came in contact with the murder weapon?'

'You can't rule it out,' she droned.

'It's too silly,' Morgan said, 'for words.' He sat down without another word.

She'd come all the way from Kent to be made to look like a fool. But she had her uses. Her dour tones were put to work as a voice-over artist. Hislop asked her to provide a running commentary on a film he wished to play in the court. It was the police video taken at the crime scene. I leaned forward.

It was a silent movie, and that made it immediately frightening. There was the weatherboard house, and there was a policeman standing outside on the pavement. There was a daisy bush and a set of swings and a police tape that shook in the wind. The green paintwork on the windowsills was chipped and peeling. It matched the colour of the letterbox.

The camera went up the driveway and around the back, and examined the window that the police claim Lundy jemmied open to make it look like a burglary. There was an oil drum and a green corrugated-iron fence and a ladder with six rungs. Pallets from Lundy's kitchen sink business were leaning in an untidy pile against the house. The back yard had a small scruffy lawn, a trailer, a sock on a clothesline. And then the camera moved into the house.

The kitchen was small, with blue cupboards. There was a coffee cup on a bench, and three cans of Lion Brown. The film lasted about six minutes. It was badly lit and badly edited, and the camera shook, and all that just made it terrifying. It went up the hallway. There was Amber. She lay on the carpet. She wore a nightgown. Her small hand was curled beside her hair.

There was Christine. Everything was shadows and blood, a dark room, a missing person — the murderer. Who was it? Who was it who made that happen, who created that bleak scene so badly filmed, so horrifying? 'If you think about it,' said Leak, 'the assailant is part of the scene.'

Leak meant that his body interrupted the various flights and parabolas of the blood when he smashed Christine's and Amber's brains in, and indicated where he was standing, and the length of his weapon. The waterbed looked like it took up most of the bedroom, leaving the killer only a narrow space to stand by the side of the bed and start swinging his axe or some such weapon that killed Christine and chopped at the headboard.

She said Christine would have been lying on the left side of the bed when the first blow hit her. She tried to defend herself, and moved to the right, where she was killed.

'Amber,' said Leak, 'wasn't in bed with her mum.' That was a heartbreaking thing to hear: 'her mum'. Leak's expertise in the field of blood splatter recreated that slaughter of an innocent. 'She was upright long enough after the first blow for the blood to run down her shoulder ... The final blows came when she was face-down on the floor.'

The police video continued to move around Christine's bedroom. There was her body and there was the floral bedspread and there were the curtains. On the floor was a cloth doll. The killer had dropped it there. It used to sit on top of Christine's jewellery box, which had been taken from the house and never recovered. The camera moved closer. The doll had a smile on its face.

So this was what I had wanted to see: a six-minute horror movie, set in a home in Palmerston North, with a white electric jug on the kitchen bench and a child, dead, on a patterned carpet. It was a winter's day. The sky was grey, and the officer outside the house looked as though he was freezing. Someone had already left a bunch of flowers beside the letterbox — an offering of love for the family that no longer existed.

8

Leak's appearance as a defence witness interrupted Morgan's narrative. Justice France had allowed her to jump the queue because it was the only time she was available to travel from England to New Zealand. No matter; Morgan returned to his own witness list after she gave evidence, and arrived at the hot molten core of his story, the central drama of his narrative, the centre of his journey to establish guilt and win the trial — Lundy's shirt.

It was fixed to an exhibit board at the front of the courtroom. Made in China, 65 per cent polyester, 35 per cent cotton garment, sort of grey–blue, size XXL, as vast as a tent — its former owner would likely disappear inside it now, and not find his way out. It was like a weight-watcher's exhibit. The shirt was the 'before', Lundy was the 'after'. He still took up a lot of room, but he wasn't half the man he used to be; regardless, the shirt was like a shadow hanging over him, a ghost come back to haunt him. He wore it the night of the murders. That much was agreed by all parties. According to the Crown, he wore it under some kind of protective clothing — a pair of overalls, perhaps — and Christine's brain somehow landed on the chest and sleeve of the polo shirt while he was engaged in the process of killing.

He changed into a white shirt the next morning. He ironed it in the motel room, and put the polo shirt, inside-out, in a travel bag with a pair of green underpants and some socks. The police took the bag and its contents after he sped to Palmerston North when he heard of the murders. It was placed in a forensic bag the following week, and was finally examined by Bjorn Sutherland 59 days after the killings. That was when he noticed the two suspicious stains. The shirt was labelled exhibit number C3003; the stain on the pocket became C3003/4, and the stain on the sleeve became C3003/3. Sutherland made glass slides of the stains. What were they? How to identify their origin? And who was best equipped in the field of transferring cellular material from one slide to another? Police asked Scotland Yard and the FBI for assistance, but got nowhere. So much for those venerable palaces of forensic inquiry. But then the call went out to Texas cancer researcher Dr Rodney Miller, who had made his serendipitous appearance at a medical conference in Palmerston North just three days before the killings, and talked about his work in the field of … transferring cellular material from one slide to another.

In the event, Miller didn't bother with Sutherland's slides. He took samples directly from the shirt. Thin slices were mounted on glass slides, and embedded in wax, or paraffin blocks. The slides were stained with two dyes: hematoxylin and eosin. Miller examined the slides under a microscope. They suggested the presence of central nervous system tissue. Next, he applied the exquisite science of his immunostains, which provided 'conclusive evidence', as he said in the 2002 trial, of human brain. Case closed.

Except that Levick's dogged investigations long after the trial led him to other experts in the field who totally rejected Miller's findings. Miller, in turn, scorned their views. A bitter war of words — Miller had a flair for name-calling, later describing one eminent chemist as 'blowing smoke from his arse' — was recorded in their affidavits placed with the Privy Council in 2013. The stage was set for a showdown at the retrial. Miller versus his critics, who would tear into the validity of his immunostains and denounce the Texan as inept, wrong-headed, a bum.

Except it didn't work out that way. I said to Hislop while we were waiting for the verdict, 'Miller — he's been vindicated in this trial, hasn't he?'

He said, 'He has, to be honest.'

I filched a photocopy from Levick's den to take with me to Wellington. I felt it was necessary to have on hand. It was an enlarged image of C3003/3 — that microscopic stain on Lundy's shirt, magnified many times. It was purple with hematoxylin and eosin dyes, and looked vaguely artistic, like an interesting abstract. The image was shaped something like the North Island. Miller wrote in a report, 'Cell nuclei were clearly visible, and the morphologic appearance was compatible with brain tissue ... A subsequent battery of immunostains showed that this tissue reacted positively with GFAP, S100 protein, neurofilament, and synaptophysin. This pattern of immunoreactivity is that of tissue originating from the central nervous system (brain or deep spinal cord) ... It provided unequivocal evidence that Mark Lundy had brain tissue on his shirt from an area that also contained Christine Lundy's DNA.'

Miller appeared at the second trial by videolink from his home in Dallas. There wasn't much of a cross-examination. Hislop challenged him on the cleanliness of his laboratory, and questioned him about the possibility of contamination. In his evidence to Morgan, Miller revealed that he had made new immunostains on Lundy's shirt with the same result: clear evidence of central nervous system tissue. He also carried out the same tests on a fresh brain. They made for an interesting — and revealing — comparison with the stuff on Lundy's shirt. The Lundy samples were taken from the paraffin blocks. 'They will remain stable for decades, if not hundreds of years,' Miller said. No one contested that; the issue with his immunostains had always been that the stain on Lundy's shirt would have been so degraded that it was 'impossible' to determine the nature of the cells. They had simply been on the shirt for too long — 159 days had passed before Miller cut away the fabric, and tested the stains. Nonsense, Miller countered, and came up with a brilliant argument in the shape of his testing on a fresh brain. He took tissue from it and smeared it on fabric. He left it to dry in a cupboard. He tested it with his immunostains after 28 days, and his markers showed positive for central nervous system tissue. He tested it after 159 days, matching his forensic examination of Lundy's shirt, and his markers showed positive for central nervous system tissue. He tested it after 365 days, and his markers showed positive for central nervous system tissue.

Case closed, in essence; despite Levick's furious arguments to the contrary, Hislop felt there was no longer any evidential basis to challenge Miller in court. Their own expert agreed with Miller. Dr Colin Smith, a small, chubby neuropathologist from the University of Edinburgh, was called to the stand. Och, the poor wee man had a terrible cold. He snuffled and wheezed, and his nose glowed red. Did he agree that the tests on Lundy's shirt revealed the presence of central nervous system tissue? He held a paper tissue to his dripping snoot, and dredged up his devastating answer through piles of phlegm: 'There's no question that's what it is.'

I'd caught up with Levick the previous week at a foodhall in west Auckland. He was receiving regular updates from Lundy, and felt confident of Lundy's chances of acquittal. He said: 'They haven't landed a punch yet.' I texted him when prosecution witness Daniel du Plessis gave evidence: 'They've landed a punch.'

Du Plessis, a forensic neuropathologist at the University of Edinburgh, regretted to say he'd had plenty of opportunity to study the brains of homicide victims in his native South Africa: 'We are awash in crime.' Gillian Leak had made mention of her work on the Yorkshire Ripper investigation. Du Plessis made mention of his work on the tragedy of the 96 people killed at the Hillsborough football stadium.

The New Zealand police had contacted him in 2013 to look into the Lundy case. They asked him whether he could establish the nature of the stains on Lundy's polo shirt: 'If it was tissue, which part of the body this tissue came from.' He set about replicating Miller's immunostains.

Morgan: 'And what was the outcome?'

'His observations were correct.'

Du Plessis was a very direct witness. He explained complex methodology in a simple and authoritative manner. He said, 'I was impressed by the quality of [Miller's] tests. I made the same observations as he did. All the boxes you expect to be positive for central nervous system tissue were ticked. None of the results were dubious or ambivalent.'

There you had it. It was all over bar the pretty pictures. Beautiful images of the staining techniques filled the big screens in the courtroom. They were psychedelic abstracts, in deep purples and feminine pinks, magnified 200,000 times — one was shaped like a map of the North Cape, another was like a pencil drawing. Du Plessis took the role of art historian, helpfully pointing out salient features: 'Here, we see the fine meshwork of nerve fibres … Here, we can see layered stacks of myelin. It looks like a stack of pancakes.' He explained that myelin was a fatty sheath, or membrane, which insulates nerve fibres in the brain.

The whole question of the degraded quality of the stain, said du Plessis, was a nonsense. He compared dried brain tissue to the wonderful preservation of Egyptian mummies, and the tasty preservation of biltong, those dried strips of leather which in South Africa are considered to be food.

When his exhibition of slides came to an end, Morgan asked him, 'In your opinion, what was found on the shirt?'

The next PowerPoint slide came up on the screen. It had words on it. It was headlined, CONCLUSION. Du Plessis read it out: 'Incontrovertible evidence of tissue of central nervous system origin (brain or spinal cord).'

The punchline was much the same as his opening statement, but it felt even more damning to see it written on a screen. And then du Plessis, unequivocal to the end, told the jury: 'The evidence is overwhelming and incontestable.'

What are you left with after 'overwhelming and incontestable'? It was all down to the shirt, and the shirt was like a noose around Lundy's neck. But I had forgotten a small detail. It was something Levick had come up with way back in 2003, not long after he'd taken an interest in the whole saga. He'd read up on Miller's immunostains, and wrote in an email to Lundy's closest friend, 'The chemical markers used to test positive for brain signals only recognise mammalian tissue … There is no differentiation between human, dog, horse, sheep etc.'

Hislop slowly got to his feet to begin cross-examination. He looked away — he rarely made eye contact with witnesses — and appeared lost in thought. 'Dr du Plessis,' he said after a while, 'you can't say, can you, if the central nervous system tissue that you say you found is human, or non-human?'

Du Plessis: 'No.'

Human, or animal? Christine, or food? I looked again at my filched photocopy of Miller's immunostained image of C3003/3. What was I looking at? What was the true nature of the cells on the sleeve of Lundy's stupid polo shirt? Police searching Lundy's car found a wrapper for a beef and chilli pie. Was all of that testing — 'it's extremely labour-intensive work', du Plessis remarked — conducted on the spilled remains of a meat pie? Did Lundy kill his own wife and daughter, or was he just a fat slob with pie down his shirt?

9

Police saw the vexed question coming. Just as they had scoured the world back in 2001 to find someone who could test whether the stains on Lundy's shirt were tissue fragments from Christine's brain, and their prayers were answered in the shape of Dr Rodney Miller and his amazing dancing immunostains, which were criticised as 'novel ... innovative', so they scoured the world in 2014 to find someone who could test whether the stains were human, and their prayers were answered in the shape of Netherlands Forensic Institute head Dr Laetitia Sijen and her amazing dancing RNA molecular experiments, which were criticised as 'novel ... innovative'.

It was imperative for Lundy's defence to stop Sijen in her tracks. Hislop had tried, and failed, to convince a pre-trial hearing and the Court of Appeal that Sijen's evidence should be ruled inadmissible. A third attempt was made during the trial at a closed hearing in front of Justice France. Hislop once again referred to Professor Stephen Bustin's considered opinion that Sijen's testing was 'novel', invalid, no better than a 'pseudo-science'. It shouldn't be put in front of a jury, Hislop argued; it was prejudicial to a fair trial. The appeal failed. In his ruling, France duly noted that one of the three judges at the Court of Appeal hearing had voted to rule out Sijen's evidence: 'The novelty of the work was a matter that influenced Ellen France in her dissent.' He meant his wife. No doubt Mr and Mrs France have many differences of opinion. 'In my view,' France ruled, 'Professor Bustin's evidence is simply another opinion.'

The genie was out of the bottle. Sijen had her day — several days — in court. Like Leak with the Yorkshire Ripper, Sijen began by talking of her encounters with human depravity. She had investigated war crimes in the former Yugoslavia. There was something fragile about Sijen. She had slightly pleading eyes, and a nervous disposition. She brought along a colleague from the Netherlands Forensic Institute to support her in court.

It sounded like a fun place to work. There were 700 people in its offices in The Hague, working across a range of forensic disciplines; Sijen was head of research and development in the department of human biological traces. She explained that RNA was a molecular material found in human and animal tissue cells. That was about as simple as it got, and Justice France intervened to get her to talk in lay terms. He said to her, 'You and I will have different DNA, but our blood cells will have the same RNA?'

'Exactly.'

'Thank you,' he said.

She went on to describe the method of RNA analysis which she'd developed at her laboratory. It was used, she said, to identify the origin of organ tissue — whether it came from the liver, lung, brain, etc. When she was contacted by the New Zealand police to identify whether the tissue on Lundy's shirt came from the human brain, she developed a new model. Sijen introduced four markers that would signal the presence of RNA molecules found exclusively in the human brain. She tested them on the Lundy shirt sample, as well as brain tissue taken from a cow, a sheep, a chicken, a cat, a dog, a rabbit, a pig and a guinea pig. 'You can order their brains online,' she pointed out.

Her initial tests showed no sign of human brain RNA in the sheep, cat, dog and guinea pig. Interestingly, though, signals were picked up in samples taken from the cow, the rabbit and the pig. Another test was taken. This time the temperature was raised from 64 to 68 degrees, and the signals disappeared. There you have it: the difference between the human race and the cow, rabbit and pig is four degrees of separation.

The four markers were used on the C3003/3 tissue on Lundy's sleeve, and the test was repeated three times. This was the moment of truth. What would the test reveal from a possible 12 positive reactions to human brain? The score: seven reactions out of 12, or 58 per cent. 'From the results,' said Sijen, 'we infer that human central nervous system tissue was present.' Sijen had arbitrarily decided that 50 per cent was a pass rate. Her tests had only narrowly passed. The evidence, then, was that Lundy wore his wife's brain on his shirt.

Hislop roared at Sijen that her tests were unreliable, prone to error, 'greatly flawed', B-grade forensic science, and a work in progress that had never actually been performed before. Why hadn't the Crown found anyone to support her work, like du Plessis had with Miller? Could it be that no one was prepared to be seen with her in public? How dared she pass off her tests as valid? There was a sense that she copped the kind of attack meant for Miller until it seemed apparent that his immunostaining tests were vindicated and Hislop felt he had to back off. He said to me in the wait for the verdict, 'Taking on Miller would have done us all sorts of credibility damage, especially when we had to fight Sijen's testing as well. We needed credibility for that fight.'

After her long mauling on the witness stand, Sijen could be seen weeping as she was led away by her colleague. No doubt it was brutal. But a greater damage had been inflicted on Lundy's defence. The science did for him. The shirt did for him. It had Christine's DNA on it, although that was to be expected, and no one knew whether it originated from the tissue or had arrived independently — a cough, a sneeze. It had central nervous system origin (brain or spinal cord) on it, according to Miller, backed up by du Plessis as well as the defence's own expert witness, the coughing Scotsman Dr Colin Smith. And now, according to the nervous, weepy Sijen — although the defence later called two scientists of obvious genius who tore her work to sheds, and although the Crown had no one to back her up, no one to agree with her, no one who sided with her in the slightest — it had human brain on it. One, two, three. *Gotcha*.

10

The myth of scientific fact got a terrible battering at the trial. It was a parade of brilliant minds, and there were times when the mere appearance of an expert lifted the ambient IQ in the courtroom. But everywhere you looked there was dispute, rancour, denial, bitter attack, weary acceptance, name-calling, tears — everywhere you looked was mere opinion. Or not even that. The forensic nadir of the trial looked as though it had been reached early on when police computer 'expert' Maarten Kleintjes tried to distance himself from the crackpot theory that Lundy had fiendishly manipulated the clock on his home computer. But in the second week of March, one of the strangest characters in the Lundy saga arrived on the witness stand.

Dr James Pang conducted the autopsies on the bodies of Christine and Amber. It was his crackpot theory that their stomach contents, and the absence of the tell-tale smell of gastric juices, meant that they had died pretty much exactly one hour after their last meal. The whole charade of trying to prove they were killed at around 7pm began with Pang's nose. When Lundy's conviction was quashed by the Privy Council, one of the main reasons was its rejection of the time of death: 'New evidence eradicates scientific support for the claim.'

Its origins were recorded by a witness who preceded Pang on the stand. In 2000, Inspector Brett Calkin was put in charge of Amber's body. He talked about going to the house and putting on paper overalls. Amber's body lay in the hallway. Calkin and two other officers approached her. The winter's day, the police caravan parked outside; the silent house, the murdered seven-year-old girl, the big footsteps of strangers in the Lundy hallway; there was such kindness in the way Calkin said her name.

'We placed Amber in the back of a hearse ... Her body was stored in a refrigerator, and I locked the door and used a padlock which only has one key that I held on to ... I removed Amber from the fridge and took her to the main room.'

She was weighed at 9.25pm. Her body was washed at 10.52pm prior to the autopsy. At 12.45am, Dr Pang opened her stomach, and Calkin wrote down what Pang said: 'The contents are possibly potato, maybe fish, maybe meat, no apparent vegetables.' Maybe food: her last meal was from McDonald's. And then Calkin read out Pang's assessment: 'Most likely death has occurred within one hour of the meal.'

Pang was next on the stand. He was small, even rather petite, with very black hair for a man in his sixties, and a puffy face. Most witnesses leaned forward. Pang leaned back in his chair. The microphone had to be bent towards him. He was like a little sultan.

Vanderkolk, making a rare speaking appearance in court, questioned him for an hour. Most of the time Pang talked about the appalling injuries that Amber and Christine suffered. Vanderkolk led Pang into intimate detail. 'Seven large gaping cut wounds ... 80 millimetres in length and 5 centimetres in depth ... The wounds had sharp, clean-cut edges ... They shattered the bones of the face ... The major portion of the front half of the brain was missing,' etc.

The issue of stomach contents was raised twice, briefly; and both times Pang's voice came out in a terrible croak, and he guzzled down water to soothe his troubled throat.

He drank quite a lot during the afternoon when he was cross-examined. It began so tenderly. 'Sir,' said Hislop, 'if I can take you through your postmortem of Amber Grace Lundy? Thank you.'

Pang was quick to state that his theory of a 7pm time of death was, in fact, only a 'rough estimate'. He said: 'At present, the only thing I can say with any certainty is that Christine and Amber died sometime in the 14 hours between when they were last known to be alive, and when their bodies were discovered.'

Hislop: 'Your position now is markedly different.'

'Not entirely.'

'Are you saying that your 14-hour window, which you tell us today, is consistent with your position in 2000, that they died one hour after the meal?'

'That's right. Yes.'

'When was it you changed your mind? When did you change your mind? Do you accept you changed your mind?'

'No. The one-hour estimate is within the 14-hour certainty.'

He smiled, and appeared to wag his head from side to side.

Hislop said, 'Are you familiar with the code of expert witnesses? It says you're not here to bat for one side. You have a duty to be impartial.'

'That's correct, yes,' Pang croaked.

Justice France stepped in, and asked Pang if he still accepted that Christine and Amber were killed an hour after their meal. Pang answered, 'Now I would not give that as an estimate.'

Hislop thanked the judge, and said to Pang, 'You have accepted to His Honour that you changed your position. When was it you changed your mind? Do you understand the question?'

Pang licked his lips, and croaked, 'I think so.'

'Well, could you answer it?'

'I gave an estimate, but the only certainty is in the 14-hour bracket.'

'Let's just try again. When was it you changed your mind?'

And then Pang said, 'I would think it was after reading the Privy Council judgment.'

It was 4pm. He had taken two hours to answer the question. But Hislop hadn't quite finished. He said, 'Who made you change your mind? Was it put to you that you should say what you're telling us, that the only certainty of time of death is in the 14-hour bracket?'

'I have not been talked into changing my mind by anyone.'

'Tell me this,' said Hislop. 'You say it was after the Privy Council judgment in 2013. Did you ring the police, and say, "Hey, I got it wrong"? Did you say, "I'm dreadfully sorry, but having reflected on the Privy Council judgment, I got it wrong"?'

'No.'

'On January 26 this year, the prosecution advised us they had changed the time of death. Is that when you changed your mind, too? And would that be a coincidence?'

He croaked, almost noiselessly. It sounded like a 'no'. Hislop had conducted the cross-examination through rather clenched teeth. It might have had something to do with the fact that the first he'd been informed that Pang had a Damascene experience and changed his view on the time of death was the previous night. Things finally came to an end, and Pang was excused. When he left, the ambient IQ of the courtroom seemed to lift.

11

His name had become like a rumour. He was talked about, a lot, but never seen. Witness after witness mentioned him, sometimes in passing, sometimes under questioning. It was always in the past tense. Perhaps he was dead. They were talking about something that happened a long time ago. Perhaps he was only a ghost, his name haunting the courtroom.

But then he was summoned, and there stood Police Inspector Ross Grantham, a tall man with silver hair and a superb posture in his blue police uniform with three pips on each shoulder and a merit award pinned to his chest. It's likely the award was presented to him in recognition of his massive role as officer in charge of the investigation into the murders of Christine and Amber Lundy.

Grantham, who busted Lundy; Grantham, who led the inquiry into one of the worst prosecutions in modern New Zealand criminal history, when stomach contents, computer manipulations, and hallucinating psychics were used to bolster his fanatical belief that Christine and Amber were killed at about 7pm. How could he have got it so wrong? What was he thinking? What did it say about the rest of the investigation? There was a very keen sense of anticipation among the media when Grantham approached the stand. The expectation was that the defence would attempt to tear him a new one.

He came prepared. He brought five journals with him to the stand. They formed an impressive stack, but that was nothing compared to his back-up — another police officer entered the court dragging a two-wheeler trolley loaded with journals and folders containing goodness knows how many pages of various assorted memoranda.

Vanderkolk stood for the prosecution. He knew Grantham well — they were respected establishment figures together in Palmerston North, and had worked closely together on the trial in 2002. He asked Grantham, 'Do you remember a meeting with Mark Lundy on December 4, 2000?'

Grantham said, 'Can I refer to my notes?'

He was told that he could. He searched his pockets, and wailed, 'In my hurry to get here I left behind my glasses!'

It was interesting to note his anxiety, his small wave of panic. A police officer was sent to search for the glasses in an office outside the courtroom. He didn't return. The judge gave Grantham permission to track down the spectacles. The three pips and the merit award were lost in a blur of blue as he legged it out of the court. He was away a few minutes. He returned, triumphant. He took his seat, put on his spectacles, peered inside a folder, and said to Vanderkolk: 'Yes.'

They discussed the December 4 meeting. Lundy had called it, to check on the police investigation into the murders. Grantham asked him whether police could search his car and some belongings, and Lundy said sure, no problem. 'The accused said he wanted to help us any way he could.'

Vanderkolk then asked Grantham a series of questions about the slides containing samples taken from Lundy's polo shirt. Grantham said he kept the slides in a safe in his office. He packed them — and the polo shirt — for the visit to Dallas, Texas, where Dr Miller snipped out the stained areas on the fabric, embedded them in paraffin wax, removed small slices, and exposed them to his immunostaining technique. Grantham took the paraffin blocks back to New Zealand, and put them in his safe.

'Thank you,' said Vanderkolk. 'That will be all.'

Grantham was on the stand for all of 15 minutes. Justice France called for a break; the defence would go at Grantham after lunch.

But the defence did not go at Grantham after lunch. Ross Burns treated him with great courtesy, and asked him not especially detailed questions in a pleasant and respectful manner for 45 minutes. It was all over so fast the prosecution were unable to call their next witness. 'I've been caught short,' Morgan told the judge. He had plainly expected that Grantham would remain on the stand for all that Thursday afternoon and probably into the following week.

The five journals, the two-wheeler trolley supporting millions of words about Mark Lundy — none of it was needed. Grantham floated out of the courtroom.

What just happened? What was Burns playing at? He hadn't done much more than engage Grantham in small talk. There were a few questions about potentially suspicious activity reported in Lundy's neighbourhood on the night of the murders — a woman screaming, dogs going berserk, the sound of breaking glass. That didn't go very far.

Things looked more promising when Burns raised the controversial subject of Grantham's meeting with pathologist Dr Heng Teoh. Grantham arranged the meeting in January 2001 to ask Teoh whether he could identify tissue on the slides taken from Lundy's shirt. He wrote at the time, 'He [Teoh] would only commit to saying the cells are tissue cells. He opined that the time lapse between the murders and the preparation of the slide (59 days) was too long. The cells had degenerated badly. What concerned me about Dr Teoh was that he was quite clear that he did not want to be involved in a police investigation and did not want to have to give evidence in any court proceedings. When he looked at the slide he commented that he did not think Mark Lundy should be convicted on the strength of the cells in the slide. He then pointed out that just because Christine Lundy's DNA was on his shirt didn't mean a lot, as she was his wife. He later commented that this case may have to remain an unsolved mystery.'

Grantham's failure to disclose his report to the defence at the first trial was only made known three days before the Privy Council hearing in 2013. 'Out of the woodwork it came,' as Hislop put it, during our interview in the Wellington High Court. 'It was absolutely incredible that it had not seen the light of day.' Surely, then, Burns would demand Grantham explain the omission. But he didn't. Well, what about the curious business of Grantham keeping extremely sensitive evidence — the glass slides — in the safe in his office? What sort of practice was that? And did it have anything to do with the mystifying fact that the tissue on Sutherland's glass slides was very poorly degraded after 59 days, but the tissue that Miller took from Lundy's shirt after 159 days, in Grantham's presence, was in a much better condition?

Leaving aside the science, what about the focus of the investigation? How soon did Grantham decide it was Lundy? Was he obsessive in his determination to bust Lundy, and was this at the expense of failing to investigate other options? Minor example: did police ever follow up the presence of small rubber fragments found in Christine's bedroom, as recorded in the notebooks of two police officers? A tomahawk with a rubber handle was stolen from a neighbouring property that night. Did police look into the possibility of a match? Was the information somewhere among the suitcases and folders and volumes that Grantham wore like an armour into Courtroom 1?

There were other, much better questions that could have been put to Grantham. But there was no rough-housing, no inquisition. It was more like a genteel conversation which eventually petered out. After Morgan admitted that he didn't have any witnesses on standby, France announced with great pleasure that court was adjourned for a long weekend.

I bailed up Burns outside the courtroom, and demanded of him, 'WTF?'

He smiled most charmingly, puckishly even, and said, 'Oh, come now. He's a very senior policeman. It wouldn't do to try to undermine his credibility. It wouldn't do at all.' At least he resisted the temptation to wink.

Yes, Hislop said later, it was a deliberate tactic. 'We didn't need to attack him; and it's hard to know how juries are going to react when you confront a copper.'

I said, 'Behrens did that in 2002 when he accused Grantham of planting brain tissue on Lundy's shirt.'

'Yeah. Catastrophic. It blew up in their faces. It's pretty desperate unless you have evidential basis. Keeping it in the safe was a bit odd, but apart from that … We weren't going to attack the man just because some of our supporters didn't like him. Geoff and others blamed him for Mark's incarceration. I'm sure Grantham thought he was in for a royal roasting, but we didn't need to go there.'

Grantham's release brought an end to week four of the trial. Mary from Epsom reluctantly went to Singapore; it was an annual holiday, and she'd booked it well in advance, but it pained her to miss even a day of the trial. She'd made a friend, Anne, from up the Hutt railway line in Woburn. Anne said: 'He's guilty, isn't he?' Mary regarded it as a mystery and a tragedy. I regarded it in much the same way. I went home for a week. I loved the strange half-life I was leading in Wellington, a detached observer in Courtroom 1, quietly roaming the waterfront and the town belt at day's end, honeypuffs for breakfast and garlic prawns for dinner, but I longed for my family, too. I was caught between love and an interest that went beyond professional curiosity. Important events took place outside of the Wellington High Court. Local and possibly international news led with the story that Natalia Kills had said mean things to some drip on *X Factor New Zealand*. I remained preoccupied with the the trial. They have a rhythm, Justice France had said. They have a momentum. The weeks had gone by like carriages on a railway track, creaking and thumping along, twisting and turning, always moving forward. You never knew what would happen next, or who the cat would drag out from under a rock.

12

There he was, at last, in person, his presence advertised on the very first day of the trial when the prosecution stated in its opening address that it would call on the services of one of the most fabled and despised characters in criminal history — a jailhouse snitch. Witness X, as he must be known, was asked to swear on oath. 'Aw yeah,' said X.

This was how the Crown prepared to come to the end of its massive effort to prosecute Lundy for a second time: not yet with a bang, in the meantime with a snitcher. The court was cleared, the door locked, the TV cameras switched off. Outside, a fresh autumn day in the capital; inside, a murky little sub-plot to the trial. The police did their best to conceal signs of shame. Detective Andy Partridge, who was always the coolest man in the room with his long black hair and pretty shirts, tried to assume a poker face. It was hard not to laugh. X was a comical and gnome-like character, tattooed, smirky, who wore his shirt buttoned tight up to his neck. He had a wide chest and looked as though he might be handy with his fists, but his record of violence was restricted to acts of despicable cowardice — domestic assault, beating partners and children. He listed his CV — his criminal vitae — by way of admitting to stretches in numerous prisons. He met Lundy at Rimutaka in March 2002.

Lundy showed no sign of recognition as X was led into the court. Perhaps he didn't remember him. It was a long time since they had met, and the two men hadn't actually spent a lot of quality time together. But X remembered Lundy.

In fact, he remembered him in some detail. He said Lundy wore shorts, a jersey, and white trainers. They were in a prison yard. They sat opposite each other on benches. X sat astride the bench.

There were two other inmates and the four of them were going to play cards, but the other two just sort of jumped up and wandered off. It was getting on to lunch. X and Lundy talked about what was on the menu. Probably sandwiches, X remembered. Peanut butter sandwiches.

They'd never met before and they never talked again other than to say hi, how's it going, during the two weeks they were in the same segregation unit of the prison. 'He looked familiar,' said X, 'but I didn't know who he was. I knew his first name was Mark.' The whole country knew that, too. Lundy was a household name, and one of the most recognisable people in New Zealand. He was enormous, a big fatty with Coke-bottle glasses and a bland, round face.

They started talking. Morgan asked X, 'What did the two of you chat about?'

X said, 'He asked me what I was in for. I told him it was a bank robbery and I wouldn't be in there if it wasn't for my mum telling the police. He said he wouldn't be in there if his daughter hadn't come in and seen what he was doing to his wife. He told me he'd been planning it for a while and she had it coming to her.'

And there it was. Startlingly, frankly, absolutely: the confession. Lundy had denied it to police, to family, to friends, to everyone, but blurted it out to a small-time crook he had only just met in a prison yard.

X didn't find it particularly interesting. He said, 'I just thought he was in there for beating his wife up or something like that.' He added that Lundy mentioned he was waiting for his appeal to go through.

The years passed. Curiously, they didn't keep in touch. X went back to prison, got released, went back inside again, over and over. The stretches were usually about three months. He once told a parole officer, 'Some people go to Paris every year. I go to prison.'

He was quite a funny guy; he had an appealing kind of smile, and his comic timing was excellent. The court was played a farcical telephone recording of his call to the police in 2013 when he'd seen his old mate Mark on TV — the Privy Council had overturned Lundy's conviction, and ordered his release from jail.

X: 'I hadn't really thought about what he'd said to me for a long time, but when I saw him on TV I had a flashback.' He decided to inform the authorities of that conversation of old. Morgan said, 'Why?'

X said, piously, 'It was the right thing to do.'

He went about it in a haphazard way, though. X chose to call the motorway traffic number *555 ('It just popped into my head') and asked to be put through to police because he had vital information about Mark Lundy. The operator said she couldn't do that. A recording of the call was played in court.

X: 'If you can't put me through, sweet as, I won't bother about it.'

Operator: 'Okay.'

X, under his breath: 'Fucken hell.'

Later, X sat down and wrote a letter to a judge. It began: 'Sir. I have the smoking gun to end all smoking guns. I have information about a cold-blooded murderer ...' The rest of the letter was a whining demand to be released on bail.

His lawyer advised him not to send the letter if he wanted to be a credible witness.

For the defence, Burns asked, 'Have you ever taken any advice on being a credible witness?'

'Nah,' said X.

'Perhaps you should have,' said Burns.

X, Burns pointed out, constantly elected to be in segregation in prison. It offered a better chance of protection from harm. Burns: 'You probably saw Mark Lundy as a really good opportunity to get segregation for life, I suggest. Narking on him would get you favours. This is one of the biggest trials this country has ever seen, do you agree with that?'

'You probably know better than me,' said X.

'One way of ensuring segregation is to say, "I'm the one who narked on Mark Lundy." That's right, isn't it?'

'Nah.'

'To put it bluntly, in order for you to have a comfortable time in prison, you're prepared to put another man in prison for the rest of his life, aren't you?'

'Nah.'

Burns talked about X's long criminal history ('I've made some bad decisions'), which included about 30 dishonesty offences, and read from reports which described his character as 'manipulative ... with multiple personality disorders'. X couldn't even lie straight in his little cot. A good liar sometimes tells the truth; X was compulsive. Those peanut butter sandwiches he remembered having for lunch in prison — was it Eta or Sanitarium, smooth or crunchy? Burns should have asked, because X had an answer for everything.

The subject returned to that amazing conversation between X and Lundy back in 2002. Burns said he had some interesting documents that he wanted to share with the court. He searched manila folders, bound volumes, his briefcase. 'Perhaps we should adjourn for afternoon tea,' France sighed.

'Thank you, Your Honour.'

When court resumed, Burns had found his documents. He was right. They were very interesting. They placed X and Lundy in the yard together on four occasions. The dates were all during the weekend.

And then Burns said, 'Do you know why you weren't together between Monday and Friday? It's because Mr Lundy was in court. He was on trial in 2002. He hadn't even been convicted. He couldn't possibly have been waiting for his appeal, as you have told us. Everything you've said is a lie, isn't it?'

X said, 'Nah! Cos he said he was waiting for an appeal!'

Snitch, squirming; snitch, stitched.

13

There was one last witness for the prosecution: Lundy. Lundy, as he was in 2000 and 2001, when he was interviewed by Detective Inspector Steve Kelly in a small interview room in the Palmerston North police station. The films were played in court. They were long, rambling, inconsequential, pedantic, humourless, boring — then suddenly chilling and apparently deeply incriminating.

The first interview was filmed on 14 September 2000, a fortnight after the murders, and the day before Lundy would be taken back to the house for the first time since he had left to travel to Petone. He was nervous about it. 'I don't know how I'm going to handle that,' he told Kelly towards the end of the interview. 'I did a sort of practice run the other night. I drove round the roundabout [near the house] and had an anxiety attack. It was too close.'

Lundy subsequently described the visit at his first trial: 'They opened the ranchslider. It took courage but I went in … There was a half-bottle of Crossroads merlot on the kitchen bench. I was asked if it was cooking wine. Crossroads would have been disgusted at the thought, and I made that comment … I then had to go up the hallway. I saw blood on the floor outside my bedroom door and I lost control. I'd put a scenario in my head where Christine and Amber had not suffered, and not seen each other die.'

A police officer gave this eyewitness account: 'We made our way to [the] start of the hallway and that's where he stopped. He became very upset. He was breathing very heavily, and I recall him holding the arm of the Victim Support guy and I recall him placing his hands over his face, and taking every possible last gasp of breath. He didn't walk up the hallway, he sidled up against the wall, like you would if you were creeping.'

Genuine, awful horror and despair, or the over-actor at it again, making an exhibition of anguish? Keen observers of body language no doubt picked up signals or whatever in the film of the police interview, too. Lundy and Kelly sat at a small table. There was a clock on the wall. Kelly was a compact man in his thirties. He wore a white shirt and tie. Lundy slumped forward in a grey tracksuit. He had a smooth, round face, a fringe, and was huge, a whopper. This was the Lundy everyone remembered. This was the Lundy everyone loathed. Kelly said, 'How are you feeling, mate?'

'Truthfully? Absolute shit. Honestly, I am an absolute wreck.'

'Can I ask how you've been sleeping?'

'Badly. Last night I ended up watching cricket and fell asleep on the couch. Sometime after three I got up and went to bed. It took probably about three-quarters of an hour to an hour to get to sleep and I slept for about an hour. Then just lay in bed.'

'Mate, do you want a drink of water or coffee?'

'Yeah, water if you could.'

Kelly asked Lundy about his movements in Petone on the night of the murders. He said he had dinner in his motel room, and then drove across the road to read a book. His favourite author was Wilbur Smith: 'I've read all except one of his books.' When it got too dark, he went back to the room and polished off most of a 1.125-litre bottle of rum mixed with Diet Coke. He was celebrating the launch of a new kitchen product. 'It's going to be extremely profitable.' He talked about phoning the escort.

'Where do you use an escort, just in Wellington?'

'No, I've used one in Napier and New Plymouth. I'd estimate a couple of times in each place in the last five years.' He stayed at the Marineland Motel and the Snowgoose Lodge in Napier, and the Carrington and Braemar in New Plymouth.

'The other thing, Mark. Sometime back, your cleaner found something similar to a girlie magazine under the bed.'

'Yeah.'

'Do you know anything about that?'

'Christine actually was reading articles in them.'

'Wasn't yours?'

'Not mine. I wouldn't want to waste my money to be honest.'

'Well, having said that, what about the pornography that was in your briefcase in your car?'

'That was given to me.'

'By who?'

'I can't even remember now. It's actually been there for a couple of years. I forgot it was in there ...'

Not a word of that particular exchange rings true. It sounds more like he was caught red-handed with porn, and airily tried to pin it on his dead wife and someone whose name escaped him. The stick mags and the escorts were probably deeply shaming, but what do they prove? Kelly moved on. The two men talked about the home computer, the ranchslider, Amber's bedtimes, a bracelet found in Lundy's car, the insurance money. You could see Kelly gently ferreting around for evidence, but it was a sympathetic interview. Lundy liked Kelly; he said later that he saw him as a friend.

'Mark, it's a bit over two weeks since your wife and daughter were murdered,' Kelly said towards the end of the interview. 'You've done a lot of thinking and we've done a lot of investigating. It's not often I do this, but I'm going to ask you, what's your theory on it?'

'I haven't got one. I have absolutely no bloody idea. The only thing I can think of is, maybe it was a burglary gone wrong … I don't know. Who the hell could kill — who could take a life, but kill a beautiful little girl especially, it's …' He said he'd tried to imagine what happened. The best he could hope happened, he said, was that 'neither of them saw each other die and they died quickly. That's getting me through.' He put his head in his hands. He didn't know what tomorrow would bring when he went back to the house.

And then he asked Kelly, 'Have you guys had any luck, any suspects?'

'There's a lot of suspects, Mark.'

'Oh, is there?'

'You can take it as a personal thing from me, Mark, whoever murdered your wife and daughter will be caught.'

'Cool.'

'There's absolutely no way they won't be caught. We will catch them.'

'Excellent.'

14

The second interview was filmed on 23 February 2001, six months after the murders, and the day Lundy was placed under arrest and charged with the murders. Kelly escorted him to Manawatu Prison. He said at the first trial, 'While waiting for the large electronic gate to open, I said, "Mark, I and many other people are very disappointed."' Lundy's response was not recorded.

The interview room seemed smaller, and was filmed at a strange, oblique angle. The only props were the same — a table and two chairs. The clock had gone. As for the wardrobe department, Kelly was once again in white shirt and tie, while Lundy opted for baggy shorts and a vast yellow T-shirt. It was just after 9am and he was hung-over. He mentioned a drinking session the previous night; the last guest left in a taxi at 1.30am. 'I'll get an early night tonight,' he said.

Again, they talked about the home computer ('I can do the basics'), the ranchslider, Amber's bedtimes, a bracelet found in Lundy's car, the insurance money. It was a three-hour interview and the first half of it was innocuous in tone, although it's obvious that Kelly, in part, was pursuing the crackpot theory of the 7pm time of death. There was a detailed inventory of Lundy's car: popcorn, $1.55 in coins, four metal plumbing bolts, Sellotape, a wire coat-hanger, Pepsi, a pie wrapper. Lundy confirmed his travel bag contained a pair of brown socks, green Rio underwear, and a striped XXL polo shirt — the shirt which had been taken to Texas earlier that month for Miller's historic tests.

Kelly introduced a subtle change of tone to the interview when he told Lundy that a witness — Margaret Dance, the musing psychic — had seen him near his house at about 7.15pm on the night of the murders. 'You never went back to your home address that night?'

'Definitely not.'

Kelly asked about Lundy's debts in the wine venture, and whether Christine was concerned. Lundy said they were both concerned. Kelly asked if they argued, and Lundy replied that they hadn't.

'I'm trying to solve the murder involving Christine and your daughter, Amber.'

'Yes, I know.'

'Be truthful with me.'

'I am.'

'I think perhaps you had argued about it.'

Lundy replied they hadn't. The interview had picked up pace. Kelly said Lundy didn't have an alibi between 5.30pm and 8.30pm on the night of the murders. 'There's a big window there,' he said. Lundy said he was in Petone. Kelly then asked about Lundy's marriage, and said it didn't appear as though he and Christine were very close. They didn't sit together at the wine club evenings. Kelly then said Lundy's behaviour since their deaths 'has not portrayed a loving, caring relationship'. The interview had arrived at a tipping point.

'You think,' Lundy said, 'that I've killed them.'

'All right, that's what I'm thinking. You murdered your wife and daughter. How do you feel about me saying that, Mark?'

'Bloody terrible, to be honest. Like, I'm bloody lost for words. It's got to be the most heinous, heinous thought that I could come up with. It's— I have told so many people, right, that I really like you, and said, "Steve, he's a really good top bloke, he's really neat", until now.'

'I'm doing my job.'

'I know you are, I know you are.'

'Let me say something. You're dealing with a team of detectives that have worked well in excess of 20,000 hours trying to find who killed your wife and daughter. That equates to one man working for 10 years, a quarter of his working life, and we're not finished.'

'Yeah.'

'In order for me to explain to you what happened there,' said Kelly, arriving at the moment of truth in his interview, at its central drama, its leap of faith, 'I'm going to have to show you some photographs.'

'I didn't want this,' said Lundy, with a kind of whimper.

Kelly said, 'The day has come.' He opened up a folder and took out a photograph from the crime scene. 'That is Christine.'

Lundy's response to the appalling photographs Kelly showed him of the massacre were to prove crucial the following week. It was the things he said and the things he didn't, and the way he behaved and the way he didn't. The film brought the viewer into that small room, with its askew camera angle, its bare walls, its heaving fatty in yellow — it had something to do with his guilt or innocence.

It finished with Lundy's arrest, off-camera. The interview had lasted three hours. Towards the end, Kelly sang a kind of aria, with Lundy as his prompt.

'I can fully understand why you think I did it, I really can,' said Lundy.

'Mark, I don't think you did it, I know you did it. I'm telling you I know you murdered your wife and daughter. I don't think it, I damn well know it. And I have conclusive, absolutely irrefutable evidence that you did it. You will not get out of this, Mark. You murdered both of them.'

'I did not murder them. I was not there.'

'That is a load of bollocks, mate. Absolute bullshit. If you want to know what we've been doing for six months, we have been working on you. For six months, from day one, the number-one suspect on my spreadsheet is you. Now that's the way it's been for all those man-hours, all of those going to work at six in the morning and working till nine at night, seven days a bloody week, with cops thinking that you killed your wife and daughter.'

'I didn't. I was not in Palmerston.' Lundy's whinings that the lacuna in the whole story was himself — that he wasn't in Palmerston North, that he was whoring in Petone — failed to impress Kelly.

'You are a liar. That there is the evidence.' He showed Lundy the images of stains on the polo shirt. It's possible that one of the pictures was the same one I carried with me in Wellington — that purple outline a shape like the North Island, stained purple with hematoxylin and eosin dyes, its cell nuclei and nerve fibres revealing the apparent presence of Christine's brain. Lundy peered at it, baffled. Kelly said, 'This is the fragments in the shirt. This is what they look like close up. This is the conclusion, that either brain or deep spinal cord is present on your shirt. Caught you, buddy, absolutely caught you. You deny it till the cows come home, mate.'

The interview came to a halt at 10 past 12. Lundy called his lawyer, Mike Behrens. Hung-over, busted, a blob in yellow, he was taken to the gates of Manawatu Prison ('I and many others are disappointed in you') in long, flat Camp Road, just past the Linton army camp. Somewhere nearby flowed the Manawatu River. The gates opened. There endeth Lundy's freedom for the next 13 years.

15

The trial had now fast approached its own moment of truth. What were the jury thinking? Had they already made up their minds? It was time for Morgan and Hislop to stand and deliver their closing addresses. Morgan delivered: the guy deserved a standing ovation. Perhaps not from Lundy, whom he smote with cold fury for two days, but when it was over the first person to rush to his side with unseemly haste and thrust out his hand in congratulations was defence lawyer Ross Burns. 'I couldn't help it,' he said, when I invited him into my parlour in the courtroom during our wait for the verdict. 'It was a tour de force. I went from feeling very confident about an acquittal, to thinking, "Oh, shit. This is now on a knife edge."'

Morgan dressed like he bought his suits from Hallensteins, and his only hint of flamboyance was the silver streak of his widow's peak. He was quite charmless, but his manner in closing was direct and compelling. He made a very, very good case. He told powerful stories. He spoke loudly, unhesitatingly, seriously. It was interesting to compare his speech to Vanderkolk's closing address in 2002; much of the material was the same, but where Vanderkolk's speech impressed with its elegant, thoughtful sentences, Morgan preferred hard-boiled prose.

'This is not a killing by a random burglar. All of the evidence indicates it's an inside job. This is a person who went there with a purpose. This purpose was to kill Christine Lundy. He set about killing her with a vengeance. He chops at her face. Multiple times. He even misses two or three times and strikes the headboard because of the frenzy of the attack. All the blows are focused on her face. He was trying to obliterate her face. This was committed by someone who wanted to wipe Christine Lundy off the face of the Earth. He strikes her so hard that he drives the weapon 5 centimetres into her skull.'

Not a comma in sight, none of the effete scaffolding of colons and such. Physically, too, Morgan was a model of containment. He kept his hands to himself, didn't indulge in any miming of the dreadful attack. He stood straight and maintained steady eye contact. 'And what threat was Amber to anyone? Was she really going to recognise a random burglar in the dark? She was seven for heaven's sake.'

Yes, said Hislop, Morgan was right. The killings weren't rational. 'There are violent and deranged people in the world. Deranged psychotic attacks — it happens. Sadly, it happens.' A monster did it. 'He bashes out Christine's brain. He turns, and there's Amber. She's standing between the killer and his exit. She was in the way. Bang, she's dead.'

Hislop's address was half as long as Morgan's. He kept it simple, and numerical. He called it 'the three impossible things'. He said it was impossible for Lundy to be the killer because he simply didn't have enough petrol in his car, and because he couldn't have been in Palmerston North at the most likely time of death. Impossibility one: Lundy simply didn't have enough petrol. Police Sergeant Danny Johanson — the giant who looked like a couple of Dan Carters — made the return trip from Petone to Palmerston North six times during the first police investigation. His test drives showed that to be able to make the extra trip, Lundy would have needed 85 litres of petrol when he last filled up his Ford Fairmont. But the tank's capacity was only 68 litres. Hislop: 'It dispels the myth of the secret journey.' Impossibility two: Christine and Amber's last supper was from McDonald's, at about 6pm. It takes about six hours for the stomach to empty. They couldn't have been killed much after midnight because the postmortem showed that their stomachs were full. But the earliest Lundy could have got to his home was about 2.30am — he'd been tied up until just before 1am, boring a prostitute in his motel room with talk of his kitchen sink business. Hislop: 'It makes it impossible he was in Palmerston North killing his family.' Impossibility three was that a neighbour testified that he'd seen the sliding door wide open at around 11pm on the night of the murders. The murderer was inside the house, waiting in darkness, to strike. Hislop: 'We know Mr Lundy was in Petone then, don't we? You remember the escort.'

Well, Morgan said, the neighbour's testimony was sketchy at best, and Christine and Amber must have eaten later than 6pm — there was a banana peel in the kitchen, and maybe they reheated the remains of the Happy Meal later that night. As for the car, police evidence suggested that about 300 kilometres were 'missing' on the speedo during Lundy's recent travels — and could only be accounted for because Lundy had made his 297-kilometre 'killing journey'.

The drive was made in stealth and began in secrecy. Lundy parked on the street to make a quiet getaway. Morgan scorned Lundy's claim that he'd parked there after driving across the street earlier that night to read his Robert Ludlum thiller ('The silhouetted figure in the doorway rushed into the dark, windowless room', etc.) under a streetlight. Morgan: 'Why would you do such a thing? It's winter! It's twilight at 6.20pm! And why drive across the street? Why not just walk? Does it have the ring of truth?'

Yes, certainly, said Hislop. 'Any of us who stay in motels regularly know that after a while you've just got to get out of the room. But why would you sit outside and read your book in winter? Wouldn't you get in your car, park up, and read?'

The public gallery was full, due in part to a delegation from Vanderkolk's law offices in Palmerston North. He'd given them the day off to attend the trial, and to watch their boss, a splendid and regal figure in his pinstriped flannels, idle away the hours while inspecting his fingernails. In fact, he wasn't the best-dressed man in court any more. That distinction now belonged to the most unlikely candidate — the juror who had spent the first few weeks in jandals, shorts, and the T-shirt that stated IF IT AIN'T BEAM, IT AIN'T BOURBON. Suddenly, the face-pulling munter showed up in polished shoes, and a suit and tie. The radical makeover became the central mystery in court. Had someone said something? Was he trying to score? He scrubbed up well. He looked like the most powerful man in the room, like he owned it. Justice France and everyone else were his tenants.

Morgan and Hislop gave competing arguments about the bracelet found in the car, Lundy's finances, the police investigation — and, of course, the shirt. The shirt, the shirt. Lundy's short-sleeved XXL polo tent — pinned like some vast moth in its exhibit case — should take its place alongside David Bain's jersey and Ewen McDonald's dive boots in a kind of fashion parade in the history of New Zealand murder. Morgan delivered perhaps the best of his pithy hard-boiled zingers: 'No husband should have his wife's brain on her shirt.' Hislop didn't say too much about the stupid shirt. He briefly raised the possibility of contamination, accidental or otherwise ('Did something happen to it in Miller's lab?'), and made a few noises about the stain possibly being food — it got there from cooking neck chops or sausages, or from Lundy slobbering on a pie. He said he wasn't much fussed about the stain. He affected an air of nonchalance. This was the best he could come up with, and it was kind of lame: 'If it was impossible for Mark Lundy to be in Palmerston North at the time of the murders, then whatever had got on the shirt, whatever it is, got there in a way consistent with his innocence.'

Hislop's manner in closing was gentle, self-effacing. He wore a pale tie and a pale shirt. He was rumpled in his silks, and presented himself as a pleasant coot and figure of quiet reason. He fluttered over the science, and alighted on the fact that there was no blood or tissue found on Lundy's shoes, his glasses, his rings, or in his car. That didn't make sense, he said. Nor did the Crown's assertion that the mysterious weapon was one of Lundy's tools. 'What tool do they say he used? A hammer? A chisel? A screwdriver? We waited, and waited, and waited. No answer was ever forthcoming. The silence was deafening.' At least two of his impossibilities introduced significant reasonable doubt. He made a very good case. He got the last word. 'The only safe verdict,' he said, 'is not guilty.' It lacked the impact of Morgan's final sentence: 'The killer is the accused.'

The processing of a man's fate had come to an end. The trial had reached its point of no return. No more fine talk from lawyers, no more evidence from witnesses, nothing left to give except for Justice France to sum up on the Monday morning, and direct the jury to leave Courtroom 1 and decide. Every minute of their deliberations would be a familiar agony — been there, suffered that — for the man accused for a second time of killing his wife and child. I saw Lundy outside court later that afternoon. The autumn light lay tenderly on the row of pohutukawa trees across the road. He was talking with his sister, Caryl, and looked in good spirits.

16

We know more about their deaths — the violence of it, the executioner swinging some sort of axe in the dark bedroom — than their lives. But we know and remember their names. Christine and Amber Lundy have been given the same kind of wretchedly sad immortality as Ben and Olivia, Sophie Elliott, the Crewes, the Bains.

Once upon a time they walked to school together. It took three blocks from their home to the end of the street, then around the corner and over the railway line to Roslyn Primary School — the same familiar journey, the same deep happiness of mother and child together. They last walked it on a Tuesday morning in late winter.

The flatlands of cold, rivery Manawatu, the edge of town in Palmerston North. 'They lived in a modest little home,' as Morgan described it, 'in a blue-collar suburb.' The letterbox and windowsills had matching green trim. There was a set of swings and a trampoline in the front yard, a trailer parked out the back.

Amber was seven. She was born on 9 July 1993, at 1.25am, by emergency Caesarian after Christine had been in labour for 20 hours. Everyone said that her parents adored her; no one needed to point out that she adored them. Mark Lundy told police, 'She used to put on little concerts for us. We would be watching TV and she would appear in a pair of plastic shoes, and dressed up with a little feather boa around her neck, and do a little dance.'

She was enrolled at Rocket dance studios when she was three and a half. Christine took her there on that Tuesday, after school. She wore her favourite outfit — a pink and orange leotard with blue tights — and Christine waited in the same seat where she always sat. There was a show coming up, and the girls tried on their costumes.

The class lasted an hour. After it finished, Amber was due at Pippins. Amber was the third generation in her family to go guiding; her grandmother, Christine's mother, Helen Weggery, was active in the movement in Tokomaru, and Christine, too, had gone through Guides, and met her husband at the 1978 Gang Show. 'Fantastic dancer,' he said of her. They were engaged in Easter 1982, and married in May the next year.

There was $11.19 in change in the kitchen, and a collection of 83 bottles of wine. Mark and Christine belonged to the Manawatu and Bacchus wine clubs, but she didn't drink much. She liked the company. They were a popular couple. They'd had the Durhams, Stewart and Caroline, over for a barbecue the previous Saturday night; they'd played cards, and stayed until midnight.

Mark Lundy's favourite author was Wilbur Smith, Christine was an avid reader of Mills & Boon. Her habit was to read in the conservatory with her lunch. She also read *New Idea* and *Woman's Day*, sometimes the *Australian Women's Weekly*. The TV shows she enjoyed most were light ent — *Changing Rooms, Taste New Zealand, Shortland Street*.

After she had walked back to the house, having taken Amber to school on Tuesday morning, Christine and Mark had driven in separate cars to Lighting Direct. She wanted a lightshade for the spare bedroom. Mark had to drive to Petone, on a business trip; they kissed goodbye in the store.

Last kiss, last walk to school, last supper at 5.48pm when Christine and Amber ordered McDonald's. Pippins had been cancelled. They ordered nine chicken nuggets, a chicken burger, a filet-o-fish burger, large fries, and two apple pies. The owners of a nearby dairy remembered Christine coming into their shop almost every day for a 1.5-litre bottle of Diet Coke and a Sante chocolate bar. The family were big people. Christine weighed 112 kilograms, Amber 45 kilograms. A verbose pathologist who wore snowdrop-patterned socks said at the trial, fairly unnecessarily, 'They had a body mass of 44 and 31, which you would say is obese.'

Christine didn't cook. Her friends conceded she wasn't the tidiest person in the world, either. But she was brilliantly organised. She ran her husband's kitchen sink business from an office in the house, and worked on the accounts until late at night. Afterwards, she'd play Patience and Solitaire on the computer to wind down.

She turned off the PC at 10.52pm that Tuesday. Christine was a night owl, and often stayed up late to read or watch TV. Amber had her routines — pyjamas on at 7pm, bed at 7.30pm, lights out by 8pm. 'She was the easiest child to babysit,' Helen Weggery told police. Sometimes her parents read her a bedtime story, sometimes she read it to them. She slept with a soft toy of Rolly, a jowly dog who featured on TV commercials for toilet paper. Lundy had fixed a net in her bedroom for her stuffed toys and her dolls. There were bunk beds in her room. She slept in the bottom bunk.

The dance lessons and swimming lessons, Pippins, friends, school, family — she loved her life. It was safe. Her mum and dad looked after her.

She spoke to her father for the last time on Tuesday, when she asked him over the phone whether it was okay to have McDonald's for dinner. 'Of course you can,' he told her. The exchange was read out in court. A smile touched Lundy's face, the memory reaching back to him after 15 years of a little girl saying, 'Please, Daddy?'

After she put Amber to bed, Christine worked on her brother's GST accounts. Glenn Weggery had called around that morning to see whether she'd finished. He'd called around the previous morning, too, and then on Wednesday morning, when the curtains were still closed.

Mark Lundy appeared on the witness stand the first time he was found guilty, at his trial in 2002, and was asked, 'What do you miss most about Amber?'

'Everything,' said her father, who will be known and remembered for the rest of his days as her murderer.

17

Lundy was found guilty at two minutes to four on April Fool's Day. The last I saw of him — the last time he might ever be seen in public — was when he was led from the courtroom after the jury were dismissed. He was a man in shock, in disbelief, in agony. The judge promptly sent him back to rot in jail for the remainder of his life. It was over. He was made to disappear.

I left Wellington the next day. It felt strange to be leaving Wellington for good. The brand-new paving at the Cenotaph war memorial beside Parliament was nearly finished; when I left court that afternoon, it was to the sharp, loud clang of the bell at the Old Government House. The flight was called, and I found myself in line with David Hislop. He was on his way home, too, to London; he was in jeans and a groovy shirt, and was glum, beaten, quiet. He'd emailed early that morning, 'Just a word of thanks for your commiserations and support yesterday.' I'd found him after the verdict, standing in a room in the High Court with Ross Burns and Julie-Anne Kincade, the three of them devastated. I didn't stay long. He wrote, 'I am unshaken in my belief that the jury got it wrong but perhaps 12 years of entrenched belief in his guilt was just one hurdle too high to clear. After four years on the case I am bowing out and others with more energy can carry on if they can.' Burns was finished with it, too, but he'd made it plain all along that this was his swan-song — he'd come out of retirement for the case.

Hislop was at the airport with Kincade. She'd resolved to carry on, and was soon at work on Lundy's appeal. Her lead argument was that the RNA evidence — Dr Sijen's test in support of the Crown's case that Lundy wore Christine's brain on his polo shirt — should never have been allowed in court. The defence had bungled that one, made a poor submission at the pre-trial hearing when they had tried to get it thrown out of court. Their subsequent pleas to the Court of Appeal, and then directly to Justice France, had also failed. What chance of that same exact appeal finally working the fourth time around? And what difference had it made to the verdict, anyway? Did the jury seriously consider anything remotely scientific?

'You are anonymous,' Justice France had said to the chosen 12 on the opening day of the trial. Fine. I don't want to know their names. I don't want to see any of them ever again — yes, I'm sure the feeling is mutual. I think I probably hate them. I hadn't really thought all that much about them during the trial. The pretty forewoman took a lot of notes. The cripple seemed as though he was asleep most of the time, and the callow youth looked as though he didn't have a clue what was being said. The munter was in his own amazing production — that radical makeover had transformed him, but his face remained in a state of agitation. Were there little alliances, important cliques? The forewoman seemed on especially good terms with the hipster. He sat directly behind her, and now and then she'd turn and they'd exchange a knowing smile. They were sometimes seen sharing a joke as they entered court, and they were also sighted together on the morning of the verdict at Tank Juice Bar on Lambton Quay. They walked through the grounds of Parliament on the way to court. Their relationship took on a sinister turn at the precise moment Lundy's chances of an acquittal went from extremely likely to zero.

The verdict was on a Wednesday. Justice France summed up on Monday. It drew a crowd, with every seat taken in the public gallery. People were excited to be there, to witness the end of a truly horrible saga in New Zealand history. Mary from Epsom was there, and Anne from Woburn was there, and they were joined by Nathan from Plimmerton, who had a court-watching speciality — he only appeared during the wait for the verdict. He loved the tension, the uncertainty. He loved the verdict most of all, its power on a room. He was in Courtroom 1 when Ewen McDonald was found not guilty of the murder of Scott Guy, and he said he'd never forget that moment. He worked as a gardener; he was strong, with big hands, and there was a sensitivity to him. He was separated from the mother of his children. He said to me that Monday, after the judge had given his summing up, that he was in a new relationship, and things were going as well as could be expected. A radio journalist came over and made a long speech about his history of failed relationships. It was a very long history. I escaped outside, where tui sang in the flax bush. Glenn Weggery was there, standing with detectives from Palmerston North; they weren't happy. Things looked bad for the prosecution. After the jubilation of Morgan's exhilarating closing defence, their mood had been brought crashing down by Justice France's summing up.

France was most famous as the judge who had ordered journalist Laura McQuillan off the media bench during the Ewen McDonald trial for wearing an apparently distracting pair of gold lamé sequinned 'disco pants'. He was a stickler for a dress code during the Lundy trial, too; no man could sit before him without a tie. He presided over the court with good grace and unflagging attention to detail. He ruled it with a silver bouffant. But his greatest contribution was his summing up, when he established himself as the most brilliant jurist at the trial. He'd spoken for nearly three hours. He maintained his flair for the malapropism, the flat-out blunder. He referred to Hislop as a character by the name of 'Mr Wislop', claimed that Lundy's first trial was in 2003 (it was 2002), and called the accused 'Mr Lundry'. Dirty Lundry, or clean Lundry? The remainder of France's address was a masterclass, a model of clear and nuanced thinking. It was balanced and judicious, as you'd expect. But it was also an instruction to ignore much of what the Crown had put forward, and to acquit.

He told the jury to reject Morgan's hard-boiled term 'the killing journey'. That had no place in court, he said. The prosecution kept returning to the bracelet found in Lundy's car, saying that it had fallen out of the jewellery box which he had taken from the crime scene.

France dismissed it as an unproven nonsense. On the matter of no one in the scientific community coming forward to back Dr Sijen's critical evidence that the stain contained human RNA, he said: 'Sijen stands alone.' The best he could say in support of the tests: 'If you accept that it is human brain, then the Crown's case is considerably strengthened ... Mrs Lundy's brain tissue is obviously a very significant thing.'

He ticked off Hislop's 'three impossible things' that ruled out Lundy being the killer. France was in support of Lewis Carroll. 'One can't believe impossible things,' says Alice in *Through the Looking-Glass*. 'If you accept he did not have enough petrol to make the trip,' France said of the defence's first impossibility, 'you must acquit.'

And then he trashed the motive. The Crown said that Lundy did it for the oldest cliché in homicide — an insurance cheque. They examined the accounts of his sink business, and declared that it was on the verge of collapse. Lundy was in serious debt. Really? France told the jury: 'You may be drawn to the view that the business wasn't hopeless, wasn't great, but they had no real reason to think they wouldn't at least stay the same and maybe get better quite soon. I think it fair if I say to those of you who haven't had business experience that owing money to people, and being owed by others, is not unusual for small businesses. It is to be noted equally the Lundys were owed money.' As for the insurance pay-out, France said, 'It's important to remember the change in insurance was nothing to do with him. The $200,000 had been in place for a while; the idea of increasing it came from the broker, not Mr Lundy. He knew it would not go up until it was all settled and that had not been done yet, so why kill her now?'

He gave Kleintjes a bad review. He gave Pang a bad review. He gave his worst review to dear old X, the jailhouse snitch, the comedian with his thick neck bursting out of his tightly buttoned shirt. 'You saw him in the witness box. I don't know — maybe in one sense he seemed to you in his own way an engaging witness,' he said of the wretch. 'But you should think about things such as the likelihood of Mr Lundy admitting this to a relative stranger, and the error the witness seemingly made about Mr Lundy waiting for an appeal. You also heard of his past offending and how others have called him manipulative. These are matters to weigh in the mix.' He smiled sweetly, and said: 'Great care is needed.'

The evidence of Detective Inspector Kelly, too, caused him to make comments on 'misleading witnesses'. Kelly was the officer who conducted the filmed interviews with Lundy, leading to his dramatic arrest. Kelly had denied to Hislop that Lundy was always the number-one suspect. But France took the trouble to point out to the jury that Kelly had said the complete opposite to Lundy himself, during the interview, 'in a bit of the video you didn't see'.

The police had tunnel vision. There wasn't any motive. There was concern that several prosecution witnesses were 'misleading'. There was no support for Sijen's claims. X was a wretch. And: 'If you accept the analysis that Mr Lundy could not do it because he did not have enough fuel, then you should stop there and acquit.'

Thus the glum faces of the police. Thus Lundy in good spirits outside court that afternoon; thus the celebratory night out on the piss for Hislop and Burns. I caught them on the way out. I said to Hislop, 'How would you describe things as they are right now? Are they finely poised?'

He said, 'I would have thought it was finely poised at nine this morning. But having heard the summing up, and watched the jury — and I was looking at them carefully — I think we're a few yards ahead. I've seen some long faces on the other side.' He meant the police and the prosecution. Hislop's laugh was like a happy woof; the thought of those long faces made him bark.

I said, 'What did you see when you watched the jury?'

'I was seeing them writing down all the right stuff. But also, it was just that the summing up was much better than I expected. The judge was making some pretty sound remarks. He basically told them to forget the NFI [Netherlands Forensic Institute] stuff. He steered them.'

'He said something like, "Sijen stands alone."'

'Yeah, exactly. And he's right of course.'

Hislop had never heard of Lundy or his case when he took it on in 2010. I said, 'What do you make of your client?'

He said, 'He's probably one of the least likely murderers I've come across. He does genuinely seem like a gentle, rather soft kind of guy. It's one of the things that just doesn't add up. I genuinely don't think he did it. I don't think he's got the balls. You need big balls to do that.'

Burns had been on holiday in Cyprus with his wife, about to have his first beer of the midday, when he had opened up his emails to find Hislop asking him to join the defence team. He knew all about the case. 'Like everybody else, I assumed he was as guilty as sin.'

I said, 'You're an officer of the court and your feelings about guilt or innocence don't come into it. But did you cross that line, and say, "My client is not guilty"?'

'I had that epiphany when I was going through the petrol consumption evidence and realised he couldn't have done it,' Burns said. 'I remember sitting down — I was at home, at our house in Mangawhai Heads — and then getting up and saying to my wife, "This is an innocent man." And that's frightening.'

He didn't think the Crown had presented enough evidence for a conviction. He didn't think it had the jury onside. He said, 'The body language of three, four people tell me they're prepared to give Mark Lundy a free ticket home. That may change in deliberation …'

I said to Hislop, 'If your guy didn't do it, then what the hell happened?'

'I don't know,' he said. 'Was it a hit wrapped up with the aborted sale of purchase, or the root stock … You just don't know. There's no evidence that that's right. There are nutters out there.

Was it purely a case of mistaken identity? A hit on the wrong house? We'll never know.'

I asked him to comment again on France's summing up, and he said, 'Just his tone seemed to me to be very, very weighted towards the defence. He concentrated quite a bit on the burden of proof, which was nice. He kept coming back to our three impossibilities, especially the petrol. I mean, what are you going to do? The guy couldn't drive there to do it. He didn't fly.'

'Well, Morgan talked about discrepancies in the mileage.'

'Ahhh, that's a pile of shit. No. This jury is hot on the petrol. Hot on it. A lot of serious note-taking on the petrol. But, hey,' he said, and raised his palms to Heaven, 'I could be dead wrong.'

He was dead wrong. The verdict was unanimous. 'Guilty,' said the foreperson, twice, in a small, childish voice on that beautiful afternoon in autumn. The word fell from her lips. It floated around the courtroom. It was the damnation everyone had expected since the jury had made an extraordinary request the previous day at about 2pm. Word went around that they had something to ask Justice France. It's not uncommon for juries to seek clarification on particular issues; the difficult science at the Lundy trial meant that it was inevitable that a question would be asked of some arcane matter. But then the word went around that they didn't have anything to ask about science whatsoever. They wanted to see films. They'd requested repeat screenings of two police videos — that frightening six-minute tour of the crime scene, and much of the second, climactic interview between Lundy and his nemesis, Detective Inspector Kelly.

There was a particular moment in the crime scene that they obviously wanted to see again. Three of them leaned forward when the camera showed the bloody glove print on the conservatory window. It was Christine's blood, and the killer had left it there. I remember Levick miming his theory — the killer wore paper booties, and leaned his hand against the window for balance as he bent to take off the protective shoes.

The police argued that the fact that it was on the inside of the window showed that Lundy had staged the break-in. When the film zoomed in on the close-up of the glove print, the foreperson turned to the juror behind her, and exchanged a knowing smile. Interesting. Even more interesting was the psychodrama which two members of the jury seemed to play out during the film of Lundy's police interview with Kelly. When the film began, everyone in the room looked at it on the big screen – except for two jurors, who kept their eyes on Lundy in the dock, and watched him watching the film.

What was that about? It felt like the funeral all over again. It felt like another journey into the bullshit science of body language. Did the way Lundy behave in court, and in the police interview, somehow reveal something about his guilt? The film of Kelly's interview took a sudden and alarming turn when he said to Lundy, 'I'm going to have to show you some photographs.'

'I didn't want this,' Lundy complained.

Kelly said, 'The day has come.' He opened up a folder and took out a photograph from the crime scene. 'That is Christine.'

Lundy turned away in horror, and cried out: 'No!'

'Christine has got severe head injuries to her arms and head area. There's blood everywhere.'

Lundy slid his chair across the floor to get away from the pictures, and said, 'Oh yuck.'

'Oh yuck' didn't quite cover it. 'Oh yuck' didn't really measure up to the graphic slaughter of his wife. 'Oh yuck.' Who says 'Oh yuck'?

'The blows have gone across the head, Mark,' said Kelly.

'Oh God. I hate you now, I really do,' said Lundy — and his response once again seemed significant to some jurors.

Kelly got up and awkwardly rubbed Lundy's shoulders. It was a strange piece of male bonding. He said, 'Mark, the thing about this is that Amber would have been killed with the same instrument.'

'Oh God, you're not going to show me that, too, are you?'

Lundy talked in whimpers. He turned his head away from the pictures. He was in some distress. But when Kelly asked him questions about other subjects — the bracelet found in his car, his tools — Lundy reverted to making casual conversation. It was as though he couldn't maintain his grief and horror. It came and went. Lundy recoiled, groaned loudly, made strangled kinds of screams. He covered his face. He bowed his head. Was it horror, or a lame attempt to mime the response expected of an innocent man?

Kelly showed him a picture of Amber lying dead in the doorway to his bedroom, and said, 'If you look back at the photograph of her brains, they went everywhere, up the wall, up the bed, across the dresser, up the curtain, every-bloody-where but right there, and the reason why they didn't go there, Mark, is cos that's where you were standing.'

'No,' Lundy sobbed.

'Don't even think about lying to me, do not think about lying to me.'

'I am not lying.'

'You are.'

'I was not in Palmerston North!'

'I'll show you something else, and you're going to have to look at this because this is how it works. That is a picture of your beautiful daughter. That's a picture of your beautiful daughter in the doorway with her head cut. That there is a close-up of it. Don't make faces, because I'm saying you did this. And you hit her that hard, that's her skull.'

'I didn't, Steve, I did not, I was not in Palmerston North, I was in Wellington, I did not kill my wife and daughter. Please, cover those up — please?'

'Mark, why would I cover them up? You did it, for God's sake.'

'I bloody well didn't.'

It was the funeral all over again … He showed too much grief, he didn't show enough. He wailed and whimpered, a hung-over fatty confronted with appalling photographs, pleading, crying, then talking matter-of-factly about bracelets and such. It looked bad. Or was it just footage of a man in shock? It had absolutely nothing to do with the murders, it didn't place him at the crime, it offered nothing in the way of evidence, it didn't point to motive, to opportunity, to anything that suggested that he killed his wife and daughter. But was it what the jury wanted to see; was it what they needed to convict?

The mood in the courtroom changed completely after that. Hislop looked like he'd seen a ghost. I found him pacing outside on the pavement, his head bowed. I said, 'With respect, you're fucked.'

He gave one of his barking laughs, and said, 'Well.'

I said, 'No. You're fucked.'

He said, 'Fuck off. Okay?' He stomped off, his head still bowed.

The end was nigh. Mike White from *North & South* read it that way, too; he was shocked. Mike, to his vast professional credit, was largely responsible for everyone coming to this room in Wellington to hear six weeks of evidence. His investigative story on the murders challenged the Crown case against Lundy with sufficient power to attract not just Hislop but also some of the world's leading forensic scientists to the cause. It had led to the first conviction being quashed. His own views on Lundy's guilt or innocence provided a model of rational thinking which I tried to follow. He said, 'All I can do is approach it from the angle the judge instructed the jury to: can you be sure he did it? If not, then you've got to acquit because there's not sufficient evidence, and thinking it's possible, or even likely he did it, isn't good enough. Does the evidence show he did it for sure? I've never been able to get to that point, personally.'

The police started to look more relaxed. Ben Vanderkolk sat with one of his sons, who worked up the road at The Backbencher pub, and put his arm around his shoulders. I was glad Geoff Levick had decided against coming to Wellington for the verdict. I had emailed him on the weekend, and he'd replied, 'No, I've decided not to come down as I will be seeing Mark anyway probably on the same day as the Not Guilty verdict. Mark is informed and is ok with that.'

I mucked around Thorndon waiting for the verdict. I foraged for delicious golden peaches growing wild in a tree in the carpark of the Indian High Commission, and shared them in court. I stopped and chatted with the religious maniac on Lambton Quay who wore a sandwich board that advised PERILOUS TIMES WILL COME. At the Corrections Department offices on The Terrace, I walked through its entertaining prison museum — a rope made from sheets, a tattoo machine made with a ballpoint pen and a motor from an electric razor. Inevitably, there were reminders of Lundy among the museum exhibits. He would have remembered the heavy serge-green uniform that guards wore until it was retired in 2011. Beautiful penmanship in the nineteenth-century admissions register at Invercargill Gaol recorded the execution of James Welsh for the murder of his wife.

On Wednesday afternoon I was sitting around at the courthouse with Mike White when Julie-Anne Kincade approached us, and said, 'It's time.' Her face was intensely serious. The lawyers and the families and the media and the curious filed into the court. Justice France took his throne. The jury entered; they kept their eyes down. The registrar said, 'Place Mark Edward Lundy before the court.' He entered and gave his sister a smile; she sat behind him with her husband. He stood with his hands behind his back.

Detective Inspector Marc Hercock, a nice man who favoured Blues Brothers dark glasses, gave a press conference outside court. A police wagon took Lundy away. I stood around in a daze for a while. I said goodbye to Mary of Epsom. She said, 'Thank you for all your support.' What? I commiserated with Hislop, I said so long to Mike White. He emailed a few days later: 'Were we the only two people in court other than the defence and Lundy family that were unsettled by the decision?'

Before I left, I received permission to sit in Courtroom 1 and study the crime scene photographs shown to the jury. I wanted to see what the case was all about. I wanted to see what had happened to Christine and Amber, in colour, not in the creepy black and white photocopies I'd studied at Kumeu. Many of the photos were pixillated. They concealed the worst of Christine's injuries. But they were still very graphic and terribly sad. The little girl on her front, her head in a pool of blood on the carpet with its pattern of autumn leaves. Christine was photographed at postmortem, her face wiped clean. But it was no human face that remained. I was moved to something like a crisis of faith. I felt tired and depressed. I thought: maybe the jury got it right. They'd deliberated for 13 hours, over two nights. It can't have been easy. Twelve adults looked at the evidence. Maybe all this really was his doing, his vicious and unforgiveable act. Maybe he *did* do that. He killed his wife and, having gone that far, having arrived at that state of euphoria and madness, took one or two quick strides towards his daughter. Maybe when Amber stood at the doorway and looked in, the last word she said was 'Daddy?'

I don't know. I think it was the same horror visited upon them by someone else, someone who was already in the house that night when their neighbour saw the sliding door open; I think the stomach contents and the gas tank put Lundy in Petone, sleeping off the rum and the escort, just another travelling salesman with a wire coat-hanger in the back of his car, who got up the next morning, threw his polo shirt with a food stain on it into his bag, ate a bacon and egg sandwich on The Esplanade with a view of Wellington harbour, and set about seeing his clients, selling a tap, fixing a scratch on a sink, showing no sign of sleeplessness or mania. The evidence didn't stack up. What use was the discredited science of Sijen? The logic didn't stack up. Who the hell would order an escort as an alibi? Reasonable doubt was all over the place. How to explain the flakes of dark-blue paint at the crime scene? In the eyes of the law, his monstrousness extended beyond the killings to lying about it. The alternative monstrousness was that an innocent man grieved for his wife and daughter, and was placed under arrest — and falsely convicted, certainly once, quite likely twice.

I visited Geoff Levick after the trial. The dementia unit in Kumeu had opened, and some poor soul in a cardigan was standing outside in winter sunlight. A black shag was drying its wings on a post in front of Levick's fish pond. The mandarin trees were in fruit. There were new manila folders stuffed with documents in the room off his garage. We talked about Hislop, paint flakes, Miller, the jury. He hadn't given up fighting, and likely never will. Julie-Anne Kincade had filed notice to appeal. Lundy was back at Wanganui prison. The house where he lived with Christine and Amber was up for tender. It had been painted and renovated, but was immediately recognisable — there was the driveway someone had crept around that night in 2000, there was the kitchen still with its blue cupboards, there were the bedrooms ... I wept again to look inside that house of grief and horror, to be reminded of what had happened there, and what had happened, too, at the trial in Wellington. The house looked haunted. It felt haunted by the living: by Lundy.

Levick drove me to a foodhall in west Auckland after I visited. We talked about what would happen when Lundy's 20-year prison sentence came to an end. Without confession or remorse, he'd probably keep going back inside each time he appeared for parole. Lundy had said to Levick that his best revenge on the people who put him there would be to live to 100, and forever state his innocence.

Acknowledgements

These stories have been revised, reshaped and in most cases entirely rewritten from their original publication in the *New Zealand Herald*, *Metro*, *North & South* and the *Sunday Star-Times*. One of the abiding pleasures of working in journalism is the opportunity to learn from the best in the field; my thanks and gratitude to the editorial guidance and professional expertise of staff at those newspapers and magazines: Shayne Currie, Jared Savage, Tim Murphy, Chris Reed, Simon Wilson, Virginia Larson, Cate Brett, Miriyana Alexander, and the incomparable Donna Chisholm.

Particular thanks to the tenacious Jeremy Olds, for his additional reporting on the chapter "The killings at Stilwell Rd"; and to Mike White, whose detailed advice and wise counsel were crucial to all the chapters on Mark Lundy.

Finlay Macdonald has been my best friend since I left adolescence for early adulthood at the age of 30. His commissioning of this book, and our conversations about its thinking and its intent, are the latest evidence of his support and also his rare intelligence.

My thanks also to Rachel Dennis and Kate Stone for their skill and attentiveness in helping to shape the book and its contents.

Writing a book separates the author from their family. I was a remote creature preoccupied with thoughts of violent crime while I wrote this book, but my heart always was and always will be with Emily and Minka.